Qt 6 C++ GUI Programming Cookbook

Practical recipes for building cross-platform GUI applications, widgets, and animations with Qt 6

Lee Zhi Eng

Qt 6 C++ GUI Programming Cookbook

Assistant Group Product Manager: Kunal Sawant

Associate Publishing Product Manager: Teny Thomas

Senior Editor: Rounak Kulkarni

Book Project Manager: Deeksha Thakkar

Technical Editor: Rajdeep Chakraborty and Jubit Pincy

Copy Editor: Safis Editing

Proofreader: Rounak Kulkarni

Indexer: Manju Arasan

Production Designer: Prashant Ghare

Senior DevRel Marketing Executive: Shrinidhi Monaharan

Business Development Executive: Samriddhi Murarka

First published: July 2016

Third edition: March 2024

Production reference: 1280324

Published by Packt Publishing Ltd.

Grosvenor House

11 St Paul's Square

Birmingham

B3 1RB, UK.

ISBN 978-1-80512-263-0

www.packtpub.com

In loving memory of my late brother, Lee Zhi Zheng, whose introduction to the world of computing ignited my passion for technology. I extend my heartfelt gratitude to my parents and dear friends for their unconditional love, encouragement, and inspiration throughout my journey.

– Lee Zhi Eng

Contributors

About the author

Lee Zhi Eng is a self-taught programmer who worked as an artist and programmer at several game studios before becoming a part-time lecturer for two years at a university, teaching game development subjects related to Unity and Unreal Engine. He has taken part in various projects related to games, interactive apps, and virtual reality and has also participated in multiple projects that are more oriented toward software and system development. When he is not writing code, he enjoys traveling, photography, and exploring new technologies.

About the reviewer

Nibedit Dey is a seasoned software engineer-turned-serial entrepreneur with over 14 years of experience crafting sophisticated software-based products adorned with captivating user interfaces. Prior to venturing into entrepreneurship, he honed his skills at Larsen & Toubro and Tektronix in various R&D capacities, leveraging his expertise in biomedical engineering and embedded systems. Specializing in Qt and embedded technologies, Nibedit currently spearheads two innovative start-ups, ibrum technologies and AIDIA Health, where he oversees the entire product life cycle from conception to delivery. Not content with mere entrepreneurial pursuits, Nibedit is also an accomplished author, having penned the acclaimed book *Cross-Platform Development with Qt 6 and Modern C++*. His contributions to the tech community extend beyond literature, as he serves as a respected reviewer of technical works and imparts knowledge as a sought-after trainer in Qt and C++. Fueled by an unwavering passion for embracing new technologies, Nibedit continues to push the boundaries of innovation, driving transformative change in the digital landscape.

Table of Contents

3

States and Animations with Qt and QML   67

4

QPainter and 2D Graphics   93

5

OpenGL Implementation   127

6

Transitioning from Qt 5 to Qt 6   159

12

13

14

Performance Optimization 375

Preface

With the growing need to develop GUIs for multiple targets and screens, improving the visual quality of your application becomes important so that it stands out from your competitors. With its cross-platform ability and the latest UI paradigms, Qt makes it possible to build intuitive, interactive, and user-friendly user interfaces for your applications.

Qt 6 C++ GUI Programming Cookbook, Third Edition, teaches you how to develop functional and appealing user interfaces using the latest version of QT6 and C++. This book will help you learn a variety of topics such as GUI customization and animation, graphics rendering, and implementing Google Maps. You will also explore advanced concepts such as asynchronous programming, event handling using signals and slots, network programming, and various aspects of optimizing your application.

By the end of the book, you will be confident to design and customize GUI applications that meet your client's expectations and understand the best practice solutions for common problems.

Who this book is for

This intermediate-level book is designed for those who want to develop software using Qt 6. If you want to improve the visual quality and content presentation of your software application, this book is for you. Prior experience in C++ programming is required.

What this book covers

Chapter 1, Look-and-Feel Customization with Qt Designer, shows you how to design your program's user interface using both Qt Creator and Qt Design Studio.

Chapter 2, Event Handling – Signals and Slots, covers topics related to the signals and slots mechanism provided by Qt 6, which allows you to handle your program's event callbacks with ease.

Chapter 3, States and Animations with Qt and QML, explains how to animate your user interface widgets by empowering the state machine framework and the animation framework.

Chapter 4, QPainter and 2D Graphics, covers how to draw vector shapes and bitmap images on screen using Qt's built-in classes.

Chapter 5, OpenGL Implementation, demonstrates how to render 3D graphics in your program by integrating OpenGL into your Qt project.

Chapter 6, Transitioning from Qt5 to Qt6, covers how you can transition your Qt 5 project to Qt 6 and discusses the differences between the two versions.

Chapter 7, Using Network and Managing Large Documents, shows you how to set up an FTP file server and then create a program that helps you to transfer files to and from it.

Chapter 8, Threading Basics – Asynchronous Programming, covers how to create multithreading processes in your Qt 6 application and run them simultaneously to process heavy calculations.

Chapter 9, Building a Touchscreen Application with Qt 6, explains how to create a program that works on a touchscreen device.

Chapter 10, JSON Parsing Made Easy, shows how to process data in the JSON format and use it together with the Google Geocoding API to create a simple address finder.

Chapter 11, Conversion Library, covers how to convert between different variable types, image formats, and video formats using Qt's built-in classes as well as third-party programs.

Chapter 12, Accessing Databases with SQL Driver and Qt, explains how to connect your program to a SQL database using Qt.

Chapter 13, Develop Web Applications Using Qt WebEngine, covers how to use the web rendering engine provided by Qt and develop programs that empower web technology.

Chapter 14, Performance Optimization, shows you how to optimize your Qt 6 application and speed up its processing.

To get the most out of this book

You will need the following software/hardware to try the learnings from this book:

Software/hardware covered in the book	Operating system requirements
Qt Creator 12.0.2	Windows, macOS, or Linux
Qt Design Studio	Windows, macOS, or Linux
SQLiteStudio	Windows, macOS, or Linux

If you are using the digital version of this book, we advise you to type the code yourself or access the code from the book's GitHub repository (a link is available in the next section). Doing so will help you avoid any potential errors related to the copying and pasting of code.

Download the example code files

You can download the example code files for this book from GitHub at `https://github.com/PacktPublishing/QT6-C-GUI-Programming-Cookbook---Third-Edition-/tree/main`. If there's an update to the code, it will be updated in the GitHub repository.

We also have other code bundles from our rich catalog of books and videos available at `https://github.com/PacktPublishing/`. Check them out!

Conventions used

There are a number of text conventions used throughout this book.

`Code in text`: Indicates code words in text, database table names, folder names, filenames, file extensions, pathnames, dummy URLs, user input, and Twitter handles. Here is an example: "A slot function called `on_pushButton_clicked()` will now appear in both `mainwindow.h` and `mainwindow.cpp`."

A block of code is set as follows:

```
import QtQuick
import QtQuick.Window
Window {
    visible: true
    width: 640
    title: qsTr("Hello World")
}
```

When we wish to draw your attention to a particular part of a code block, the relevant lines or items are set in bold:

```
width: 128;
    height: 128;
    x: -128;
    y: parent.height / 2;
```

Any command-line input or output is written as follows:

```
find_package(Qt6 REQUIRED COMPONENTS Network)
target_link_libraries(mytarget PRIVATE Qt6::Network)
```

Bold: Indicates a new term, an important word, or words that you see onscreen. For instance, words in menus or dialog boxes appear in **bold**. Here is an example: "Select **Application (Qt)** under the **Projects** window, and then select **Qt Widgets Application**."

> **Tips or important notes**
> Appear like this.

Get in touch

Feedback from our readers is always welcome.

General feedback: If you have questions about any aspect of this book, email us at customercare@ packtpub.com and mention the book title in the subject of your message.

Errata: Although we have taken every care to ensure the accuracy of our content, mistakes do happen. If you have found a mistake in this book, we would be grateful if you would report this to us. Please visit www.packtpub.com/support/errata and fill in the form.

Piracy: If you come across any illegal copies of our works in any form on the internet, we would be grateful if you would provide us with the location address or website name. Please contact us at copyright@packtpub.com with a link to the material.

If you are interested in becoming an author: If there is a topic that you have expertise in and you are interested in either writing or contributing to a book, please visit authors.packtpub.com.

Share Your Thoughts

Once you've read *Qt 6 C++ GUI Programming Cookbook*, we'd love to hear your thoughts! Scan the QR code below to go straight to the Amazon review page for this book and share your feedback.

https://packt.link/r/1805122630

Your review is important to us and the tech community and will help us make sure we're delivering excellent quality content.

Download a free PDF copy of this book

Thanks for purchasing this book!

Do you like to read on the go but are unable to carry your print books everywhere?

Is your eBook purchase not compatible with the device of your choice?

Don't worry, now with every Packt book you get a DRM-free PDF version of that book at no cost.

Read anywhere, any place, on any device. Search, copy, and paste code from your favorite technical books directly into your application.

The perks don't stop there, you can get exclusive access to discounts, newsletters, and great free content in your inbox daily

Follow these simple steps to get the benefits:

1. Scan the QR code or visit the link below

https://packt.link/free-ebook/978-1-80512-263-0

2. Submit your proof of purchase
3. That's it! We'll send your free PDF and other benefits to your email directly

1

Look-and-Feel Customization with Qt Designer

Qt 6 allows us to easily design our program's user interface through a method most people are familiar with. Qt not only provides us with a powerful user interface toolkit, called **Qt Designer**, which enables us to design our user interface without writing a single line of code, but it also allows advanced users to customize their user interface components through a simple scripting language called **Qt Style Sheet**.

In this chapter, we're going to cover the following recipes:

- Using style sheets with Qt Designer
- Customizing basic style sheets
- Creating a login screen using style sheets
- Using resources in style sheets
- Customizing properties and sub-controls
- Styling in **Qt Modeling Language** (**QML**)
- Exposing the QML object pointer to C++

Technical requirements

The technical requirements for this chapter include having **Qt 6.1.1 MinGW 64-bit** and **Qt Creator 12.0.2**. The code that's used in this chapter can be downloaded from this book's GitHub repository: `https://github.com/PacktPublishing/QT6-C-GUI-Programming-Cookbook---Third-Edition-/tree/main/Chapter01`.

Using style sheets with Qt Designer

In this example, we will learn how to change the look and feel of our program and make it look more professional by using style sheets and resources. Qt allows you to decorate your **graphical user interfaces (GUIs)** using a style sheet language called **Qt Style Sheets**, which is very similar to **Cascading Style Sheets (CSS)**, something that's used by web designers to decorate their websites.

How to do it...

Let's get started by learning how to create a new project and get ourselves familiar with Qt Designer:

1. Open up **Qt Creator** and create a new project. If this is the first time you have used Qt Creator, you can either click the big button, which reads **Create Project...**, or simply go to **File | New Project...**.

2. Select **Application (Qt)** from the **Projects** window and select **Qt Widgets Application**.

3. Click the **Choose...** button at the bottom. A window will pop out and ask you to insert the project's name and its location.

4. Click **Next** several times, then click the **Finish** button to create the project. We will stick with the default settings for now. Once the project has been created, the first thing you will see is a panel with tons of big icons on the left-hand side of the window, which is called the mode selector panel; we will discuss this in more detail in the *Dissecting Qt Designer* recipe.

5. You will see all your source files listed on the sidebar panel, which is located next to the mode selector panel. This is where you can select which file you want to edit. In this case, this is `mainwindow.ui`, because we are about to start designing the program's UI.

6. Double-click the `mainwindow.ui` file; you will see an entirely different interface appear out of nowhere. Qt Creator helped you switch from the script editor to the UI editor (Qt Designer) because it detected the `.ui` extension on the file you're trying to open.

7. You will also notice that the highlighted button on the mode selector panel has changed from **Edit** to **Design**. You can switch back to the script editor or change to any other tools by clicking one of the buttons located in the upper half of the mode selector panel.

8. Let's go back to Qt Designer and look at the `mainwindow.ui` file. This is the main window of our program (as the filename implies) and it's empty by default, without any widget on it. You can try to compile and run the program by pressing the **Run** button (the green arrow button) at the bottom of the mode selector panel; you will see an empty window pop up once the compilation is complete.

9. Let's add a push button to our program's UI by clicking on the **Push Button** item in the **Widget Box** area (under the **Buttons** category) and dragging it to our main window in the form editor. Keep the push button selected; you will see all the properties of this button inside the **Property Editor** area on the right-hand side of your window. Scroll down to the middle and look for a property called **styleSheet**. This is where you will apply styles to your widget, which may or may not be inherited from its children or grandchildren recursively, depending on how you set your style sheet. Alternatively, you can right-click on any widget in your UI at the form editor and select **Change styleSheet...** from the pop-up menu.

10. You can click on the input field of the **styleSheet** property to directly write the style sheet code, or click on the **...** button beside the input field to open up the **Edit Style Sheet** window, which has a bigger space for writing longer code for style sheets. At the top of the window, you can find several buttons, such as **Add Resource**, **Add Gradient**, **Add Color**, and **Add Font**, that can help you kickstart your coding if you can't remember the properties' names. Let's try to do some simple styling with the **Edit Style Sheet** window.

11. Click **Add Color** and choose a color.

12. Pick a random color from the color picker window – let's say, a pure red color. Then, click **OK**.

13. A line of code has been added to the text field in the **Edit Style Sheet** window, which in my case is as follows:

```
color: rgb(255, 0, 0);
```

14. Click the **OK** button; the text on your push button should change to red.

How it works...

Let's take a bit of time to get familiar with Qt Designer's interface before we start learning how to design our own UI:

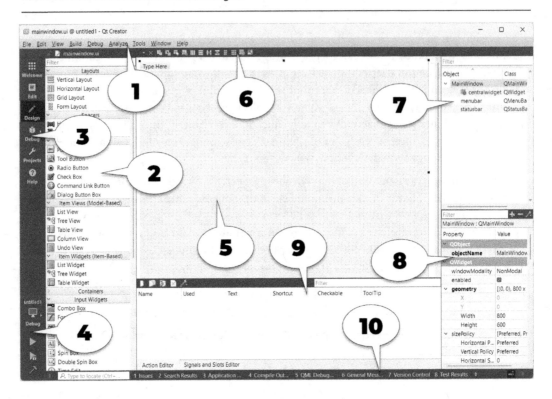

Figure 1.1 – Overview of Qt Designer's interface

The explanation for the preceding screenshot is as follows:

1. **Menu bar**: The menu bar houses application-specific menus that provide easy access to essential functions, such as creating new projects, saving files, undoing, redoing, copying, and pasting. It also allows you to access development tools that come with Qt Creator, such as the compiler, debugger, and profiler.

2. **Widget Box**: This is where you can find all the different types of widgets provided by Qt Designer. You can add a widget to your program's UI by clicking one of the widgets from the **Widget Box** area and dragging it to the form editor.

3. **Mode selector**: The mode selector is a side panel that places shortcut buttons for easy access to different tools. You can quickly switch between the script editor and form editor by clicking the **Edit** or **Design** button on the mode selector panel, which is very useful for multitasking. You can also easily navigate to the debugger and profiler tools at the same speed and manner.

4. **Build shortcuts**: The build shortcuts are located at the bottom of the mode selector panel. You can build, run, and debug your project easily by pressing the shortcut buttons here.

5. **Form editor**: The form editor is where you edit your program's UI. You can add different widgets to your program by selecting a widget from the **Widget Box** area and dragging it to the form editor.

6. **Form toolbar**: From here, you can quickly select a different form to edit. Click the drop-down box located at the top of the **Widget Box** area and select the file you want to open with Qt Designer. Beside the drop-down box are buttons to switch between the different modes of the form editor, and also buttons to change the layout of your UI.

7. **Object Inspector**: The **Object Inspector** area lists all the widgets within your current .ui file. All the widgets are arranged according to their parent-child relationship in the hierarchy. You can select a widget from the **Object Inspector** area to display its properties in the **Property Editor** area.

8. **Property Editor**: The **Property Editor** area will display all the properties of the widget you selected from either the **Object Inspector** area or the form editor window.

9. **Action Editor** and **Signals & Slots Editor**: This window contains two editors: **Action Editor** and **Signals & Slots Editor**. Both can be accessed from the tabs beneath the window. **Action Editor** is where you create actions that can be added to a menu bar or toolbar in your program's UI.

10. **Output panes**: Output panes consist of several different windows that display information and output messages related to script compilation and debugging. You can switch between different output panes by pressing the buttons that carry a number before them, such as **1 Issues**, **2 Search Results**, or **3 Application Output**.

There's more...

In this recipe, we discussed how to apply style sheets to Qt widgets through C++ coding. Although that method works well, most of the time, the person who is in charge of designing the program's UI is not the programmer, but rather a UI designer who specializes in designing user-friendly UI. In this case, it's better to let the UI designer design the program's layout and style sheet with a different tool and not mess around with the code. Qt provides an all-in-one editor called **Qt Creator**.

Qt Creator consists of several different tools, such as a script editor, compiler, debugger, profiler, and UI editor. The UI editor, which is also called **Qt Designer**, is the perfect tool for designers to design their program's UI without writing any code. This is because Qt Designer adopted the *what you see is what you get* approach by providing an accurate visual representation of the final result, which means whatever you design with Qt Designer will turn out the same visually when the program is compiled and run.

The similarities between Qt Style Sheets and CSS are as follows:

- This is how a typical piece of CSS code looks:

```
h1 { color: red; background-color: white;}
```

- This is how Qt Style Sheets look, which is almost the same as the preceding CSS:

```
QLineEdit { color: red; background-color: white;}
```

As you can see, both of them contain a selector and a declaration block. Each declaration contains a property and a value, separated by a colon. In Qt, a style sheet can be applied to a single widget by calling the `QObject::setStyleSheet()` function in C++ code.

Consider the following, for example:

```
myPushButton->setStyleSheet("color : blue");
```

The preceding code will turn the text of a button with the `myPushButton` variable name to blue. You can achieve the same result by writing the declaration in the style sheet property field in Qt Designer. We will discuss Qt Designer more in the *Customizing basic style sheets* recipe.

Qt Style Sheets also supports all the different types of selectors defined in the CSS2 standard, including the **universal selector**, **type selector**, **class selector**, and **ID selector**, which allows us to apply styling to a very specific individual widget or group of widgets. For instance, if we want to change the background color of a specific line-edit widget with the `usernameEdit` object name, we can do this by using an ID selector to refer to it:

QLineEdit#usernameEdit { background-color: blue }

> **Note**
> To learn about all the selectors available in CSS2 (which are also supported by Qt Style Sheets), please refer to this document: `http://www.w3.org/TR/REC-CSS2/selector.html`.

Customizing basic style sheets

In the previous recipe, you learned how to apply a style sheet to a widget with Qt Designer. Let's go crazy and push things further by creating a few other types of widgets and changing their style properties to something bizarre for the sake of learning.

This time, however, we will not apply the style to every single widget one by one; instead, we will learn to apply the style sheet to the main window and let it inherit down the hierarchy to all the other widgets so that the style sheet is easier to manage and maintain in the long run.

How to do it...

In the following example, we will format different types of widgets on the canvas and add some code to the style sheet to change its appearance:

1. Remove the style sheet from `PushButton` by selecting it and clicking the small arrow button beside the **styleSheet** property. This button will revert the property to its default value, which in this case is the empty style sheet.

2. Add a few more widgets to the UI by dragging them one by one from the **Widget Box** area to the form editor. I've added a line edit, combo box, horizontal slider, radio button, and a check box.

3. For the sake of simplicity, delete **menuBar**, **mainToolBar**, and **statusBar** from your UI by selecting them in the **Object Inspector** area, right-clicking, and choosing **Remove**. Now, your UI should look similar to this:

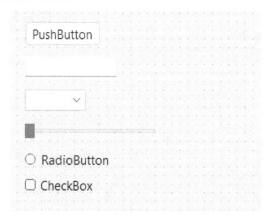

Figure 1.2 – Dragging and dropping some widgets onto the form editor

4. Select the main window from either the form editor or the **Object Inspector** area, then right-click and choose **Change styleSheet...** to open the **Edit Style Sheet** window. Insert the following into the style sheet:

```
border: 2px solid gray;
border-radius: 10px;
padding: 0 8px;
background: yellow;
```

5. You will see a bizarre-looking UI with everything covered in yellow with a thick border. This is because the preceding style sheet does not have a selector, which means the style will apply to the children widgets of the main window down the hierarchy. To change that, let's try something different:

```
QPushButton {
        border: 2px solid gray;
        border-radius: 10px;
        padding: 0 8px;
        background: yellow;
}
```

6. This time, only **PushButton** will get the style described in the preceding code, and all the other widgets will return to the default styling. You can try to add a few more push buttons to your UI; they will all look the same:

Figure 1.3 – Changing the push buttons to yellow

7. This happens because we specifically tell the selector to apply the style to all the widgets with the QPushButton class. We can also apply the style to just one of the push buttons by mentioning its name in the style sheet, as shown in the following code:

```
QPushButton#pushButton_3 {
        border: 2px solid gray;
        border-radius: 10px;
        padding: 0 8px;
        background: yellow;
}
```

8. Once you understand this method, we can add the following code to the style sheet:

```
QPushButton {
    color: red;
    border: 0px;
    padding: 0 8px;
    background: white;
}
QPushButton#pushButton_2 {
    border: 1px solid red;
    border-radius: 10px;
}
```

9. This code changes the style of all the push buttons, as well as some properties of the pushButton_2 button. We keep the style sheet of pushButton_3 as-is. Now, the buttons will look like this:

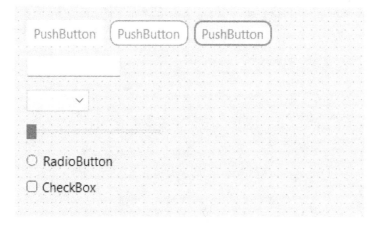

Figure 1.4 – Applying a different style to each button

10. The first set of style sheets will change all widgets of the QPushButton type to a white rectangular button with no border and red text. The second set of style sheets only changes the border of a specific QPushButton widget called pushButton_2. Notice that the background color and text color of pushButton_2 remain white and red, respectively, because we didn't override them in the second set of style sheets, hence it will return to the style described in the first set of style sheets since it applies to all the QPushButton widgets. The text of the third button has also changed to red because we didn't describe the **Color** property in the third set of style sheets.

11. Create another set of style sheets that use the universal selector by using the following code:

```
* {
    background: qradialgradient(cx: 0.3, cy: -0.4, fx: 0.3, fy:
-0.4, radius: 1.35, stop: 0 #fff, stop: 1 #888);
    color: rgb(255, 255, 255);
    border: 1px solid #ffffff;
}
```

12. The universal selector will affect all the widgets, regardless of their type. Therefore, the preceding style sheet will apply a nice gradient color to all the widgets' backgrounds and set their text to white with a one-pixel solid outline that is also white. Instead of writing the name of the color (that is, white), we can use the rgb function (rgb(255, 255, 255)) or hex code (#ffffff) to describe the color value.

13. As before, the preceding style sheet will not affect the push buttons because we have already given them their own styles, which will override the general style described in the universal selector. Just remember that in Qt, the more specific style will ultimately be used when there is more than one style with an influence on a widget. This is how the UI will look now:

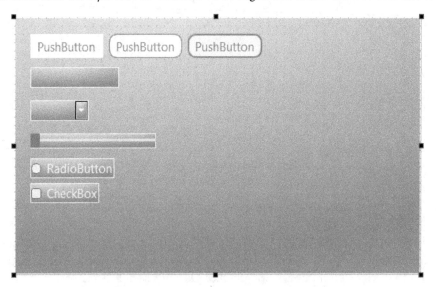

Figure 1.5 – Applying a gradient background to all the other widgets

How it works...

If you are ever involved in web development using HTML and CSS, Qt's style sheets work the same way as CSS. Style sheets provide the definitions to describe the presentation of the widgets – what the colors are for each element in the widget group, how thick the border should be, and so on. If you specify the name of the widget to the style sheet, it will change the style of the particular `PushButton` widget with the name you provide. None of the other widgets will be affected and will remain as the default style.

To change the name of a widget, select the widget from either the form editor or the **Object Inspector** area and change the **objectName** property in the property window. If you used the ID selector previously to change the style of the widget, changing its object name will break the style sheet and lose the style. To fix this problem, simply change the object name in the style sheet as well.

Creating a login screen using style sheets

Next, we will learn how to put all the knowledge we learned in the previous recipe together and create a fake graphical login screen for an imaginary operating system. Style sheets are not the only thing you need to master to design a good UI. You will also need to learn how to arrange the widgets neatly using the layout system in Qt Designer.

How to do it...

Let's get started by following these steps:

1. We need to design the layout of the graphical login screen before we start doing anything. Planning is very important to produce good software. The following is a sample layout design I made to show you how I imagine the login screen will look. Just a simple line drawing like this is sufficient, so long as it conveys the message clearly:

Figure 1.6 – A simple drawing depicting the login screen

2. Go back to Qt Designer again.

3. We will be placing the widgets at the top panel first, then the logo and the login form beneath it.

4. Select the main window and change its width and height from 400 and 300 to 800 and 600, respectively – we'll need a bigger space in which to place all the widgets.

5. Click and drag a label under the **Display Widgets** category from the **Widget Box** area to the form editor.

6. Change the **objectName** property of the label to `currentDateTime` and change its text property to the current date and time for display purposes – for example, `Wednesday, 25-10-2023 3:14 PM`.

7. Click and drag `PushButton` under the **Buttons** category to the form editor. Repeat this process once more because we have two buttons on the top panel. Rename the two buttons `restartButton` and `shutdownButton`.

8. Select the main window and click the small icon button on the form toolbar that says **Lay Out Vertically** when you mouse over it. You will see that the widgets are automatically arranged on the main window, but that's not exactly what we want yet.

9. Click and drag a **Horizontal Layout** widget under the **Layouts** category to the main window.

10. Click and drag the two push buttons and the text label into the horizontal layout. You will see the three widgets being arranged in a horizontal row, but vertically, they are located in the middle of the screen. The horizontal arrangement is almost correct, but the vertical position is off.

11. Click and drag a **Vertical Spacer** widget from the **Spacers** category and place it beneath the **Horizontal Layout** widget we created in *Step 9* (under the red rectangular outline). All the widgets will be pushed to the top by the spacer.

12. Place a **Horizontal Spacer** widget between the text label and the two buttons to keep them apart. This will ensure the text label always sticks to the left and the buttons align to the right.

13. Set both the **Horizontal Policy** and **Vertical Policy** properties of the two buttons to **Fixed** and set the **minimumSize** property to 55 x 55. Set the **text** property of the buttons to empty, as we will be using icons instead of text. We will learn how to place an icon in the button widgets in the *Using resources in style sheets* recipe.

14. Your UI should look similar to this:

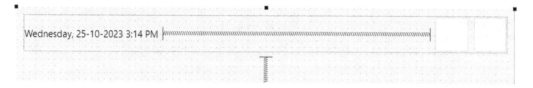

Figure 1.7 – Pushing apart the text and buttons using a horizontal spacer

Next, we will be adding the logo. Follow these steps:

1. Add a **Horizontal Layout** widget between the top panel and a **Vertical Spacer** widget to serve as a container for the logo.

2. After adding the **Horizontal Layout** widget, you will find that the layout is way too thin in height (almost zero height) for you to add any widgets to it. This is because the layout is empty and it's being pushed by the vertical spacer under it into zero height. To solve this problem, we can set its **vertical margin** (either **layoutTopMargin** or **layoutBottomMargin**) to be temporarily bigger until a widget is added to the layout.

3. Add a **Label** value to the **Horizontal Layout** widget that you just created and rename it logo. We will learn more about how to insert an image into the label to use it as a logo in the *Using resources in style sheets* recipe. For now, just empty out the **text** property and set both its **Horizontal Policy** and **Vertical Policy** properties to **Fixed**. Set the **minimumSize** property to 150 x 150.

4. Set the vertical margin of the layout back to zero if you haven't already done so.

5. The logo will now appear to be invisible, so we will just place a temporary style sheet to make it visible until we add an image to it in the *Using resources in style sheets* recipe. The style sheet is really simple:

```
border: 1px solid;
```

Your UI should look similar to this:

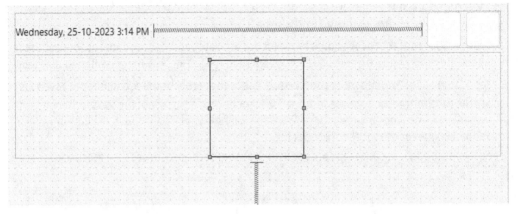

Figure 1.8 – Putting the placeholder logo in the middle

Now, let's create the login form:

1. Add a **Horizontal Layout** widget between the logo's layout and the **Vertical Spacer** widget. Set the **layoutTopMargin** property to a large number (that is, 100) so that you can add a widget to it more easily.

2. Add a **Vertical Layout** widget inside the **Horizontal Layout** widget you just created. This layout will be used as a container for the login form. Set its **layoutTopMargin** property to a number lower than that of the horizontal layout (that is, 20) so that we can place widgets in it.

3. Right-click the **Vertical Layout** widget you just created and choose **Morph into | QWidget**. Here, **Vertical Layout** is converted into an empty widget. This step is essential because we will be adjusting the width and height of the container for the login form. A layout widget does not contain any properties for width and height, only margins, since a layout will expand toward the space surrounding it. This makes sense considering that it does not have any size properties. Once you have converted the layout into a QWidget object, it will automatically inherit all the properties from the widget class, which means we can now adjust its size to suit our needs.

4. Rename the QWidget object, which we just converted from the layout, loginForm and change both its **Horizontal Policy** and **Vertical Policy** properties to **Fixed**. Set the **minimumSize** parameter to 350 x 200.

5. Since we already placed the loginForm widget inside **Horizontal Layout**, we can set its **layoutTopMargin** property back to zero.

6. Add the same style sheet that you did for the logo to the loginForm widget to make it visible temporarily. However, this time, we need to add an ID selector in front so that it will only apply the style to loginForm and not its children widgets:

```
#loginForm { border: 1px solid; }
```

Your UI should look something like this:

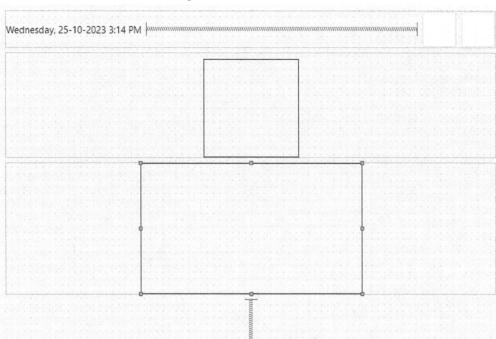

Figure 1.9 – Constructing the frame for the login form

We are not done with the login form yet. Now that we have created the container for the login form, it's time to put more widgets into the form:

1. Place two horizontal layouts in the login form container. We need two layouts: one for the username field and another for the password field.

2. Add **Label** and **Line Edit** properties to each of the layouts you just added. Change the **text** property of the upper label to Username: and the one beneath to Password:. Rename the two line edits to username and password, respectively.

3. Add a push button beneath the password layout and change its **text** property to Login. Rename it loginButton.

4. You can add a **Vertical Spacer** widget between the password layout and the Login button to distance them slightly. After the **Vertical Spacer** widget has been placed, change its **sizeType** property to **Fixed** and change its **Height** property to 5.

5. Select the loginForm container and set all its margins to 35. This is to make the login form look better by adding some space to all its sides.

6. Set the **Height** property of the Username, Password, and loginButton widgets to 25 so that they don't look so cramped.

    Your UI should look something like this:

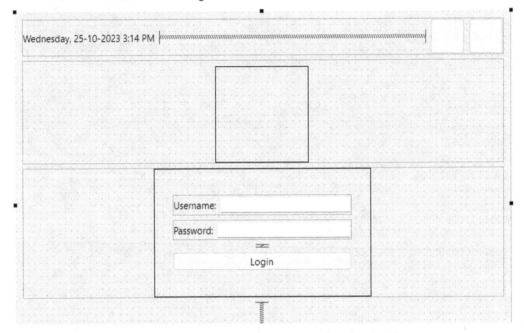

Figure 1.10 – Adding widgets to the login form

> **Note**
> Alternatively, you can use a grid layout for the **Username** and **Password** fields to keep their sizes uniform.

We're not done yet! As you can see, the login form and the logo are both sticking to the top of the main window due to the **Vertical Spacer** widget beneath them. The logo and the login form should be placed at the center of the main window instead of the top. To fix this problem, follow these steps:

1. Add another **Vertical Spacer** widget between the top panel and the logo's layout. This will counter the spacer at the bottom to balance out the alignment.

2. If you think that the logo is sticking too close to the login form, you can add a **Vertical Spacer** widget between the logo's layout and the login form's layout. Set its **sizeType** property to **Fixed** and its **Height** property to 10.

3. Right-click the top panel's layout and choose **Morph into | QWidget**. Rename it `topPanel`. The layout must be converted into **QWidget** because we cannot apply style sheets to a layout. This is because a layout doesn't have any properties other than margins.

4. There is a little bit of a margin around the edges of the main window – we don't want that. To remove the margins, select the **centralWidget** object from the **Object Inspector** window, which is right under the **MainWindow** panel, and set all the margin values to zero.

5. Run the project by clicking the **Run** button (with the green arrow icon) to see what your program looks like. If everything goes well, you should see something like this:

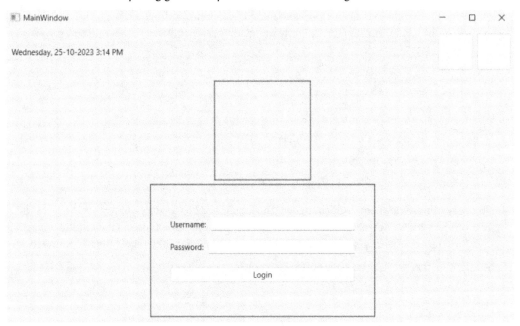

Figure 1.11 – We're done with the layout – for now

6. Now, let's decorate the UI using style sheets! Since all the important widgets have been given object names, it's easier for us to apply the style sheets to them from the main window since we will only write the style sheets to the main window and let them inherit down the hierarchy tree.

7. Right-click on **MainWindow** from the **Object Inspector** area and choose **Change styleSheet...**.

8. Add the following code to the style sheet:

```
#centralWidget { background: rgba(32, 80, 96, 100); }
```

9. The background of the main window will change color. We will learn how to use an image for the background in the *Using resources in style sheets* recipe. So, the color is just temporary.

10. In Qt, if you want to apply styles to the main window itself, you must apply them to its **centralWidget** widget instead of the main window since the window is just a container.

11. Add a nice gradient color to the top panel:

```
#topPanel {
        background-color: qlineargradient(spread:reflect, x1:0.5,
y1:0, x2:0, y2:0, stop:0 rgba(91, 204, 233, 100), stop:1
rgba(32, 80, 96, 100));
}
```

12. Apply the black color to the login form and make it look semi-transparent. We will also make the corners of the login form container slightly rounded by setting the border-radius property:

```
#loginForm {
        background: rgba(0, 0, 0, 80);
        border-radius: 8px;
}
```

13. Apply styles to the general types of widgets:

```
QLabel { color: white; }
QLineEdit { border-radius: 3px; }
```

14. The preceding style sheets will change all the labels' texts to a white color; this includes the text on the widgets as well because, internally, Qt uses the same type of label on the widgets that have text on them. Also, we made the corners of the line edit widgets slightly rounded.

15. Apply style sheets to all the push buttons on our UI:

```
QPushButton {
        color: white;
        background-color: #27a9e3;
        border-width: 0px;
        border-radius: 3px;
}
```

16. The preceding style sheet changes the text of all the buttons to a white color, then sets its background color to blue, and makes its corners slightly rounded.

17. To push things even further, we will make it so that the color of the push buttons changes when we mouse over it by using the hover keyword:

```
QPushButton:hover { background-color: #66c011; }
```

18. The preceding style sheet will change the background color of the push buttons to green when we mouse over them. We will talk more about this in the *Customizing properties and sub-controls* recipe.

19. You can further adjust the size and margins of the widgets to make them look even better. Remember to remove the border line of the login form by removing the style sheet that we applied directly to it in *step 6*.

20. Your login screen should look something like this:

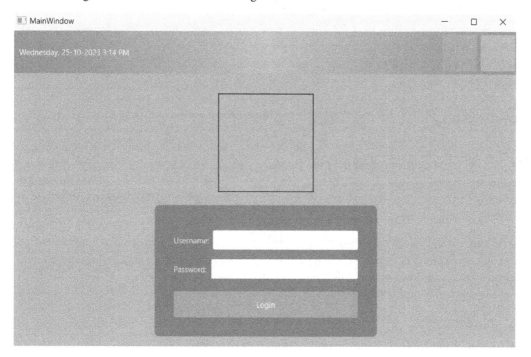

Figure 1.12 – Applying colors and styles to the widgets

How it works...

This example focused more on the layout system of Qt. Qt's layout system allows our application GUI to automatically arrange itself within the given space by arranging the children objects of each widget. The spacer items that we used in this recipe help push the widgets contained in a layout outward to create spacing along the width of the spacer item.

To locate a widget in the middle of the layout, we must put two spacer items into the layout: one on the left-hand side of the widget and one on the right-hand side of the widget. The widget will then be pushed to the middle of the layout by the two spacers.

Using resources in style sheets

Qt provides us with a platform-independent resource system that allows us to store any type of file in our program's executable for later use. There is no limit to the types of files we can store in our executable – images, audio, video, HTML, XML, text files, binary files, and so on are all permitted.

The resource system is really useful for embedding resource files (such as icons and translation files) into the executable so that it can be accessed by the application at any time. To achieve this, we must tell Qt which files we want to add to its resource system in the .qrc file; Qt will handle the rest during the build process.

How to do it...

To add a new .qrc file to our project, go to **File | New File**. Then, select **Qt** under the **Files and Classes** category and select **Qt Resources File**. After that, give it a name (that is, resources) and click the **Next** button, followed by the **Finish** button. The .qrc file will now be created and automatically opened by Qt Creator. You don't have to edit the .qrc file directly in XML format as Qt Creator provides you with the user interface to manage your resources.

To add images and icons to your project, you need to make sure that the images and icons are being placed in your project's directory. While the .qrc file is opened in Qt Creator, click the **Add** button, followed by the **Add Prefix** button. The prefix is used to categorize your resources so that they can be better managed when you have a ton of resources in your project:

1. Rename the prefix you just created to /icons.

2. Create another prefix by clicking **Add**, followed by **Add Prefix**.

3. Rename the new prefix /images.

4. Select the /icon prefix and click **Add**, followed by **Add Files**.

5. A file selection window will appear; use that to select all the icon files. You can select multiple files at a time by holding the *Ctrl* key on your keyboard while clicking on the files to select them. Click **Open** once you're done.

6. Select the /images prefix and click the **Add** button, followed by the **Add Files** button. The file-selection window will pop up again; this time, we will select the background image.

7. Repeat the preceding steps, but this time, we will add the logo image to the /images prefix. Don't forget to save once you're done by pressing *Ctrl + S*. Your .qrc file should now look like this:

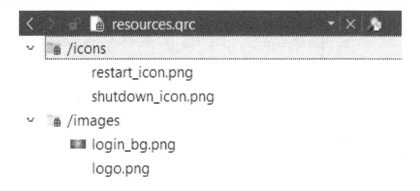

Figure 1.13 – Showing the structure of the resource file

8. Go back to the mainwindow.ui file; let's make use of the resources we have just added to our project. Select the restart button located on the top panel. Scroll down the **Property Editor** area until you see the **icon** property. Click the little button with a drop-down arrow icon and click **Choose Resources** from its menu.

9. The **Select Resource** window will pop up. Click on the icons prefix on the left panel and select the restart icon on the right panel. Press **OK**.

10. A tiny icon will appear on the button. This icon looks very tiny because the default icon size is set to 16 x 16. Change the **iconSize** property to 50 x 50; you will see that the icon appears bigger. Repeat the preceding steps for the shutdown button, except this time, choose the shutdown icon instead.

11. The two buttons should now look like this:

Figure 1.14 – Applying icons to the push buttons

12. Let's use the image we added to the resource file as our logo. Select the logo widget and remove the style sheet that we added earlier to render its outline.

13. Scroll down the **Property Editor** area until you see the **pixmap** property.

14. Click the little drop-down button behind the **pixmap** property and select **Choose Resources** from the menu. Select the logo image and click **OK**. The logo size no longer follows the dimension you set previously; it follows the actual dimension of the image instead. We cannot change its dimension because this is simply how the **pixmap** property works.

15. If you want more control over the logo's dimension, you can remove the image from the **pixmap** property and use a style sheet instead. You can use the following code to apply an image to the icon container:

```
border-image: url(:/images/logo.png);
```

16. To obtain the path of the image, right-click the image's name in the file list window and choose **Copy path**. The path will be saved to your operating system's clipboard; now, you can just paste it into the preceding style sheet. Using this method will ensure that the image fits the dimensions of the widget that you applied the style to. Your logo should now appear like what's shown in the following screenshot:

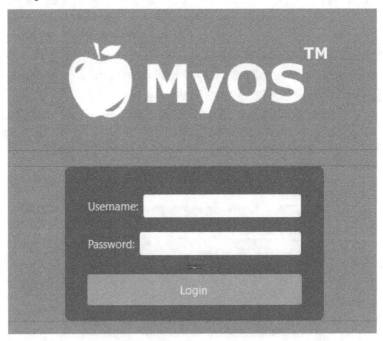

Figure 1.15 – The logo is now appearing at the top of the login form

17. Apply the wallpaper image to the background using a style sheet. Since the background dimension will change according to the window size, we cannot use **pixmap** here. Instead, we will use the `border-image` property in a style sheet. Right-click the main window and select **Change styleSheet...** to open the **Edit Style Sheet** window. We will add a new line under the style sheet of the **centralWidget** widget:

```
#centralWidget {
    background: rgba(32, 80, 96, 100);
    border-image: url(:/images/login_bg.png);
}
```

18. It's really that simple and easy! Your login screen should now look like this:

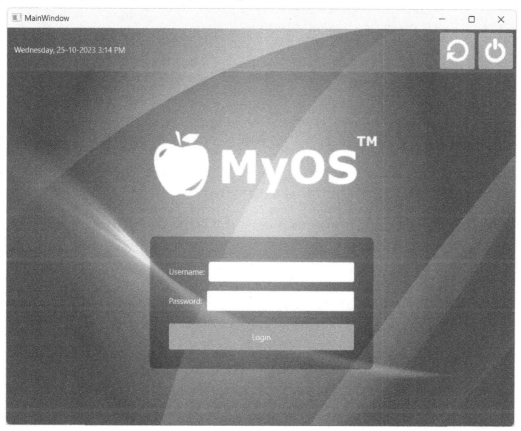

Figure 1.16 – The final result looks neat

How it works...

The resource system in Qt stores binary files, such as images and translation files, in the executable when it gets compiled. It reads the **resource collection files** (.qrc) in your project to locate the files that need to be stored in the executable and include them in the build process. A .qrc file looks something like this:

```
<!DOCTYPE RCC>
<RCC version="1.0">
    <qresource>
        <file>images/copy.png</file>
        <file>images/cut.png</file>
        <file>images/new.png</file>
        <file>images/open.png</file>
        <file>images/paste.png</file>
        <file>images/save.png</file>
    </qresource>
</RCC>
```

It uses **XML format** to store the paths of the resource files, which are relative to the directory that contains them. The listed resource files must be located in the same directory as the .qrc file, or one of its subdirectories.

Customizing properties and sub-controls

Qt's style sheet system enables us to create stunning and professional-looking UIs with ease. In this example, we will learn how to set custom properties for our widgets and use them to switch between different styles.

How to do it...

Follow these steps to customize widget properties and sub-controls:

1. Let's create a new Qt project. I have prepared the UI for this purpose. The UI contains three buttons on the left-hand side and a **tab widget** with three pages located on the right-hand side, as shown in the following screenshot:

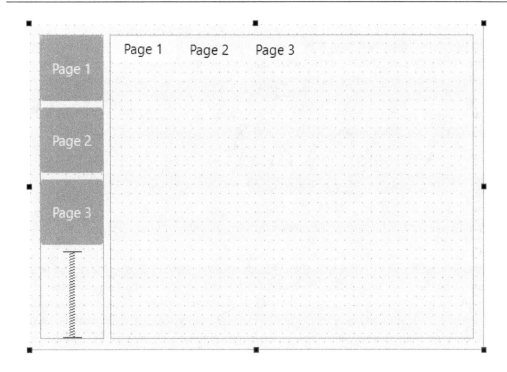

Figure 1.17 – Basic user interface with three tabs and buttons

2. The three buttons are blue because I've added the following style sheet to the main window (not to the individual button):

```
QPushButton {
    color: white;
    background-color: #27a9e3;
    border-width: 0px;
    border-radius: 3px;
}
```

3. I will explain what **pseudo-states** are in Qt by adding the following style sheet to the main window. You might be familiar with this:

```
QPushButton:hover {
    color: white;
    background-color: #66c011;
    border-width: 0px;
    border-radius: 3px;
}
```

4. We used the preceding style sheet in the *Creating a login screen using style sheets* recipe, to make the buttons change color when there is a mouse-over event. This is made possible by Qt Style Sheet's **pseudo-state**, which in this case is the word hover separated from the QPushButton class by a colon. Every widget has a set of generic pseudo-states, such as **active**, **disabled**, and **enabled**, and also a set of pseudo-states that apply to their widget type. For example, states such as **open** and **flat** are available for QPushButton, but not for QLineEdit. Let's add the **pressed** pseudo-state to change the buttons' color to yellow when the user clicks on it:

```
QPushButton:pressed {
    color: white;
    background-color: yellow;
    border-width: 0px;
    border-radius: 3px;
}
```

5. Pseudo-states allow the users to load a different set of style sheets based on the condition that applies to them. Qt pushes this concept further by implementing **dynamic properties** in Qt Style Sheets. This allows us to change the style sheet of a widget when a custom condition has been met. We can make use of this feature to change the style sheet of our buttons based on a custom condition that we can set using custom properties in Qt. First, we will add this style sheet to our main window:

```
QPushButton[pagematches=true] {
    color: white;
    background-color: red;
    border-width: 0px;
    border-radius: 3px;
}
```

6. This changes the push button's background color to red if the pagematches property returns **true**. This property does not exist in the QPushButton class. However, we can add it to our buttons using QObject::setProperty():

    • In your mainwindow.cpp source code, add the following code right after ui->setupUi(this):

    ```
    ui->button1->setProperty("pagematches", true);
    ```

The preceding code will add a custom property called pagematches to the first button and set its value as true. This will make the first button turn red by default.

- After that, right-click on **Tab Widget** and choose **Go to slot…**. A window will pop up; select the `currentChanged(int)` option from the list and click **OK**. Qt will generate a slot function for you, which looks something like this:

```
private slots:
void on_tabWidget_currentChanged(int index);
```

- The **slot function** will be called whenever we change the page of **Tab Widget**. We can then decide what we want it to do by adding our code to the slot function. To do that, open `mainwindow.cpp`; you will see the function's declaration there. Let's add some code to the function:

```
void MainWindow::on_tabWidget_currentChanged(int
index) {
    // Set all buttons to false
    ui->button1->setProperty("pagematches", false);
    ui->button2->setProperty("pagematches", false);
    ui->button3->setProperty("pagematches", false);
    // Set one of the buttons to true
    if (0 == index)
        ui->button1->setProperty("pagematches", true);
    else if (index == 1)
        ui->button2->setProperty("pagematches", true);
    else
        ui->button3->setProperty("pagematches", true);
    // Update buttons style
    ui->button1->style()->polish(ui->button1);
    ui->button2->style()->polish(ui->button2);
    ui->button3->style()->polish(ui->button3);
}
```

7. The preceding code sets the `pagematches` properties of all three buttons to **false** when **Tab Widget** switches its current page. Be sure to reset everything before we decide which button should change to red.

8. Check the `index` variable supplied by the event signal; this will tell you the index number of the current page. Set the `pagematches` property of one of the buttons to **true**, based on the `index` number.

9. Refresh the style of all three buttons by calling `polish()`. You may also want to add the following header to `mainwindow.h`:

```
#include <QStyle>
```

10. Build and run the project. You should now see the three buttons changing to red whenever you switch **Tab Widget** to a different page. Also, the buttons will change to green when there is a mouse-over, as well as change to yellow when you click on them:

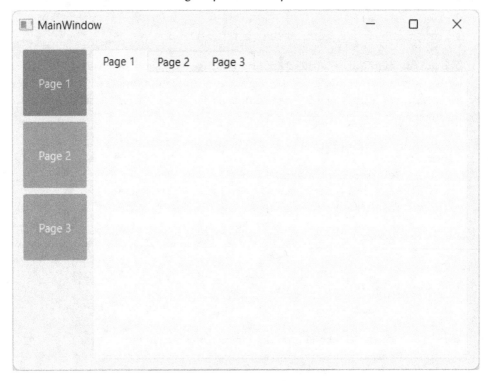

Figure 1.18 – The final result looks like this

How it works...

Qt provides users the freedom to add custom properties to any type of widget. Custom properties are very useful if you want to change a particular widget when a special condition is met, whereas Qt doesn't provide such a context by default. This allows the user to extend the usability of Qt and makes it a flexible tool for customized solutions.

For example, if we have a row of buttons on our main window and we need one of them to change its color depending on which page **Tab Widget** is currently showing, there is no way the buttons would know when they should change their color because Qt itself has no built-in context for this type of situation. To solve this issue, Qt gives us a method to add our own properties to the widgets, which uses a generic function called QObject::setProperty(). To read the custom property, we can use another function called QObject::property().

Next, we will talk about sub-controls in Qt Style Sheets. Often, a widget is not just a single object, but a combination of more than one object or control, used to form a more complex widget. These objects are called **sub-controls**.

For example, a spin box widget contains an input field, a down button, an up button, an up arrow, and a down arrow, which is quite complicated compared to some other widgets. In this case, Qt grants us more flexibility by allowing us to change every sub-control using a style sheet if we want to. We can do so by specifying the name of the sub-control behind the widget's class name, separated by a double colon. For instance, if I want to change the image of the down button to a spin box, I can write my style sheet as follows:

```
QSpinBox::down-button {
    image: url(:/images/spindown.png);
    subcontrol-origin: padding;
    subcontrol-position: right bottom;
}
```

This will only apply the image to the down button of my spin box, and not to any other parts of the widget. By combining **custom properties**, **pseudo-states**, and **sub-controls**, Qt provides us with a very flexible method to customize our user interface.

> **Note**
>
> Visit the following link to learn more about pseudo-states and subcontrols in Qt: http://doc.qt.io/qt-6/stylesheet-reference.html.

Styling in Qt Modeling Language (QML)

Qt Meta Language or **Qt Modeling Language** (QML) is a JavaScript-inspired user interface markup language that's used by Qt to design user interfaces. Qt provides you with **Qt Quick Components** (widgets powered by the QML technology) to easily design touch-friendly UI without C++ programming. We will learn more about how to use QML and Qt Quick Components to design our program's UI by following the steps provided in this recipe.

How to do it...

Follow these steps to learn about styling in QML:

1. Since Qt 6, The Qt Company has released a separate program called **Qt Design Studio** for developing Qt Quick applications. It's intended to separate the different tasks of designers and programmers. So, if you're a GUI designer, you should use **Qt Design Studio**, while sticking to Qt Creator if you're a programmer. Once you have installed and opened Qt Design Studio, create a new project by pressing on the big **Create Project...** button or by going to **File | New Project...** from the top menu:

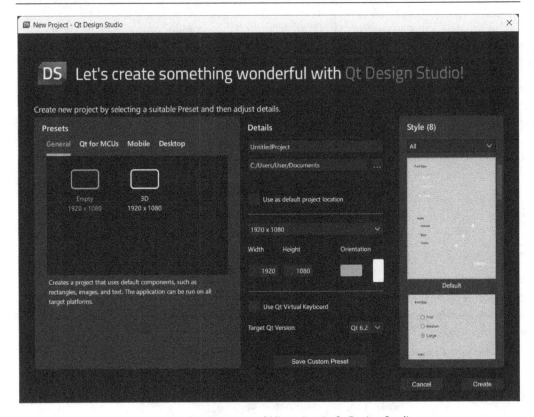

Figure 1.19 – Creating a new QML project in Qt Design Studio

2. Once the **New Project** window appears, key in the default width and height of your project window and insert a name for your project. Then, select the directory where you want your project to be created, select a default GUI style, pick a target Qt version, and click the **Create** button. Your Qt Quick project will now be created by Qt Design Studio.

3. There are some differences between a **QML project** and a **C++ Qt project**. You will see an App. qml file inside the project resource. This .qml file is the UI description file that's written using the QML markup language. If you double-click the main.qml file, Qt Creator will open the script editor and you will see something like this:

```
import QtQuick 6.2
import QtQuick.Window 6.2
import MyProject
Window {
    width: mainScreen.width
    height: mainScreen.height
    visible: true
    title: "MyProject"
```

```
        Screen01 {
            id: mainScreen
        }
    }
```

4. This file tells Qt to create a window that loads the **Screen01** user interface and a window title with your project name. The **Screen01** interface comes from another file called **Screen01.ui.qml**.

5. If you open the `main.cpp` file located in the `scr` folder in your project, you will see the following line of code:

```
QQmlApplicationEngine engine;
const QUrl url(u"qrc:Main/main.qml"_qs);
```

6. The preceding code tells Qt's QML engine to load the `main.qml` file when the program starts. If you want to load the other `.qml` file, you know where to look for the code. The `src` folder is hidden from your Qt Design Studio project; you can look for it inside your project directory.

7. If you build the project now, all you'll get is a huge window with simple text and a push button that says **Press me**. The window's background color and the text will change when you press the push button:

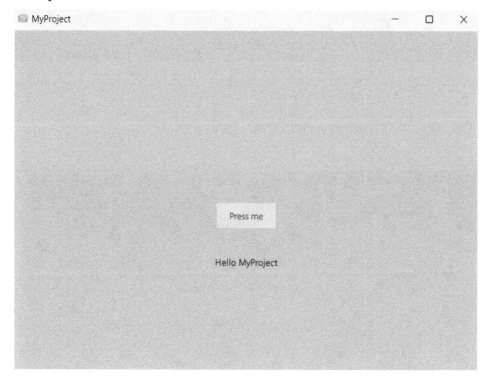

Figure 1.20 – Your first Qt Quick program

8. To add UI elements, we'll create a **Qt Quick UI File** by going to **File** | **New File…** and selecting **Qt Quick UI File** under the **Files and Classes** | **Qt Quick Files** category:

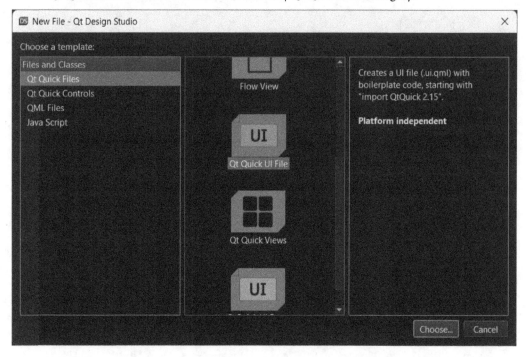

Figure 1.21 - Creating a new Qt Quick UI file

9. Set **Component name** to Main, followed by clicking the **Finish** button:

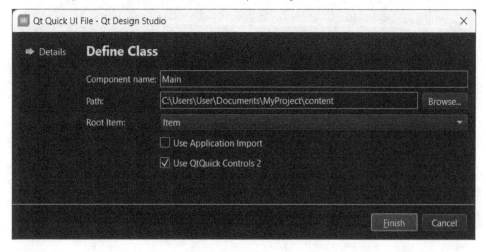

Figure 1.22 – Giving your Qt Quick component a meaningful name

10. A new file called `Main.ui.qml` has been added to your project resources. Try to open the `Main.ui.qml` file by double-clicking on it, if it hasn't been automatically opened by Qt Design Studio upon creation. You will see a completely different UI editor compared to what we had for the C++ project in the previous recipes.

11. Let's open `App.qml` and replace **Screen01** with **Main**, like so:

```
Main {
    id: mainScreen
}
```

12. When `App.qml` is loaded by the QML engine, it will also import `Main.ui.qml` into the UI since `Main` is now being called in the `App.qml` file. Qt will check whether `Main` is a valid UI by searching for its `.qml` file based on the naming convention. This concept is similar to the C++ project we completed in all our previous recipes; the `App.qml` file acts like the `main.cpp` file and `Main.ui.qml` acts like the `MainWindow` class. You can also create other UI templates and use them in `App.qml`. Hopefully, this comparison will make it easier to understand how QML works.

13. Open `Main.ui.qml`. You should see only one item listed in the **Navigator** window: **Item**. This is the base layout of the window, which shouldn't be deleted. It is similar to **centralWidget**, which we used in the previous recipe.

14. The canvas is empty at the moment, so let's drag a **Mouse Area** item and **Text** items to the canvas from the **QML Types** panel on the left. Resize **Mouse Area** so that it fills the entire canvas. Also, make sure that both **Mouse Area** and the **Text** items are being placed under the **Item** item in the **Navigator** panel, as shown in the following screenshot:

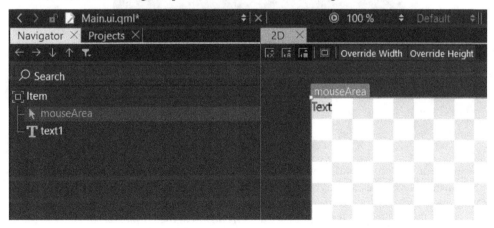

Figure 1.23 – Dragging and dropping a mouse area and text items onto the canvas

15. The **Mouse Area** item is an invincible item that gets triggered when the mouse is clicking on it, or when a finger is touching it (for mobile platforms). The **Mouse Area** item is also used in a **button** component, which we will be using in a while. The **Text** item is self-explanatory: it is a label that displays a block of text in the application.

16. On the **Navigator** window, we can hide or show an item by clicking on the icon that resembles an eye beside the item. When an item is hidden, it will not appear on the canvas or the compiled application. Just like the widgets in a C++ Qt project, Qt Quick Components are arranged in a hierarchy based on the parent-child relationship. All the child items will be placed under the parent item with an indented position. In our case, we can see that the **Mouse Area** and **Text** elements are positioned slightly to the right compared to the **Item** item because they are both children of the **Item** element. We can rearrange the parent-child relationship, as well as their position in the hierarchy, by using a click-and-drag method from the **Navigator** window. You can try clicking on the **Text** item and dragging it on top of the mouse area. You will then see that the **Text** item has changed its position and is now located beneath the mouse area with a wider indentation:

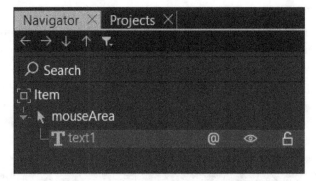

Figure 1.24 – Rearranging the parent-child relationship between items

17. We can rearrange them by using the arrow buttons located at the top of the **Navigator** window, as shown in the preceding screenshot. Anything that happens to the parent item will also affect all its children, such as moving the parent item, and hiding and showing the parent item.

> **Note**
> You can pan around the canvas view by holding the middle mouse button (or mouse scroll) while moving your mouse around. You can also zoom in and out by scrolling your mouse while holding the *Ctrl* key on your keyboard. By default, scrolling your mouse will move the canvas view up and down. However, if your mouse cursor is on top of the horizontal scroll bar of the canvas, scrolling the mouse will move the view to the left and right.

18. Delete both the **Mouse Area** item and **Text** items as we will be learning how to create a user interface from scratch using QML and Qt Quick.

19. Set the **Item** element's size to 800 x 600 as we're going to need a bigger space for the widgets.

20. Copy the images we used in the previous C++ project, in the *Using resources in style sheets* recipe, over to the QML project's folder since we are going to recreate the same login screen with QML.

21. Add the images to the resource file so that we can use them for our UI.

22. Open **Qt Design Studio** and switch to the **Resources** window. Click and drag the background image directly to the canvas. Switch over to the **Layout** tab on the **Properties** pane and click the fill anchor button, indicated here by a red circle. This will make the background image always stick to the window size:

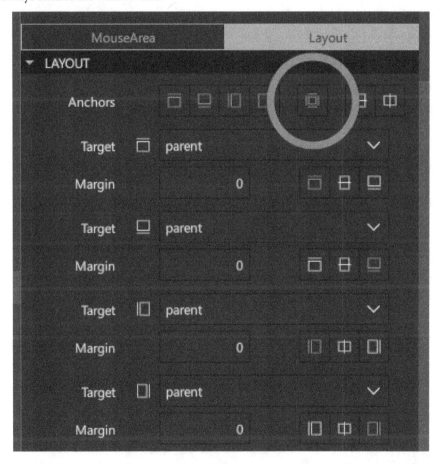

Figure 1.25 – Selecting the fill anchor button to make the item follow the size of its parent object

23. Click and drag a **Rectangle** component from the **Library** window to the canvas. We will use this as the top panel for our program.

24. For the top panel, enable the top anchor, left anchor, and right anchor so that the panel sticks to the top of the window and follows its width. Make sure all the margins are set to zero.

25. Go to the **Color** property of the top panel and select **Gradient**. Set the first color to #805bcce9 and the second color to #80000000. This will create a half-transparent panel with a blue gradient.

26. Add a **Text** widget to the canvas and make it a child of the top panel. Set its **text** property to the current date and time (for example, Wednesday, 25-10-2023 3:14 PM) for display purposes. Then, set the text color to white.

27. Switch over to the **Layout** tab and enable the top anchor and left anchor so that the text widget will always stick to the top-left corner of the screen.

28. Add a **Mouse Area** item to the screen and set its size to 50 x 50. Then, make it a child of the top panel by dragging it on top of the top panel in the **Navigator** window.

29. Set the color of the mouse area to blue (#27a9e3) and set its radius to 2 to make its corners slightly rounded. Enable the top anchor and right anchor to make it stick to the top-right corner of the window. Set the top anchor's margin to 8 and the right anchor's margin to 10 to create some space.

30. Open the **Resources** window and drag the shutdown icon to the canvas. Make it a child of the **Mouse Area** item we created a moment ago. Then, enable the fill anchor to make it fit the size of the mouse area.

31. Phew – that's a lot of steps! Now, your items should be arranged as follows in the **Navigator** window:

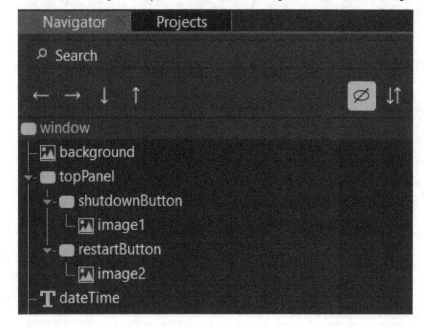

Figure 1.26 – Be cautious about the parent-child relationship between items

32. The parent-child relationship and the layout anchors are both very important to keep the widgets in the correct positions when the main window changes its size. Your top panel should look something like this:

Wednesday, 25-10-2023 3:14 PM

Figure 1.27 – Completing the top banner design

33. Let's work on the login form. Add a new **Rectangle** to the canvas by dragging it from the **Library** window. Resize the rectangle to 360 x 200 and set its radius to 15.

34. Set its color to #80000000; this will change it to black with 50% transparency.

35. Enable the vertical center anchor and the horizontal center anchor to make the rectangle always align with the center of the window. Then, set the margin of the vertical center anchor to 100 so that it moves slightly lower to the bottom. This will ensure we have the space to place the logo. The following screenshot illustrates the settings for **Anchors**:

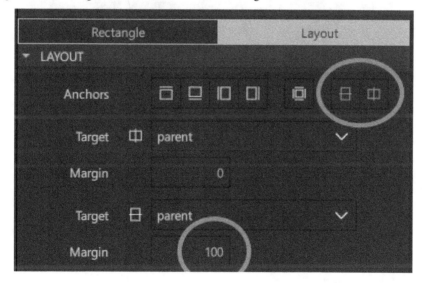

Figure 1.28 – Setting the alignment and margin

36. Add the text objects to the canvas. Make them children of the login form (the **Rectangle** widget) and set their **text** properties to Username: and Password:. Change their text color to white and position them accordingly. We don't need to set a margin this time because they will follow the rectangle's position.

37. Add two text input objects to the canvas and place them next to the text widgets we just created. Make sure the text input is also a child of the login form. Since the text input doesn't contain any background color property, we need to add two rectangles to the canvas to use as their background.

38. Add two rectangles to the canvas and make each of them a child of one of the text inputs we just created. Set the **radius** property to 5 to give them some rounded corners. After that, enable fill anchors on both of the rectangles so that they will follow the size of the text input widgets.

39. Now, let's create the login button beneath the password field. Add a mouse area to the canvas and make it a child of the login form. Resize it to your preferred dimension and move it into place.

40. Since the mouse area does not contain any background color property, we need to add a **Rectangle** widget and make it a child of the mouse area. Set the color of the rectangle to blue (#27a9e3) and enable the fill anchor so that it fits nicely with the mouse area.

41. Add a text object to the canvas and make it a child of the login button. Change its text color to white and set its **text** property to Login. Finally, enable the horizontal center anchor and the vertical center anchor so that they align with the center of the button.

42. You will now get a login form that looks pretty similar to the one we made in the C++ project:

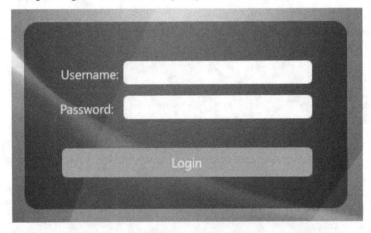

Figure 1.29 – Final design of the login form

43. Now, it's time to add the logo, which is very simple. Open the **Resources** window and drag the logo image to the canvas.

44. Make it a child of the login form and set its size to 512 x 200.

45. Position it on top of the login form. With that, you're done.

46. This is what the entire UI looks like when compiled. We have successfully recreated the login screen from the C++ project, but this time, we did it with QML and Qt Quick:

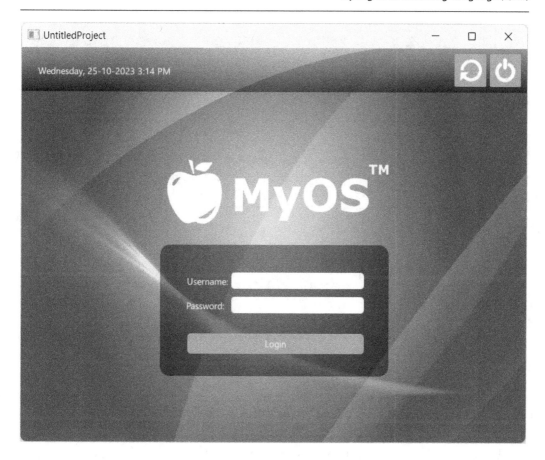

Figure 1.30 – The final result

How it works...

The Qt Quick editor uses a very different approach for placing widgets in the application compared to the form editor. The user can decide which method is best suited to their purposes. The following screenshot shows what the Qt Quick Designer looks like:

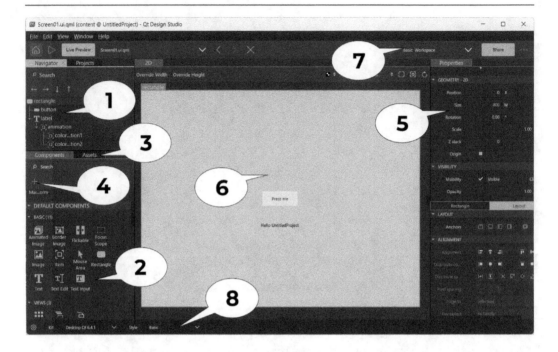

Figure 1.31 – Overview of Qt Design Studio's user interface

Let's look at the various elements of the editor's UI:

1. **Navigator:** The **Navigator** window displays the items in the current QML file as a tree structure. It's similar to the object operator window in the other Qt Designer we used in the *Using style sheets with Qt Designer* recipe.

2. **Library:** The **Library** window displays all the Qt Quick Components or Qt Quick Controls available in QML. You can click and drag it to the canvas window to add to your UI. You can also create your own custom QML components and display them here.

3. **Assets:** The **Assets** window displays all the resources in a list that can then be used in your UI design.

4. **Add Modules:** The **Add Modules** button allows you to import different QML modules into your current QML file, such as a Bluetooth module, a WebKit module, or a positioning module, to add additional functionality to your QML project.

5. **Properties:** Similar to the **Property Editor** area we used in the previous recipe, the **Properties** pane in QML Designer displays the properties of the selected item. You can also change the properties of the items in the code editor.

6. **Canvas:** The canvas is the working area where you create QML components and design applications.

7. **Workspace selector**: The workspace selector area displays the different layouts available in the Qt Design Studio editor, allowing the user to select the workspace that suits their needs.

8. **Style selector**: This selector is where you can select a different style to preview how your application will look when running on a specific platform. This is very useful when developing cross-platform applications.

Exposing the QML object pointer to C++

Sometimes, we want to modify the properties of a QML object through C++ scripting, such as changing the text of a label, hiding/showing the widget, or changing its size. Qt's QML engine allows you to register your QML objects to C++ types, which automatically exposes all its properties.

How to do it...

We want to create a label in QML and change its text occasionally. To expose the label object to C++, we can do the following:

1. Create a C++ class called MyLabel that extends from the QObject class in mylabel.h:

```
class MyLabel : public QObject {
Q_OBJECT
public:
    // Object pointer
    QObject* myObject;
    explicit MyLabel(QObject *parent = 0);
    // Must call Q_INVOKABLE so that this function can be used
in QML
    Q_INVOKABLE void SetMyObject(QObject* obj);
}
```

2. In the mylabel.cpp source file, define a function called SetMyObject() to save the object pointer. This function will later be called in QML in mylabel.cpp:

```
void MyLabel::SetMyObject(QObject* obj) {
    // Set the object pointer
    myObject = obj;
}
```

3. In `main.cpp`, include the `MyLabel` header and register it to the QML engine using the `qmlRegisterType()` function:

```
include "mylabel.h"
int main(int argc, char *argv[]) {
    // Register your class to QML
    qmlRegisterType<MyLabel>("MyLabelLib", 1, 0, "MyLabel");
}
```

4. Notice that there are four parameters you need to declare in `qmlRegisterType()`. Besides declaring your class name (`MyLabel`), you also need to declare your library name (`MyLabelLib`) and its version (`1.0`). This will be used to import your class into QML.

5. Map the QML engine to our label object in QML and import the class library we defined earlier in *Step 3* by calling `import MyLabelLib 1.0` in our QML file. Notice that the library name and its version number have to match the one you declared in `main.cpp`; otherwise, it will throw an error. After declaring `MyLabel` in QML and setting its ID as **mylabels**, call `mylabel.SetMyObject(myLabel)` to expose its pointer to C/C++ right after the label is initialized:

```
import MyLabelLib 1.0
ApplicationWindow {
    id: mainWindow
    width: 480
    height: 640
    MyLabel {
        id: mylabel
    }
    Label {
        id: helloWorldLabel
        text: qsTr("Hello World!")
        Component.onCompleted: {
            mylabel.SetMyObject(hellowWorldLabel);
        }
    }
}
```

6. Wait until the label is fully initiated before exposing its pointer to C/C++; otherwise, you may cause the program to crash. To make sure it's fully initiated, call the SetMyObject() function within Component.onCompleted and not in any other functions or event callbacks. Now that the QML label has been exposed to C/C++, we can change any of its properties by calling the setProperty() function. For instance, we can set its visibility to true and change its text to Bye bye world!:

```
// Qvariant automatically detects your data type
myObject->setProperty("visible", Qvariant(true));
myObject->setProperty("text", Qvariant("Bye bye world!"));
```

7. Besides changing the properties, we can also call its functions by calling the following code:

```
QVariant returnedValue;
QVariant message = "Hello world!";
QMetaObject::invokeMethod(myObject, "myQMLFunction",
Q_RETURN_ARG(QVariant, returnedValue), Q_ARG(QVariant,
message));
qDebug() << "QML function returned:" <<
returnedValue.toString();
```

8. Or, simply, we can call the invokedMethod() function with only two parameters if we do not expect any values to be returned from it:

```
QMetaObject::invokeMethod(myObject, "myQMLFunction");
```

How it works...

QML is designed in such a way that it can be expanded through C++ code. The classes in the Qt QML module permit QML objects to be used and operate from C++, and the capability of the QML engine united with Qt's **meta-object system** allows C++ functionality to be called directly from QML. To add some C++ data or usage to QML, it should come forward from a QObject-derived class. QML object types could be instituted from C++ and supervised to access their properties, appeal their methods, and get their signal alerts. This is possible because all QML object types are executed using QObject-derived classes, allowing the QML engine to forcibly load and inspect objects through the Qt meta-object system.

There's more...

Qt 6 comes with two different types of GUI kits – Qt Widgets and Qt Quick. Both have their strengths and advantages over the other, giving programmers the ability and freedom to design their application's interface without having to worry about feature constraints and performance issues.

Qt 6 allows you to pick the best method and programming language that suits your working style and requirements for your project. By going through this chapter, you will be able to create a good-looking and functional cross-platform application using Qt 6 in no time.

2

Event Handling – Signals and Slots

The signals and slots mechanism in Qt 6 is one of its most important features. It's a method that allows communication between objects, which is a crucial part of a program's graphical user interface. A signal can be emitted from any `QObject` object or its subclasses, which will then trigger any slot functions of any objects that are connected to the signal.

In this chapter, we're going to cover the following main topics:

- Signals and slots in a nutshell
- UI events with signals and slots
- Asynchronous programming made easier
- Function callbacks

Technical requirements

The technical requirements for this chapter include **Qt 6.6.1 MinGW 64-bit** and **Qt Creator 12.0.2**. All the code used in this chapter can be downloaded from the following GitHub repository: https://github.com/PacktPublishing/QT6-C-GUI-Programming-Cookbook---Third-Edition-/tree/main/Chapter02.

Signals and slots in a nutshell

Compared to **callbacks** (which Qt 6 also supports), the **signals and slots** mechanism is comparably more fluid and flexible for the programmer to use. It is both type-safe and not strongly coupled to the processing function, which makes it better than callback implementation.

How to do it...

Let's get started by following these steps:

1. Let's create a **Qt Widgets Application** project and open up `mainwindow.ui`.

2. Drag and drop a **PushButton** widget from the **Widget Box** to the UI canvas:

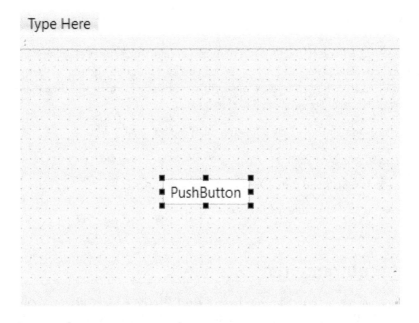

Figure 2.1 – Dragging and dropping a push button to the UI canvas

3. Right-click on the **PushButton** widget and select **Go to slot**. A window will appear:

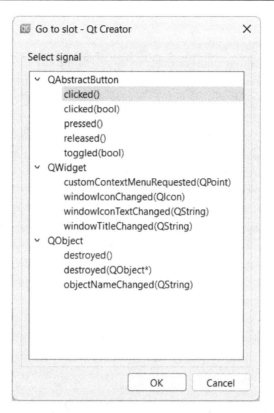

Figure 2.2 – Selecting the clicked() signal and pressing OK

4. You will see a list of built-in slot functions available for the push button. Let's select the **clicked()** option and press **OK**. A slot function called on_pushButton_clicked() will now appear in both mainwindow.h and mainwindow.cpp. Qt Creator automatically added the slot function to your source code after you pressed the **OK** button in the **Go to slot** window. If you check out mainwindow.h now, you should be able to see an extra function under the private slots keyword:

```cpp
class MainWindow : public QMainWindow {
    Q_OBJECT
public:
    explicit MainWindow(QWidget *parent = 0);
    ~MainWindow();
private slots:
    void on_pushButton_clicked();
private:
    Ui::MainWindow *ui;
};
```

5. The same goes for `mainwindow.cpp`, where the `on_pushButton_clicked()` function has been added for you:

```
void MainWindow::on_pushButton_clicked()
{
}
```

6. Now, let's add a QMessageBox header to the top of your source file:

```
#include <QMessageBox>
```

7. Then, add the following code within the `on_pushButton_clicked()` function:

```
void MainWindow::on_pushButton_clicked() {
    QMessageBox::information(this, «Hello», «Button has been
clicked!»);
}
```

8. Now, build and run the project. Then, click on the **Push** button; you should see that a message box pops out:

Figure 2.3 – A message box pops out after pressing the push button

9. Next, we want to create our own signals and slot functions. Go to **File | New File or Project**, then create a new C++ class under the **Files and Classes** category:

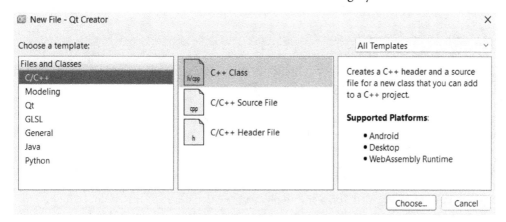

Figure 2.4 – Creating a new C++ class

10. Then, we need to name our class `MyClass` and make sure that the base class is **QObject**:

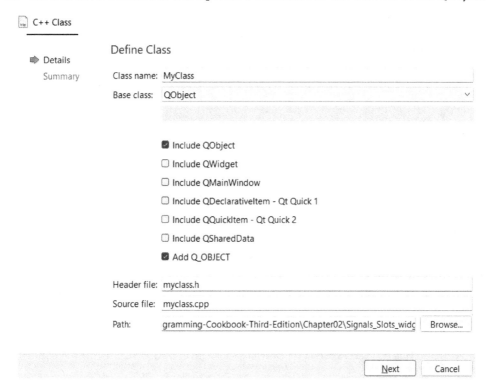

Figure 2.5 – Defining your custom class, which inherits the QObject class

11. Once you have created the class, open up `myclass.h` and add the following code, which is highlighted here for clarity:

```
#include <QObject>
#include <QMainWindow>
#include <QMessageBox>
class MyClass : public QObject {
    Q_OBJECT
public:
    explicit MyClass(QObject *parent = nullptr);
public slots:
    void doSomething();
};
```

12. Then, open up `myclass.cpp` and implement the `doSomething()` slot function. We'll copy the message box function from the previous example:

```
#include "myclass.h"

MyClass::MyClass(QObject *parent) : QObject(parent) {}
void MyClass::doSomething() {
    QMessageBox::information(this, «Hello», «Button has been
clicked!»);
}
```

13. Now, open up `mainwindow.h` and include the `myclass.h` header at the top:

```
#ifndef MAINWINDOW_H
#define MAINWINDOW_H
#include "myclass.h"
namespace Ui {
class MainWindow;
}
```

14. Also, declare a doNow() signal in `myclass.h`:

```
signals:
    void doNow();
private slots:
    void on_pushButton_clicked();
```

15. After that, open up `mainwindow.cpp` and define a `MyClass` object. Then, we'll connect the doNow() signal that we created in the previous step with our doSomething() slot function:

```
MainWindow::MainWindow(QWidget *parent) : QMainWindow(parent),
ui(new Ui::MainWindow){
    ui->setupUi(this);
```

```
      MyClass* myclass = new MyClass;
      connect(this, &MainWindow::doNow, myclass,
  &MyClass::doSomething);
  }
```

16. Then, we have to change the code of the `on_pushButton_clicked()` function to something like this:

```
void MainWindow::on_pushButton_clicked() {
    emit doNow();
}
```

17. If you build and run the program now, you will get a result that is similar to what's shown in the previous example. However, we have placed the message box code in the `MyClass` object instead of in `MainWindow`.

The preceding steps demonstrated how we can utilize the slot-and-signal feature in Qt 6 to easily link a widget action to an event function. It really is that simple.

How it works...

The signals and slots mechanism has gone through some changes in the recent version of Qt, most notably its coding syntax. Qt 6 no longer supports the older syntax; therefore, if you are trying to port your older Qt 5 project to Qt 6, you must change your code to comply with the newer syntax.

In the good old days, we would typically connect a signal to a slot like this:

```
connect(
    sender, SIGNAL(valueChanged(QString)),
    receiver, SLOT(updateValue(QString))
);
```

However, things have changed slightly since then. In the new syntax, the `SIGNAL` and `SLOT` macros are now gone, and you must specify the type of your object, as shown in the following code:

```
connect(
    sender, &Sender::valueChanged,
    receiver, &Receiver::updateValue
);
```

The new syntax also allows you to connect a signal directly to a function instead of `QObject`:

```
connect(
    sender, &Sender::valueChanged, myFunction
);
```

Additionally, you can also connect your signal to a **lambda expression**. We will talk more about this in the *Asynchronous programming made easier* recipe.

> **Note**
>
> A signal of an `arbitrary` class can trigger any private slots of an unrelated class that is going to be invoked, which is not possible with callbacks.

There's more...

All Qt projects come with a project file with the `.pro` extension. This project file is used specifically by Qt's own **qmake** build system, which helps simplify most of the complex build process by using a straightforward declarative style, defining standard variables to indicate the source and header files that are used in the project.

There's an alternative build system called **CMake**, which is also compatible with Qt. The Qt project file is not needed if you are using CMake. Instead, you can directly open `CMakeLists.txt` with Qt Creator and it will open the project just like using Qt's project file. However, it's not recommended for beginners to use CMake when developing their first application with Qt, as CMake is much more manual and it takes longer time to grasp its functionality.

> **Note**
>
> To learn more about CMake, please visit `https://doc.qt.io/qt-6/cmake-get-started.html`.

Qt categorizes its features and functionality in the form of modules and classes. Each module contains a set of related functionalities that can be added to your project separately when needed. This allows the programmer to keep their program in optimum size and performance. The Qt Core and Qt GUI modules are included in every Qt project by default. To add additional modules, you simply need to add the module keyword to your Qt project file or add the package and link its libraries in `CMakeLists.txt` if you are using CMake for your project.

For example, if I want to add the Qt `Network` module to my project, I will add the following keyword to my Qt project file:

```
QT += network
```

In CMake, however, it gets slightly longer:

```
find_package(Qt6 REQUIRED COMPONENTS Network)
target_link_libraries(mytarget PRIVATE Qt6::Network)
```

After you have added the Qt `Network` module, you can now access its C++ classes such as `QNetworkAccessManager`, `QNetworkInterface`, `QNetworkRequest`, and so on. This modular approach creates an expandable ecosystem for Qt while allowing the developers to maintain this complex and powerful framework with ease.

> **Note**
>
> To learn more about all the different Qt modules, please visit `https://doc.qt.io/qt.html`.

UI events with signals and slots

In the previous recipe, we demonstrated the use of signals and slots on a push button. Now, let's explore the signals and slots that are available in other common widget types.

How to do it...

To learn how to use signals and slots with UI events, follow these steps:

1. Let's create a new **Qt Widgets Application** project.
2. Drag and drop a **PushButton**, **Combo Box**, **Line Edit**, **Spin Box**, and **Slider** widget from the **Widget Box** into your UI canvas:

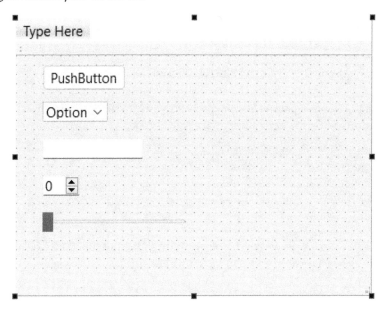

Figure 2.6 – Placing several widgets on the UI canvas

3. Then, right-click on the push button, select **clicked()**, and press the **OK** button to proceed. A slot function will be created for you by Qt Creator:

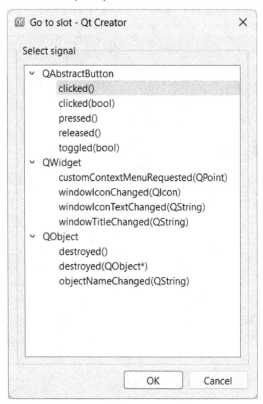

Figure 2.7 – Selecting the clicked() signal and pressing OK

4. Repeat the previous step, but this time, select the next selection until every function in `QAbstractButton` has been added to the source code:

```
void on_pushButton_clicked();
void on_pushButton_clicked(bool checked);
void on_pushButton_pressed();
void on_pushButton_released();
void on_pushButton_toggled(bool checked);
```

5. Next, repeat the same steps on the combo box until all the slot functions available under the `QComboBox` class have been added to the source code:

```
void on_comboBox_activated(const QString &arg1);
void on_comboBox_activated(int index);
void on_comboBox_currentIndexChanged(const QString &arg1);
void on_comboBox_currentIndexChanged(int index);
```

```
void on_comboBox_currentTextChanged(const QString &arg1);
void on_comboBox_editTextChanged(const QString &arg1);
void on_comboBox_highlighted(const QString &arg1);
void on_comboBox_highlighted(int index);
```

6. The same goes for `lineEdit`, all of which are under the `QLineEdit` class:

```
void on_lineEdit_cursorPositionChanged(int arg1, int arg2);
void on_lineEdit_editingFinished();
void on_lineEdit_returnPressed();
void on_lineEdit_selectionChanged();
void on_lineEdit_textChanged(const QString &arg1);
void on_lineEdit_textEdited(const QString &arg1);
```

7. After that, add the slot functions from the `QSpinBox` class for our `spin` box widget as well, which is relatively short:

```
void on_spinBox_valueChanged(const QString &arg1);
void on_spinBox_valueChanged(int arg1);
```

8. Lastly, repeat the same step for our `slider` widget, which yields similar results:

```
void on_horizontalSlider_actionTriggered(int action);
void on_horizontalSlider_rangeChanged(int min, int max);
void on_horizontalSlider_sliderMoved(int position);
void on_horizontalSlider_sliderPressed();
void on_horizontalSlider_sliderReleased();
void on_horizontalSlider_valueChanged(int value);
```

9. Once you're done with that, open up `mainwindow.h` and add the `QDebug` header, as highlighted in the following code:

```
#ifndef MAINWINDOW_H
#define MAINWINDOW_H
#include <QMainWindow>
#include <QDebug>
namespace Ui {
class MainWindow;
}
```

10. Let's implement the slot functions for our push button:

```
void MainWindow::on_pushButton_clicked() {
    qDebug() << «Push button clicked»;
}
void MainWindow::on_pushButton_clicked(bool checked) {
```

```
        qDebug() << «Push button clicked: « << checked;
    }
    void MainWindow::on_pushButton_pressed() {
        qDebug() << «Push button pressed»;
    }
    void MainWindow::on_pushButton_released() {
        qDebug() << «Push button released»;
    }
    void MainWindow::on_pushButton_toggled(bool checked) {
        qDebug() << «Push button toggled: « << checked;
    }
```

11. If you build and run the project now, and then click on the push button, you will see that a different status gets printed out but at a slightly different time. This is due to different signals being emitted at different actions during the whole clicking process:

```
Push button pressed
Push button released
Push button clicked
Push button clicked: false
```

12. Next, we will move on to the combo box. Since the default combo box is empty, let's add some options to it by double-clicking on it from `mainwindow.ui` and adding the options that are shown in the pop-up window:

Figure 2.8 – Adding more options to the combo box

13. Then, let's implement the slot functions for the combo box in `mainwindow.cpp`:

```
    void MainWindow::on_comboBox_activated(const QString &arg1) {
        qDebug() << «Combo box activated: « << arg1;
    }
```

```
void MainWindow::on_comboBox_activated(int index) {
    qDebug() << «Combo box activated: « << index;
}
void MainWindow::on_comboBox_currentIndexChanged(const QString
&arg1) {
    qDebug() << «Combo box current index changed: « << arg1;
}
void MainWindow::on_comboBox_currentIndexChanged(int index) {
    qDebug() << «Combo box current index changed: « << index;
}
```

14. We will continue to implement the rest of the slot functions for the combo box:

```
void MainWindow::on_comboBox_currentTextChanged(const QString
&arg1) {
    qDebug() << «Combo box current text changed: « << arg1;
}
void MainWindow::on_comboBox_editTextChanged(const QString
&arg1) {
    qDebug() << «Combo box edit text changed: « << arg1;
}
void MainWindow::on_comboBox_highlighted(const QString &arg1) {
    qDebug() << «Combo box highlighted: « << arg1;
}
void MainWindow::on_comboBox_highlighted(int index) {
    qDebug() << «Combo box highlighted: « << index;
}
```

15. Build and run the project. Then, try to click on the combo box, hover over the other options, and select an option by clicking on it. You should see similar results to the following in your debug output:

```
Combo box highlighted: 0
Combo box highlighted: "Option One"
Combo box highlighted: 1
Combo box highlighted: "Option Two"
Combo box highlighted: 2
Combo box highlighted: "Option Three"
Combo box current index changed: 2
Combo box current index changed: "Option Three"
Combo box current text changed: "Option Three"
Combo box activated: 2
Combo box activated: "Option Three"
```

16. Next, we will move on to line edit and implement its slot functions, as shown in the following code:

```
void MainWindow::on_lineEdit_cursorPositionChanged(int arg1, int
arg2) {
    qDebug() << «Line edit cursor position changed: « << arg1 <<
arg2;
}
void MainWindow::on_lineEdit_editingFinished() {
    qDebug() << «Line edit editing finished»;
}
void MainWindow::on_lineEdit_returnPressed() {
    qDebug() << «Line edit return pressed»;
}
```

17. We will continue to implement the rest of the slot functions of line edit:

```
void MainWindow::on_lineEdit_selectionChanged() {
    qDebug() << «Line edit selection changed»;
}
void MainWindow::on_lineEdit_textChanged(const QString &arg1) {
    qDebug() << «Line edit text changed: « << arg1;
}
void MainWindow::on_lineEdit_textEdited(const QString &arg1) {
    qDebug() << «Line edit text edited: « << arg1;
}
```

18. Build and run the project. Then, click on the line edit and type Hey. You should see results similar to the following appearing in the debug output panel:

```
Line edit cursor position changed: -1 0
Line edit text edited: "H"
Line edit text changed: "H"
Line edit cursor position changed: 0 1
Line edit text edited: "He"
Line edit text changed: "He"
Line edit cursor position changed: 1 2
Line edit text edited: "Hey"
Line edit text changed: "Hey"
Line edit cursor position changed: 2 3
Line edit editing finished
```

19. After that, we need to implement the slot functions for the spin box widget, as shown in the following code:

```
void MainWindow::on_spinBox_valueChanged(const QString &arg1){
    qDebug() << «Spin box value changed: « << arg1;
```

```
}
void MainWindow::on_spinBox_valueChanged(int arg1) {
    qDebug() << «Spin box value changed: « << arg1;
}
```

20. Try to build and run the program. Then, click the arrow buttons on the spin box, or directly edit the value in the box – you should get something similar to this:

```
Spin box value changed: "1"
Spin box value changed: 1
Spin box value changed: "2"
Spin box value changed: 2
Spin box value changed: "3"
Spin box value changed: 3
Spin box value changed: "2"
Spin box value changed: 2
Spin box value changed: "20"
Spin box value changed: 20
```

21. Lastly, we'll implement the slot functions for the horizontal slider widget:

```
void MainWindow::on_horizontalSlider_actionTriggered(int
action) {
    qDebug() << «Slider action triggered» << action;
}
void MainWindow::on_horizontalSlider_rangeChanged(int min, int
max) {
    qDebug() << «Slider range changed: « << min << max;
}
void MainWindow::on_horizontalSlider_sliderMoved(int position)
{
    qDebug() << «Slider moved: « << position;
}
```

22. Continue to implement the slot function for the slider, as shown in the following code:

```
void MainWindow::on_horizontalSlider_sliderPressed() {
    qDebug() << «Slider pressed»;
}
void MainWindow::on_horizontalSlider_sliderReleased() {
    qDebug() << «Slider released»;
}
void MainWindow::on_horizontalSlider_valueChanged(int value) {
    qDebug() << «Slider value changed: « << value;
}
```

23. Build and run the program. Then, click and drag the slider to the left and right – you should see results that are similar to the following:

```
Slider pressed
Slider moved: 1
Slider action triggered 7
Slider value changed: 1
Slider moved: 2
Slider action triggered 7
Slider value changed: 2
Slider moved: 3
Slider action triggered 7
Slider value changed: 3
Slider moved: 4
Slider action triggered 7
Slider value changed: 4
Slider released
```

Almost every widget has a set of slot functions associated with its usage or purpose. For example, a push button will start emitting signals that trigger the slot functions associated with it when it's pressed or released. These expected behaviors that define the widget have slot functions that get called when the user triggers an action. As programmers, all we need to do is implement the slot functions and tell Qt what to do when these slot functions are being triggered.

Asynchronous programming made easier

Since the signals and slots mechanism is *asynchronous* in nature, we can make use of it for things other than user interfaces. In programming terms, an *asynchronous operation* is a process that works independently, allowing the program to continue its operation without waiting for the process to complete, which may stall the whole program. Qt 6 allows you to make use of its signals and slots mechanism to easily achieve asynchronous processes without much effort. This is even more true after Qt 6 enforced the new syntax for signals and slots, which allows a signal to trigger a normal function instead of a slot function from a Qobject object.

In the following example, we will further explore this opportunity and learn how we can improve our program's efficiency by using asynchronous operations through the signals and slots mechanism that's provided by Qt 6.

How to do it...

To learn how to achieve asynchronous operations using the signals and slots mechanism, let's follow this example:

1. Create a **Qt Console Application** project:

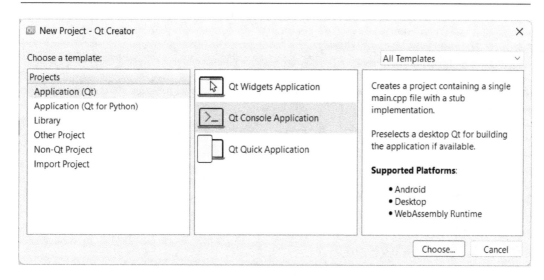

Figure 2.9 – Creating a new Qt Console Application project

2. This type of project will only provide a `main.cpp` file for you, instead of `mainwindow.h` and `mainwindow.cpp`, like our previous example projects. Let's open up `main.cpp` and add the following headers to it:

```
#include <QNetworkAccessManager>
#include <QNetworkReply>
#include <QDebug>
```

3. Then, add the following code to our `main()` function. We will be using the `QNetworkAccessManager` class to initiate a GET request to the following web URL:

```
int main(int argc, char *argv[]) {
    QCoreApplication a(argc, argv);
    QString *html = new QString;
    qDebug() << "Start";
    QNetworkAccessManager manager;
    QNetworkRequest req(QUrl("http://www.dustyfeet.com"));
    QNetworkReply* reply = manager.get(req);
```

4. Then, we use C++11's **lambda expression** to connect `QNetworkReply` signals to inline functions:

```
QObject::connect(reply, &QNetworkReply::readyRead,
  [reply, html]() {
        html->append(QString(reply->readAll()));
    });
    QObject::connect(reply, &QNetworkReply::downloadProgress,
  [reply](qint64 bytesReceived, qint64 bytesTotal) {
```

```
            qDebug() << "Progress: " << bytesReceived << "bytes /"
    << bytesTotal << "bytes";
        });
```

5. We can also use a lambda expression with `connect()` to call a function that is not under a `QObject` class:

```
QObject::connect(reply, &QNetworkReply::finished, [=]() {
        printHTML(*html);
    });
    return a.exec();
}
```

6. Lastly, we define the `printHTML()` function, as shown in the following code:

```
void printHTML(QString html) {
    qDebug() << "Done";
    qDebug() << html;
}
```

7. If you build and run the program now, you will see that it's functional even without declaring any slot function. **Lambda expressions** make declaring a slot function optional, but this is only recommended if your code is really short:

Figure 2.10 – Printing HTML source code on the terminal window

8. If the terminal window does not appear after you build and run your Qt console application project, go to **Edit | Preferences | Build & Run** and select **Enabled** for the **Default for "Run in terminal"** option.

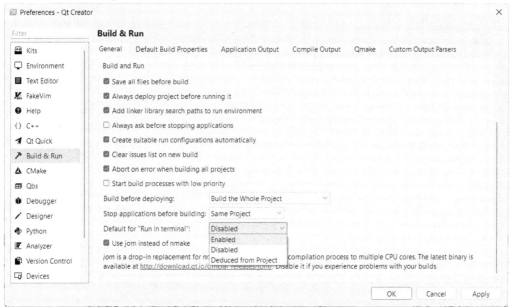

Figure 2.11 – Enabling the terminal window from the Preferences settings

The preceding example demonstrated how we can run a lambda function within the network reply slot function. This way, we can ensure that our code is shorter and easier to debug, but the lambda function is only suitable if the function is meant to be called only once.

How it works...

The preceding example is a very simple application that showcases the use of lambda expressions to connect a signal with a lambda function or a regular function without declaring any slot function and thus does not need to be inherited from a QObject class.

This is especially useful for calling asynchronous processes that are not under UI objects. Lambda expressions are functions that get defined within another function anonymously, which is quite similar to the anonymous functions in **JavaScript**. The format of a lambda function looks like this:

```
[captured variables] (arguments) {
    lambda code
}
```

You can insert variables into a lambda expression by placing them into the captured variables part, as we did in the example project in this recipe. We capture the QNetworkReply object called reply, and the QString object called html, and put them in our lambda expression.

Then, we can use these variables within our lambda code, as shown in the following code:

```
[reply, html]() {
    html->append(QString(reply->readAll()));
}
```

The argument part is similar to an ordinary function, where you input values to the arguments and use them within your lambda code. In this case, the values of bytesReceived and bytesTotal are coming from the downloadProgress signal:

```
QObject::connect(reply, &QNetworkReply::downloadProgress,
[reply](qint64 bytesReceived, qint64 bytesTotal) {
    qDebug() << "Progress: " << bytesReceived << "bytes /" <<
bytesTotal << "bytes";
});
```

You can also capture all variables that are used in your function using the = sign. In this case, we captured the html variable without specifying it in the captured variables area:

```
[=]() {
    printHTML(*html);
}
```

Function callbacks

Even though Qt 6 supports the signals and slots mechanism, some of the features in Qt 6 still use **function callbacks**, such as keyboard input, window resizing, graphics painting, and others. Since these events only need to be implemented once, there is no need to use the signals and slots mechanism.

How to do it...

Let's get started by following this example:

1. Create a **Qt Widgets Application** project, open up mainwindow.h, and add the following headers:

```
#include <QDebug>
#include <QResizeEvent>
#include <QKeyEvent>
#include <QMouseEvent>
```

2. Then, declare these functions in `mainwindow.h`:

```
public:
    explicit MainWindow(QWidget *parent = 0);
    ~MainWindow();
    void resizeEvent(QResizeEvent *event);
    void keyPressEvent(QKeyEvent *event);
    void keyReleaseEvent(QKeyEvent *event);
    void mouseMoveEvent(QMouseEvent *event);
    void mousePressEvent(QMouseEvent *event);
    void mouseReleaseEvent(QMouseEvent *event);
```

3. After that, open up `mainwindow.cpp` and add the following code to the class constructor:

```
MainWindow::MainWindow(QWidget *parent) : QMainWindow(parent),
ui(new Ui::MainWindow) {
    ui->setupUi(this);
    this->setMouseTracking(true);
    ui->centralWidget->setMouseTracking(true);
}
```

4. Then, define the `resizeEvent()` and `keyPressedEvent()` functions:

```
void MainWindow::resizeEvent(QResizeEvent *event) {
    qDebug() << "Old size:" << event->oldSize() << ", New size:"
<< event->size();
}
void MainWindow::keyPressEvent(QKeyEvent *event) {
    if (event->key() == Qt::Key_Escape) {
        this->close();
    }
    qDebug() << event->text() << "has been pressed";
}
```

5. Continue to implement the rest of the functions:

```
void MainWindow::keyReleaseEvent(QKeyEvent *event) {
    qDebug() << event->text() << "has been released";
}
void MainWindow::mouseMoveEvent(QMouseEvent *event) {
    qDebug() << "Position: " << event->pos();
}
void MainWindow::mousePressEvent(QMouseEvent *event) {
    qDebug() << "Mouse pressed:" << event->button();
}
```

```
void MainWindow::mouseReleaseEvent(QMouseEvent *event) {
    qDebug() << "Mouse released:" << event->button();
}
```

6. Build and run the program. Then, try and move the mouse around, rescale the main window, press some random keys on your keyboard, and finally press the *Esc* key on your keyboard to close the program.

You should be seeing debug texts similar to the ones that are being printed out on the application output window:

```
Old size: QSize(-1, -1) , New size: QSize(400, 300)
Old size: QSize(400, 300) , New size: QSize(401, 300)
Old size: QSize(401, 300) , New size: QSize(402, 300)
Position: QPoint(465,348)
Position: QPoint(438,323)
Position: QPoint(433,317)
"a" has been pressed
"a" has been released
"r" has been pressed
"r" has been released
"d" has been pressed
"d" has been released
"\u001B" has been pressed
```

How it works...

Qt 6 objects, especially the main window, have a dozen built-in callback functions that exist as **virtual functions**. These functions can be overridden to perform your intended behavior when called. Qt 6 may invoke these **callback functions** when its expected condition has been met, such as a keyboard button has been pressed, the mouse cursor has been moved, the window has been resized, and so on.

The functions that we declared in the `mainwindow.h` file are virtual functions that are built into the `QWidget` class. We are just overriding them with our own code to define their new behavior when they are called.

> **Note**
>
> Do take note that you must call `setMouseTracking(true)` for both `MainWindow` and `centralWidget` for the `mouseMoveEvent()` callback to work.

Without features such as function callbacks, signals and slots, we as programmers will have a more difficult time developing applications that are responsive and intuitive to use. Qt 6 shortens our development cycles and allows us to focus more on designing user-friendly applications.

3

States and Animations with Qt and QML

Qt provides an easy way to animate widgets or any other objects that inherit the QObject class through its powerful animation framework. The animation can be used either on its own or together with the **state machine framework**, which allows different animations to be played based on the current active state of the widget. Qt's animation framework also supports grouped animation, which allows you to move more than one graphics item simultaneously or move them in sequence, one after the other.

In this chapter, we're going to cover the following main topics:

- Property animation in Qt
- Using easing curves to control property animation
- Creating an animation group
- Creating a nested animation group
- State machines in Qt
- States, transitions, and animations in QML
- Animating widget properties using animators
- Sprite animation

Technical requirements

The technical requirements for this chapter include **Qt 6.6.1 MinGW 64-bit**, **Qt Creator 12.0.2**, and Windows 11. All the code used in this chapter can be downloaded from the following GitHub repository at https://github.com/PacktPublishing/QT6-C-GUI-Programming-Cookbook---Third-Edition-/tree/main/Chapter03.

Property animation in Qt

In this example, we will learn how to animate our **Graphical User Interface** (**GUI**) elements using Qt's `property animation` class, a part of its powerful animation framework that allows us to create fluid-looking animations with minimal effort.

How to do it...

In the following example, we will create a new widget project and animate the push button by changing its properties:

1. Let's create a new **Qt Widgets Application** project. After that, open up `mainwindow.ui` with Qt Designer and place a button on the main window, as shown here:

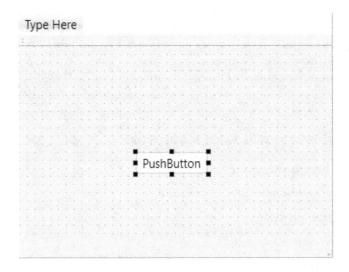

Figure 3.1 – Dragging and dropping a push button to the UI canvas

2. Open up `mainwindow.cpp` and add the following line of code at the beginning of the source code:

    ```
    #include <QPropertyAnimation>
    ```

3. After that, open up `mainwindow.cpp` and add the following code to the constructor:

    ```
    QPropertyAnimation *animation = new
    QPropertyAnimation(ui->pushButton, "geometry");
    animation->setDuration(10000);
    animation->setStartValue(ui->pushButton->geometry());
    animation->setEndValue(QRect(200, 200, 100, 50));
    animation->start();
    ```

How it works...

One of the more common methods of animating a GUI element is through the property animation class provided by Qt, known as the QPropertyAnimation class. This class is part of the animation framework and it makes use of the timer system in Qt to change the properties of a GUI element over a given duration.

What we are trying to accomplish here is animating the button from one position to another while, at the same time, enlarging the button size along the way. By including the QPropertyAnimation header in our source code in *step 2*, we will be able to access the QPropertyAnimation class provided by Qt and make use of its functionalities.

The code in *step 3* basically creates a new *property animation* and applies it to the **push button** we just created in Qt Designer. We specifically request that the property animation class changes the geometry properties of the *push button* and sets its duration to 3,000 milliseconds (3 seconds).

Then, the start value of the animation is set to the initial geometry of the *push button* because, obviously, we want it to start from where we initially placed the button in Qt Designer. The end value is then set to what we want it to become; in this case, we will move the button to a new position at x: 200 and y: 200 while changing its size to width: 100 and height: 50 along the way.

After that, call animation | start() to start the animation. Compile and run the project. You should see the button start to move slowly across the main window while expanding in size a bit at a time until it reaches its destination. You can change the animation duration and the target position and scale by altering the values in the preceding code. It is really that simple to animate a GUI element using Qt's property animation system!

There's more...

Qt provides us with several different sub-systems to create animations for our GUI, including the timer, timeline, animation framework, state machine framework, and graphics view framework:

- **Timer**: Qt provides us with *repetitive and single-shot timers*. When the timeout value is reached, an event callback function will be triggered through Qt's *signal-and-slot* mechanism. You can make use of a timer to change the properties (color, position, scale, and so on) of your GUI element within a given interval to create an animation.

- **Timeline**: The *Timeline* calls a slot periodically to animate a GUI element. It is quite similar to a *repetitive timer*, but instead of doing the same thing all of the time when the slot is triggered, the timeline provides a value to the slot to indicate its current frame index so that you can do different things (such as offset to a different space of the sprite sheet) based on the given value.

- **Animation framework**: The *animation framework* makes animating a GUI element easy by allowing its properties to be animated. The animations are controlled by using *easing curves*. Easing curves describe a function that controls what the speed of the animation should be, resulting in different acceleration and deceleration patterns. The types of easing curves supported by Qt include linear, quadratic, cubic, quartic, sine, exponential, circular, and elastic.

- **State machine framework**: Qt provides us with classes for creating and executing state graphs, which allow each GUI element to move from one state to another when triggered by signals. The *state graph* in the *state machine framework* is hierarchical, which means every state can also be nested inside of other states.

- **Graphics view framework**: The *graphics view framework* is a powerful graphics engine for visualizing and interacting with a large number of custom-made 2D graphical items. You can use the graphics view framework to draw your GUI and have them animated in a totally manual way if you are an experienced programmer.

By making use of all of the powerful features we've mentioned here, we're able to create an intuitive and modern GUI with ease. In this chapter, we will look into the practical approaches to animating GUI elements using Qt.

Using easing curves to control property animation

In this example, we will learn how to make our animation more interesting by utilizing *easing curves*. We will still use the previous source code, which uses the property animation to animate a push button.

How to do it...

In the following example, we will learn how to add an *easing curve* to our animation:

1. Define an easing curve and add it to the property animation before calling the start() function:

```
QPropertyAnimation *animation = new
QPropertyAnimation(ui->pushButton, "geometry");
animation->setDuration(3000);
animation->setStartValue(ui->pushButton->geometry());
animation->setEndValue(QRect(200, 200, 100, 50));

QEasingCurve curve;
curve.setType(QEasingCurve::OutBounce);
animation->setEasingCurve(curve);
animation->start();
```

2. Call the setLoopCount() function to set how many loops you want it to repeat for:

```
QPropertyAnimation *animation = new
QPropertyAnimation(ui->pushButton, "geometry");
animation->setDuration(3000);
animation->setStartValue(ui->pushButton->geometry());
animation->setEndValue(QRect(200, 200, 100, 50));

QEasingCurve curve;
```

```
curve.setType(EasingCurve::OutBounce);
animation->setEasingCurve(curve);
animation->setLoopCount(2);
animation->start();
```

3. Call setAmplitude(), setOvershoot(), and setPeriod() before applying the easing curve to the animation:

```
QEasingCurve curve;
curve.setType(QEasingCurve::OutBounce);
curve.setAmplitude(1.00);
curve.setOvershoot(1.70);
curve.setPeriod(0.30);
animation->setEasingCurve(curve);
animation->start();
```

It's really that easy to animate a widget or any object in Qt 6 using the built-in easing curves.

How it works...

To let an easing curve control the animation, all you need to do is define an easing curve and add it to the property animation before calling the start() function. You can also try several other types of easing curves and see which one suits you best. Here is an example:

```
animation->setEasingCurve(QEasingCurve::OutBounce);
```

If you want the animation to loop after it has finished playing, you can call the setLoopCount() function to set how many loops you want it to repeat for or set the value to -1 for an infinite loop:

```
animation->setLoopCount(-1);
```

There are several parameters that you can set to refine the easing curve before applying it to the property animation. These parameters include **amplitude**, **overshoot**, and **period**:

- **Amplitude**: The higher the *amplitude*, the higher the bounce or elastic spring effect that will be applied to the animation.

- **Overshoot**: Some curve functions will produce an *overshoot* (exceeding its final value) curve due to a damping effect. By adjusting the overshoot value, we are able to increase or decrease this effect.

- **Period**: Setting a small period value will give a high frequency to the curve. A large *period* will give it a small frequency.

These parameters, however, are not applicable to all curve types. Please refer to the Qt documentation to see which parameter is applicable to which curve type.

There's more...

While the property animation works perfectly fine, sometimes it feels a little boring to look at a GUI element being animated at a constant speed. We can make the animation look more interesting by adding an **easing curve** to control the motion. There are many types of easing curves that you can use in Qt, and here are some of them:

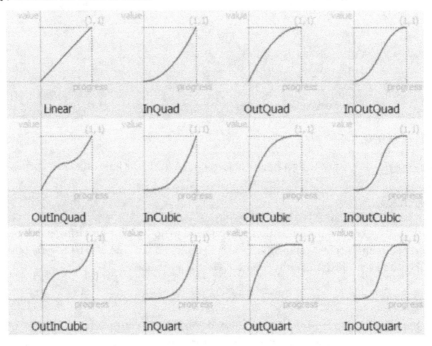

Figure 3.2 – Different types of easing curves supported by Qt 6

As you can see from the preceding diagram, each easing curve produces a different *ease-in and ease-out* effect.

> **Note**
>
> For the full list of easing curves available in Qt, please refer to the Qt documentation at http://doc.qt.io/qt-6/qeasingcurve.html#Type-enum.

Creating an animation group

In this example, we will learn how to use an *animation group* to manage the states of the animations contained in the group.

How to do it...

Let's create an *animation group* by following these steps:

1. We will use the previous example but, this time, we will add two more push buttons to the main window, as shown in the following screenshot:

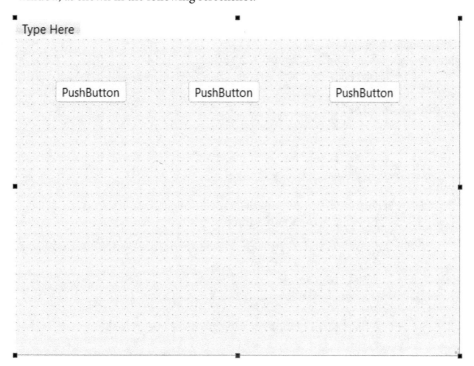

Figure 3.3 – Adding three push buttons to the main window

2. Define the *animation* for each of the push buttons in the main window's constructor:

```
QPropertyAnimation *animation1 = new
QPropertyAnimation(ui->pushButton, "geometry");
animation1->setDuration(3000);
animation1->setStartValue(ui->pushButton->geometry());
animation1->setEndValue(QRect(50, 200, 100, 50));

QPropertyAnimation *animation2 = new
QPropertyAnimation(ui->pushButton_2, "geometry");
animation2->setDuration(3000);
animation2->setStartValue(ui->pushButton_2->geometry());
animation2->setEndValue(QRect(150, 200, 100, 50));
```

```
QPropertyAnimation *animation3 = new
QPropertyAnimation(ui->pushButton_3, "geometry");
animation3->setDuration(3000);
animation3->setStartValue(ui->pushButton_3->geometry());
animation3->setEndValue(QRect(250, 200, 100, 50));
```

3. Create an *easing curve* and apply the same curve to all three animations:

```
QEasingCurve curve;
curve.setType(QEasingCurve::OutBounce);
curve.setAmplitude(1.00);
curve.setOvershoot(1.70);
curve.setPeriod(0.30);

animation1->setEasingCurve(curve);
animation2->setEasingCurve(curve);
animation3->setEasingCurve(curve);
```

4. Once you have applied the easing curve to all three animations, we will then create an *animation group* and add all three animations to the group:

```
QParallelAnimationGroup *group = new QParallelAnimationGroup;
group->addAnimation(animation1);
group->addAnimation(animation2);
group->addAnimation(animation3);
```

5. Call the start() function from the animation group we just created:

```
group->start();
```

How it works...

Qt allows us to create multiple animations and group them into an animation group. A group is usually responsible for managing the state of its animations (that is, it decides when to start, stop, resume, and pause them). Currently, Qt provides two types of classes for animation groups: QParallelAnimationGroup and QSequentialAnimationGroup:

- QParallelAnimationGroup: As its name implies, a *parallel animation group* runs all of the animations in its group at the same time. The group is deemed finished when the longest-lasting animation has finished running.

- QSequentialAnimationGroup: A *sequential animation group* runs its animations in sequence, meaning it will only run a single animation at a time and only play the next animation when the current one has finished.

There's more...

Since we are using an animation group now, we no longer call the `start()` function from the individual animation. Instead, we will be calling the `start()` function from the animation group we just created. If you compile and run the example now, you will see all three buttons being played at the same time. This is because we are using the **parallel animation group**. You can replace it with a **sequential animation group** and run the example again:

```
QSequentialAnimationGroup *group = new QSequentialAnimationGroup;
```

This time, only a single button will play its animation at a time, while the other buttons will wait patiently for their turn to come. The priority is set based on which animation is added to the animation group first. You can change the animation sequence by simply rearranging the sequence of an animation that's being added to the group. For example, if we want button 3 to start the animation first, followed by button 2, and then button 1, the code will look like this:

```
group->addAnimation(animation3);
group->addAnimation(animation2);
group->addAnimation(animation1);
```

Since property animations and animation groups are both inherited from the `QAbstractAnimator` class, it means that you can also add an animation group to another animation group to form a more complex, nested animation group.

Creating a nested animation group

One good example of using a **nested animation group** is when you have several **parallel** animation groups and you want to play the groups in sequential order.

How to do it...

Let's follow these steps to create a **nested animation group** to play different animation groups in a sequential order:

1. We will use the UI from the previous example and add a few more buttons to the main window, like so:

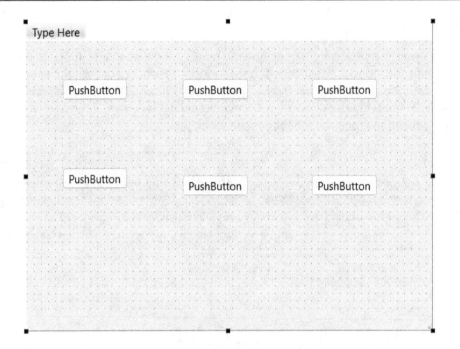

Figure 3.4 – We need even more buttons this time around

2. Create all of the animations for the buttons and then create an easing curve and apply it to all of the animations:

```
QPropertyAnimation *animation1 = new
QPropertyAnimation(ui->pushButton, "geometry");
animation1->setDuration(3000);
animation1->setStartValue(ui->pushButton->geometry());
animation1->setEndValue(QRect(50, 50, 100, 50));

QPropertyAnimation *animation2 = new
QPropertyAnimation(ui->pushButton_2, "geometry");
animation2->setDuration(3000);
animation2->setStartValue(ui->pushButton_2->geometry());
animation2->setEndValue(QRect(150, 50, 100, 50));

QPropertyAnimation *animation3 = new
QPropertyAnimation(ui->pushButton_3, "geometry");
animation3->setDuration(3000);
animation3->setStartValue(ui->pushButton_3->geometry());
animation3->setEndValue(QRect(250, 50, 100, 50));
```

3. Next, apply the following code:

```
QPropertyAnimation *animation4 = new
QPropertyAnimation(ui->pushButton_4, "geometry");
animation4->setDuration(3000);
animation4->setStartValue(ui->pushButton_4->geometry());
animation4->setEndValue(QRect(50, 200, 100, 50));

QPropertyAnimation *animation5 = new
QPropertyAnimation(ui->pushButton_5, "geometry");
animation5->setDuration(3000);
animation5->setStartValue(ui->pushButton_5->geometry());
animation5->setEndValue(QRect(150, 200, 100, 50));

QPropertyAnimation *animation6 = new
QPropertyAnimation(ui->pushButton_6, "geometry");
animation6->setDuration(3000);
animation6->setStartValue(ui->pushButton_6->geometry());
animation6->setEndValue(QRect(250, 200, 100, 50));
```

4. Then, apply the following code:

```
QEasingCurve curve;
curve.setType(QEasingCurve::OutBounce);
curve.setAmplitude(1.00);
curve.setOvershoot(1.70);
curve.setPeriod(0.30);

animation1->setEasingCurve(curve);
animation2->setEasingCurve(curve);
animation3->setEasingCurve(curve);
animation4->setEasingCurve(curve);
animation5->setEasingCurve(curve);
animation6->setEasingCurve(curve);
```

5. Create two **animation groups**, one for the buttons in the upper column and another one for the lower column:

```
QParallelAnimationGroup *group1 = new QParallelAnimationGroup;
group1->addAnimation(animation1);
group1->addAnimation(animation2);
group1->addAnimation(animation3);
```

```
QParallelAnimationGroup *group2 = new QParallelAnimationGroup;
group2->addAnimation(animation4);
group2->addAnimation(animation5);
group2->addAnimation(animation6);
```

6. We will create yet another **animation group**, which will be used to store the two animation groups we created previously:

```
QSequentialAnimationGroup *groupAll = new
QSequentialAnimationGroup;
groupAll->addAnimation(group1);
groupAll->addAnimation(group2);
groupAll->start();
```

A Nested animation group allows you to set up a more complex widget animation by combining different types of animations and executing them at your desired orders.

How it works...

What we are trying to do here is play the animation of the buttons in the upper column first, followed by the buttons in the lower column. Since both of the animation groups are **parallel animation groups**, the buttons belonging to the respective groups will be animated at the same time when the start() function is called.

This time, however, the group is a **sequential animation group**, which means only a single parallel animation group will be played at a time, followed by the other when the first one is finished. Animation groups are a very handy system that allows us to create very complex GUI animations with simple coding. Qt will handle the difficult part for us so that we don't have to.

State machines in Qt 6

A **state machine** can be used for many purposes but, in this chapter, we will only cover topics related to animation.

How to do it...

A **State machine** is not that hard to achieve in Qt at all. Let's get started by following these steps:

1. We will set up a new user interface for our example program, which looks like this:

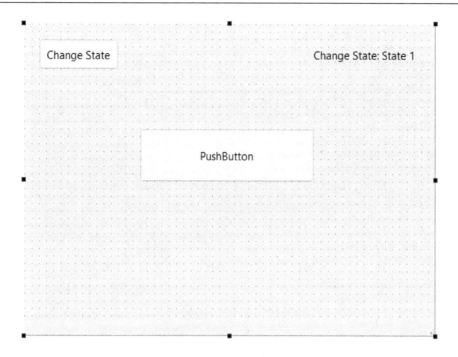

Figure 3.5 – Setting up the GUI for our state machine experiment

2. We will include some headers in our source code:

```
#include <QStateMachine>
#include <QPropertyAnimation>
#include <QEventTransition>
```

3. In our main window's constructor, add the following code to create a *new state machine* and two *states*, which we will be using later:

```
QStateMachine *machine = new QStateMachine(this);
QState *s1 = new QState();
QState *s2 = new QState();
```

4. We will define what we should do within each state, which, in this case, will be to change the label's *text* and the button's *position* and *size*:

```
QState *s1 = new QState();
s1->assignProperty(ui->stateLabel, "text", "Current state: 1");
s1->assignProperty(ui->pushButton, "geometry", QRect(50, 200,
100, 50));
```

```
QState *s2 = new QState();
s2->assignProperty(ui->stateLabel, "text", "Current state: 2");
s2->assignProperty(ui->pushButton, "geometry", QRect(200, 50,
140, 100));
```

5. Once you are done with that, let's proceed by adding `event transition` classes to our source code:

```
QEventTransition *t1 = new QEventTransition(ui->changeState,
QEvent::MouseButtonPress);
t1->setTargetState(s2);
s1->addTransition(t1);

QEventTransition *t2 = new QEventTransition(ui->changeState,
QEvent::MouseButtonPress);
t2->setTargetState(s1);
s2->addTransition(t2);
```

6. Add all of the states we have just created to the state machine and define state 1 as the **initial state**. Then, call `machine->start()` to run the state machine:

```
machine->addState(s1);
machine->addState(s2);
machine->setInitialState(s1);
machine->start();
```

7. If you run the example program now, you will notice that everything works fine, except the button is not going through a smooth transition and it simply jumps instantly to the position and size we set previously. This is because we have not used a **property animation** to create a smooth transition.

8. Go back to the event transition step and add the following lines of code:

```
QEventTransition *t1 = new QEventTransition(ui->changeState,
QEvent::MouseButtonPress);
t1->setTargetState(s2);
t1->addAnimation(new QPropertyAnimation(ui->pushButton,
"geometry"));
s1->addTransition(t1);

QEventTransition *t2 = new QEventTransition(ui->changeState,
QEvent::MouseButtonPress);
t2->setTargetState(s1);
t2->addAnimation(new QPropertyAnimation(ui->pushButton,
"geometry"));
s2->addTransition(t2);
```

9. You can also add an easing curve to the animation to make it look more interesting:

```
QPropertyAnimation *animation = new
QPropertyAnimation(ui->pushButton, "geometry");
animation->setEasingCurve(QEasingCurve::OutBounce);

QEventTransition *t1 = new QEventTransition(ui->changeState,
QEvent::MouseButtonPress);
t1->setTargetState(s2);
t1->addAnimation(animation);
s1->addTransition(t1);

QEventTransition *t2 = new QEventTransition(ui->changeState,
QEvent::MouseButtonPress);
t2->setTargetState(s1);
t2->addAnimation(animation);
s2->addTransition(t2);
```

How it works...

There are two push buttons and a label on the main window layout. The button in the top-left corner will trigger the state change when pressed, while the label in the top-right corner will change its text to show which state we are currently in. the button below will animate according to the current state. The QEventTransition classes define what will trigger the transition between one state and another.

In our case, we want the state to change from state 1 to state 2 when the **changeState** button (the one in the upper-left) is clicked. After that, we also want to change from state 2 back to state 1 when the same button is pressed again. This can be achieved by creating another event transition class and setting the target state back to state 1. Then, add these transitions to their respective states. Instead of just assigning the properties directly to the widgets, we tell Qt to use the property animation class to smoothly interpolate the properties toward the target values. It is that simple! There is no need to set the start value and end value because we have already called the assignProperty() function, which has automatically assigned the end value.

There's more...

The **state machine framework** in Qt provides classes for creating and executing state graphs. Qt's event system is used to drive the state machines, where transitions between states can be triggered by using *signals*, and then the *slots* on the other end will be invoked by the signals to perform an action, such as playing an animation.

Once you understand the basics of state machines, you can use them to do other things as well. The state graph in the state machine framework is hierarchical. Just like the animation group in the previous section, states can also be nested inside of other states:

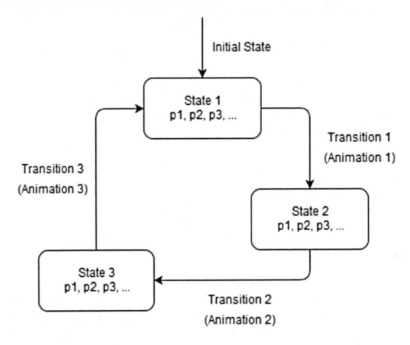

Figure 3.6 – Nested state machines explained visually

You can combine nested state machines and animations to create a very sophisticated GUI for your application.

States, transitions, and animations in QML

If you prefer to work with QML instead of C++, Qt also provides similar features in Qt Quick that allow you to easily animate a GUI element with minimal lines of code. In this example, we will learn how to achieve this with QML.

How to do it...

Let's get started by following these steps to create a window that continuously changes its background color:

1.   We will create a new **Qt Quick Application** project and set up our user interface, like so:

Figure 3.7 – A joyful application that constantly changes its background color

2. Here is what my main.qml file looks like:

```qml
import QtQuick
import QtQuick.Window
Window {
    visible: true
    width: 480;
    height: 320;
    Rectangle {
        id: background;
        anchors.fill: parent;
        color: "blue";
    }
    Text {
        text: qsTr("Hello World");
        anchors.centerIn: parent;
        color: "white";
        font.pointSize: 15;
    }
}
```

3. Add the *color animation* to the Rectangle object:

```qml
Rectangle {
    id: background;
    anchors.fill: parent;
    color: "blue";
```

```
SequentialAnimation on color {
    ColorAnimation { to: "yellow"; duration: 1000 }
    ColorAnimation { to: "red"; duration: 1000 }
    ColorAnimation { to: "blue"; duration: 1000 }
    loops: Animation.Infinite;
}
}
```

4. Add a *number animation* to the `text` object:

```
Text {
    text: qsTr("Hello World");
    anchors.centerIn: parent;
    color: "white";
    font.pointSize: 15;
    SequentialAnimation on opacity {
        NumberAnimation { to: 0.0; duration: 200}
        NumberAnimation { to: 1.0; duration: 200}
        loops: Animation.Infinite;
    }
}
```

5. Add another *number animation* to it:

```
Text {
    text: qsTr("Hello World");
    anchors.centerIn: parent;
    color: "white";
    font.pointSize: 15;
    SequentialAnimation on opacity {
        NumberAnimation { to: 0.0; duration: 200}
        NumberAnimation { to: 1.0; duration: 200}
        loops: Animation.Infinite;
    }
    NumberAnimation on rotation {
        from: 0;
        to: 360;
        duration: 2000;
        loops: Animation.Infinite;
    }
}
```

6. Define two *states*, one called the PRESSED state and another called the RELEASED state. Then, set the default state to RELEASED:

```
Rectangle {
    id: background;
    anchors.fill: parent;
    state: "RELEASED";
    states: [
    State {
        name: "PRESSED"
        PropertyChanges { target: background; color: "blue"}
    },
    State {
        name: "RELEASED"
        PropertyChanges { target: background; color: "red"}
    }
    ]
}
```

7. After that, create a mouse area within the Rectangle object so that we can click on it:

```
MouseArea {
    anchors.fill: parent;
    onPressed: background.state = "PRESSED";
    onReleased: background.state = "RELEASED";
}
```

8. Add some transitions to the Rectangle object:

```
transitions: [
    Transition {
        from: "PRESSED"
        to: "RELEASED"
        ColorAnimation { target: background; duration: 200}
    },
    Transition {
        from: "RELEASED"
        to: "PRESSED"
        ColorAnimation { target: background; duration: 200}
    }
    ]
```

How it works...

The main window consists of a blue rectangle and static text that says **Hello World**. We want the background color to change from blue to yellow, then to red, and back to blue in a loop. This can be easily achieved by using the *color animation* type in QML. What we are doing in *step 3* is basically creating a *sequential animation group* within the `Rectangle` object, then creating three different *color animations* within the group, which will change the color of the object every 1,000 milliseconds (1 second). We also set the animations to loop infinitely.

In *step 4*, we want to use the *number animation* to animate the alpha value of the static text. We created another *sequential animation group* within the `Text` object and created two *number animations* to animate the alpha value from 0 to 1 and back. Then, we set the animations to loop infinitely.

Then, in *step 5*, we rotate the `Hello World` text by adding another **number animation** to it. In *step 6*, we wanted to make the `Rectangle` object change from one color to another when we clicked on it. When the mouse is released, the `Rectangle` object will change back to its initial color. To achieve that, we first need to define the two states, one called the `PRESSED` state and another called the `RELEASED` state. Then, we set the default state to `RELEASED`.

Now, when you compile and run the example, the background will instantly change color to blue when pressed and change back to red when the mouse is released. That works great, and we can further enhance it by giving it a little transition when switching color. This can be easily achieved by adding transitions to the `Rectangle` object.

There's more...

In QML, there are eight different types of property animation you can use, and these are as follows:

- **Anchor animation**: Animates changes in anchor values
- **Color animation**: Animates changes in color values
- **Number animation**: Animates changes in qreal-type values
- **Parent animation**: Animates changes in parent values
- **Path animation**: Animates an item along a path
- **Property animation**: Animates changes in property values
- **Rotation animation**: Animates changes in rotation values
- **Vector3d animation**: Animates changes in QVector3D values

Just like the C++ version, these animations can also be grouped together in an animation group to play the animations in sequence or parallel. You can also control the animations using easing curves and determine when to play these animations using state machines, just like we did in the previous section.

Animating widget properties using animators

In this recipe, we will learn how to animate the properties of our GUI widgets using the animator feature that's provided by QML.

How to do it...

Animating QML objects is really easy if you perform the following steps:

1. Create a `Rectangle` object and add a *scale animator* to it:

```
Rectangle {
    id: myBox;
    width: 50;
    height: 50;
    anchors.horizontalCenter: parent.horizontalCenter;
    anchors.verticalCenter: parent.verticalCenter;
    color: "blue";
    ScaleAnimator {
        target: myBox;
        from: 5;
        to: 1;
        duration: 2000;
        running: true;
    }
}
```

2. Add a *rotation animator* and set the `running` value in the parallel animation group, but not in any of the individual animators:

```
ParallelAnimation {
    ScaleAnimator {
        target: myBox;
        from: 5;
        to: 1;
        duration: 2000;
    }
    RotationAnimator {
        target: myBox;
        from: 0;
        to: 360;
        duration: 1000;
    }
    running: true;
}
```

3. Add an *easing curve* to the *scale animator*:

```
ScaleAnimator {
    target: myBox;
    from: 5;
    to: 1;
    duration: 2000;
    easing.type: Easing.InOutElastic;
    easing.amplitude: 2.0;
    easing.period: 1.5;
    running: true;
}
```

How it works...

The *animator* type can be used just like any other *animation* type. We want to scale a rectangle from a size of 5 to a size of 1 within 2,000 milliseconds (2 seconds). We created a blue `Rectangle` object and added a *scale animator* to it. We set the `initial` value to 5 and the `final` value to 1. Then, we set the animation `duration` to `2000` and set the `running` value to `true` so that it will be played when the program starts.

Just like the animation types, animators can also be put into groups (that is, **parallel animation groups** or **sequential animation groups**). An animation group will also be treated as an animator by QtQuick and be run on the scene graph's rendering thread whenever possible. In step 2, we want to group two different animators into a **parallel animation group** so that they run together at the same time.

We will keep the **scale animator** we created previously and add another **rotation animator** to rotate the **Rectangle** object. This time, set the `running` value in the parallel animation group, but not in any of the individual animators.

Just like the C++ version, QML also supports **easing curves**, and they can be easily applied to any of the animations or animator types.

There's more...

There is something called an *animator* in QML, which is different from the usual *animation* type, even though there is some similarity between them. Unlike regular animation types, animator types are directly operated on Qt Quick's **scene graph**, rather than the QML objects and their properties. The value of the QML property will not be changed while the animation is running, as it will only change once the animation is finished. The benefit of using the animator type is that it operates directly on the scene graph's rendering thread, which means its performance will be slightly better than running on the **UI thread**.

Sprite animation

In this example, we will learn how to create a **sprite animation** in QML.

How to do it...

Let's make a horse run across our application window by following these steps:

1. We will need to add our sprite sheet to Qt's *resource system* so that it can be used in the program. Open up qml.qrc and click the **Add | Add Files** buttons. Select your sprite sheet image and save the resource file by pressing *Ctrl + S*.

2. Create a new empty window in main.qml:

```
import QtQuick 2.9
import QtQuick.Window 2.3
Window {
    visible: true
    width: 420
    height: 380
    Rectangle {
        anchors.fill: parent
        color: "white"
    }
}
```

3. Once you are done with that, we will start creating an AnimatedSprite object in QML:

```
import QtQuick 2.9
import QtQuick.Window 2.3
Window {
    visible: true;
    width: 420;
    height: 380;
    Rectangle {
        anchors.fill: parent;
        color: "white";
    }
```

4. Then, set the following:

```
    AnimatedSprite {
        id: sprite;
        width: 128;
        height: 128;
        anchors.centerIn: parent;
```

```
            source: "qrc:///horse_1.png";
            frameCount: 11;
            frameWidth: 128;
            frameHeight: 128;
            frameRate: 25;
            loops: Animation.Infinite;
            running: true;
        }
    }
```

5. Add a *mouse area* to the window and check for the `onClicked` event:

```
MouseArea {
    anchors.fill: parent;
    onClicked: {
        if (sprite.paused)
            sprite.resume();
        else
            sprite.pause();
    }
}
```

6. If you compile and run the example program now, you will see a little pony running in the middle of the window. How fun:

Figure 3.8 – A horse running across the application window

7. Next, we want to try and do something cool. We will make the horse run across the window and loop infinitely while playing its running animation! First, we need to remove `anchors. centerIn: parent` from QML and replace it with `x` and `y` values:

```
AnimatedSprite {
    id: sprite;
    width: 128;
    height: 128;
    x: -128;
    y: parent.height / 2;
    source: "qrc:///horse_1.png";
    frameCount: 11;
    frameWidth: 128;
    frameHeight: 128;
    frameRate: 25;
    loops: Animation.Infinite;
    running: true;
}
```

8. Add a *number animation* to the sprite object and set its properties, as follows:

```
NumberAnimation {
    target: sprite;
    property: "x";
    from: -128;
    to: 512;
    duration: 3000;
    loops: Animation.Infinite;
    running: true;
}
```

9. If you compile and run the example program now, you will see the pony go crazy and start running across the window!

How it works...

In this recipe, we place the animated sprite object in the middle of the window and set its image source to the sprite sheet that we have just added to the project resource. Then, we count how many frames there are in the sprite sheet that belong to the running animation, which in this case is 11 frames. We also inform Qt of the dimensions of each frame of the animation, which in this case are 128 x 128. After that, we set the frame rate to 25 to get a decent speed and then set it to loop infinitely. We then set the `running` value to `true` so that the animation will play by default when the program starts running.

Then, in *step 4*, we want to be able to pause the animation and resume it by clicking on the window. We simply check whether the sprite is currently paused when clicking on the mouse area. If the sprite animation is paused, then the animation resumes; otherwise, the animation is paused.

In *step 6*, we replace anchors.centerIn with x and y values so that the animated sprite object is not anchored to the center of the window, which would make it impossible to move around. Then, we create a *number animation* within the animated sprite to animate its x property. We set the start value to somewhere outside the window on the left side, and we set the end value to somewhere outside the window on the right side. After that, we set the duration to 3,000 milliseconds (3 seconds) and make it loop infinitely.

Lastly, we also set the running value to true so that it plays the animation by default when the program starts running.

There's more...

Sprite animation is used extensively, especially in game development. Sprites are used for character animation, particle animation, and even GUI animation. A sprite sheet consists of many images combined into one, which can then be chopped down and displayed on the screen, one at a time. The transitions between different images (or sprites) from the sprite sheet creates the illusion of animation, which we usually refer to as a sprite animation. A Sprite animation can be easily achieved in QML using the AnimatedSprite type.

> **Note**
>
> In this example program, I am using a free and open source image that was created by **bluecarrot16** under the *CC-BY 3.0/GPL 3.0/GPL 2.0/OGA-BY 3.0* license. The image can be obtained legally at http://opengameart.org/content/lpc-horse.

4

QPainter and 2D Graphics

In this chapter, we will learn how to render 2D graphics on screen with Qt. Internally, Qt uses a low-level class called QPainter to render its widgets on the main window. Qt allows us to access and use the QPainter class for drawing vector graphics, text, 2D images, and even 3D graphics.

You can make use of the QPainter class to create your own custom widgets or to create programs that rely heavily on rendering computer graphics such as video games, photo editors, and 3D modeling tools.

In this chapter, we're going to cover the following main topics:

- Drawing basic shapes on the screen
- Exporting shapes to **Scalable Vector Graphics (SVG)** files
- **Coordinate transformation**
- Displaying images on screen
- Applying image effects to graphics
- Creating a basic paint program
- Rendering a 2D canvas in QML

Technical requirements

The technical requirements for this chapter include **Qt 6.6.1 MinGW 64-bit** and **Qt Creator 12.0.2**. All the code used in this chapter can be downloaded from the following GitHub repository: https://github.com/PacktPublishing/QT6-C-GUI-Programming-Cookbook---Third-Edition-/tree/main/Chapter04.

Drawing basic shapes on the screen

In this section, we will learn how to draw simple vector shapes (a line, a rectangle, a circle, and so on) and display text on the main window using the QPainter class. We will also learn how to change the drawing style of these vector shapes using the QPen class.

How to do it...

Let's follow the steps listed here to display basic shapes in our Qt window:

1. First, let's create a new **Qt Widgets Application** project.

2. Open up mainwindow.ui and remove the menuBar, mainToolBar, and statusBar objects so that we get a clean, empty main window. Right-click on the bar widgets and select **Remove Menu Bar** from the pop-up menu:

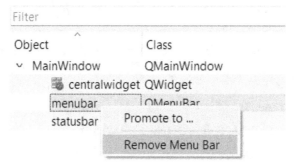

Figure 4.1 – Removing the menu bar from the main window

3. Then, open up the mainwindow.h file and add the following code to include the QPainter header file:

```
#include <QMainWindow>
#include <QPainter>
```

4. Then, declare the paintEvent() event handler below the class destructor:

```
public:
explicit MainWindow(QWidget *parent = 0);
~MainWindow();
virtual void paintEvent(QPaintEvent *event);
```

5. Next, open up the mainwindow.cpp file and define the paintEvent() event handler:

```
void MainWindow::paintEvent(QPaintEvent *event) {}
```

6. After that, we will add text to the screen using the `QPainter` class inside the `paintEvent()` event handler. We set the text font settings before drawing it on the screen at the position of `(20, 30)`:

```
QPainter textPainter;
textPainter.begin(this);
textPainter.setFont(QFont("Times", 14, QFont::Bold));
textPainter.drawText(QPoint(20, 30), "Testing");
textPainter.end();
```

7. Then, we will draw a straight line that starts from `(50, 60)` and ends at `(100, 100)`:

```
QPainter linePainter;
linePainter.begin(this);
linePainter.drawLine(QPoint(50, 60), QPoint(100, 100));
linePainter.end();
```

8. We can also easily draw a rectangle by calling the `drawRect()` function using a `QPainter` class. This time, however, we also apply a background pattern to the shape before drawing it:

```
QPainter rectPainter;
rectPainter.begin(this);
rectPainter.setBrush(Qt::BDiagPattern);
rectPainter.drawRect(QRect(40, 120, 80, 30));
rectPainter.end();
```

9. Next, declare a `QPen` class, set its color to `red`, and set its drawing style to `Qt::DashDotLine`. Then, apply the `QPen` class to `QPainter` and draw an ellipse shape at `(80, 200)` with a horizontal radius of `50` and a vertical radius of `20`:

```
QPen ellipsePen;
ellipsePen.setColor(Qt::red);
ellipsePen.setStyle(Qt::DashDotLine);
QPainter ellipsePainter;
ellipsePainter.begin(this);
ellipsePainter.setPen(ellipsePen);
ellipsePainter.drawEllipse(QPoint(80, 200), 50, 20);
ellipsePainter.end();
```

10. We can also use the `QPainterPath` class to define a shape before passing it over to the `QPainter` class for rendering:

```
QPainterPath rectPath;
rectPath.addRect(QRect(150, 20, 100, 50));
QPainter pathPainter;
pathPainter.begin(this);
```

```
pathPainter.setPen(QPen(Qt::red, 1, Qt::DashDotLine,
Qt::FlatCap, Qt::MiterJoin));
pathPainter.setBrush(Qt::yellow);
pathPainter.drawPath(rectPath);
pathPainter.end();
```

11. You can also draw any other shapes by using `QPainterPath`, such as an ellipse:

```
QPainterPath ellipsePath;
ellipsePath.addEllipse(QPoint(200, 120), 50, 20);
QPainter ellipsePathPainter;
ellipsePathPainter.begin(this);
ellipsePathPainter.setPen(QPen(QColor(79, 106, 25), 5,
Qt::SolidLine, Qt::FlatCap, Qt::MiterJoin));
ellipsePathPainter.setBrush(QColor(122, 163, 39));
ellipsePathPainter.drawPath(ellipsePath);
ellipsePathPainter.end();
```

12. `QPainter` can also be used to draw an image file onto the screen. In the following example, we load an image file called `tux.png` and draw it on the screen at the (`100`, `150`) position:

```
QImage image;
image.load("tux.png");
QPainter imagePainter(this);
imagePainter.begin(this);
imagePainter.drawImage(QPoint(100, 150), image);
imagePainter.end();
```

13. The final result should look something like this:

Figure 4.2 – Tux the penguin is overwhelmed by the shapes and lines

How it works...

If you want to draw something on screen using QPainter, all you need to do is tell it what type of graphics it should be drawing (as in text, a vector shape, an image, a polygon) with the desired position and size. The QPen class determines what the outline of the graphic should look like, such as its color, line width, line style (solid, dashed, or dotted), cap style, join style, and so on. On the other hand, QBrush sets the style of the background of the graphics, such as the background color, pattern (solid color, gradient, dense brush, and crossing diagonal lines), and pixmap.

The options for the graphics should be set before calling a draw function (such as drawLine(), drawRect(), or drawEllipse()). If your graphics do not appear on the screen and you see warnings such as QPainter::setPen: Painter not active and QPainter::setBrush: Painter not active appearing on the application output window in Qt Creator, it means that the QPainter class is not currently active and your program will not trigger its paint event. To solve this problem, set the main window as the parent of the QPainter class. Usually, if you're writing code in the mainwindow.cpp file, all you need to do is to put this in the brackets when initializing QPainter. For example, note the following:

```
QPainter linePainter(this);
```

QImage can load images from both the computer directories and from the program resources.

There's more...

Think of QPainter as a robot with a pen and an empty canvas. You just have to tell the robot what type of shape it should be drawing and its location on the canvas, then the robot will do its job based on your description.

To make your life easier, the QPainter class also provides numerous functions, such as drawArc(), drawEllipse(), drawLine(), drawRect(), and drawPie(), which allow you to easily render a predefined shape. In Qt, all the widget classes (including the main window) have an event handler called QWidget::paintEvent(). This event handler will be triggered whenever the operating system thinks that the main window should re-draw its widgets. Many things can lead to that decision, such as the main window being scaled, a widget changing its state (that is, a button being pressed), or functions such as repaint() or update() being invoked manually in the code. Different operating systems may behave differently when it comes to deciding whether or not to trigger the update event on the same set of conditions. If you're making a program that requires continuous and consistent graphical updates, call repaint() or update() manually with a timer.

Exporting shapes to SVG files

SVG is an XML-based language for describing 2D vector graphics. Qt provides classes for saving vector shapes as SVG files. This feature can be used to create a simple vector graphics editor similar to Adobe Illustrator and Inkscape. In the next example, we will continue using the same project file from the previous example.

How to do it...

Let's learn how to create a simple program that displays SVG graphics on screen:

1. First of all, let's create a menu bar by right-clicking the main window widget on the hierarchy window and selecting the **Create Menu Bar** option from the pop-up menu. After that, add a **File** option to the menu bar and a **Save as SVG** action underneath it:

Figure 4.3 – Create a Save as SVG option on the menu bar

2. After that, you will see an item called **actionSave_as_SVG** in the **Action Editor** window at the bottom of the Qt Creator window. Right-click on the item and choose **Go to slot...** from the pop-up menu. A window will now appear, which carries a list of slots available for the particular action. Choose the default signal, which is called `triggered()`, and click the **OK** button:

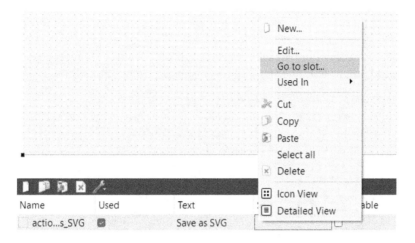

Figure 4.4 – Creating a slot function for the triggered() signal

3. Once you have clicked the **OK** button, Qt Creator will switch over to the script editor. You will realize that a slot called on_actionSave_as_SVG_triggered() has been automatically added to your main window class. At the bottom of your mainwindow.h file, you will see something like this:

```
void MainWindow::on_actionSave_as_SVG_triggered() {}
```

4. The preceding function is called when you click on the **Save as SVG** option from the menu bar. We will write our code within this function to save all the vector graphics into an SVG file. To do that, first of all, we need to include a class header called QSvgGenerator at the top of our source file. This header is very important as it's required for generating SVG files. Then, we also need to include another class header called QFileDialog, which will be used to open the save dialog:

```
#include <QtSvg/QSvgGenerator>
#include <QFileDialog>
```

5. We also need to add the svg module to our project file, like so:

```
QT += core gui svg
```

6. Then, create a new function called paintAll() within the mainwindow.h file, as shown in the following code:

```
public:
    explicit MainWindow(QWidget *parent = 0);
    ~MainWindow();
    virtual void paintEvent(QPaintEvent *event);
    void paintAll(QSvgGenerator *generator = 0);
```

7. After that, in the `mainwindow.cpp` file, move all the code from `paintEvent()` to the `paintAll()` function. Then, replace all the individual `QPainter` objects with a single, unified `QPainter` for drawing all the graphics. Also, call the `begin()` function before drawing anything and call the `end()` function after finishing drawing. The code should look like this:

```cpp
void MainWindow::paintAll(QSvgGenerator *generator) {
    QPainter painter;
    if (engine)
        painter.begin(engine);
    else
        painter.begin(this);
    painter.setFont(QFont("Times", 14, QFont::Bold));
    painter.drawText(QPoint(20, 30), "Testing");
    painter.drawLine(QPoint(50, 60), QPoint(100, 100));
    painter.setBrush(Qt::BDiagPattern);
    painter.drawRect(QRect(40, 120, 80, 30));
```

8. We go on to create **ellipsePen** and **rectPath**:

```cpp
    QPen ellipsePen;
    ellipsePen.setColor(Qt::red);
    ellipsePen.setStyle(Qt::DashDotLine);
    painter.setPen(ellipsePen);
    painter.drawEllipse(QPoint(80, 200), 50, 20);
    QPainterPath rectPath;
    rectPath.addRect(QRect(150, 20, 100, 50));
    painter.setPen(QPen(Qt::red, 1, Qt::DashDotLine,
Qt::FlatCap, Qt::MiterJoin));
    painter.setBrush(Qt::yellow);
    painter.drawPath(rectPath);
```

9. Then, we go on to create `ellipsePath` and `image`:

```cpp
    QPainterPath ellipsePath;
    ellipsePath.addEllipse(QPoint(200, 120), 50, 20);
    painter.setPen(QPen(QColor(79, 106, 25), 5, Qt::SolidLine,
Qt::FlatCap, Qt::MiterJoin));
    painter.setBrush(QColor(122, 163, 39));
    painter.drawPath(ellipsePath);
    QImage image;
    image.load("tux.png");
    painter.drawImage(QPoint(100, 150), image);
    painter.end();
}
```

10. Since we have moved all the code from paintEvent() to paintAll(), we shall now call the paintAll() function inside paintEvent(), like so:

```
void MainWindow::paintEvent(QPaintEvent *event) {
    paintAll();
}
```

11. Then, we will write the code for exporting the graphics as an SVG file. The code will be written inside the slot function called on_actionSave_as_SVG_triggered(), which was generated by Qt. We start by calling the save file dialog and obtain the directory path with the desired filename from the user:

```
void MainWindow::on_actionSave_as_SVG_triggered() {
    QString filePath = QFileDialog::getSaveFileName(this, «Save
SVG», «», «SVG files (*.svg)»);
    if (filePath == "")
        return;
}
```

12. After that, create a QSvgGenerator object and save the graphics to an SVG file by passing the QSvgGenerator object to the paintAll() function:

```
void MainWindow::on_actionSave_as_SVG_triggered() {
    QString filePath = QFileDialog::getSaveFileName(this, "Save
SVG", "", "SVG files (*.svg)");
    if (filePath == "")
        return;
    QSvgGenerator generator;
    generator.setFileName(filePath);
    generator.setSize(QSize(this->width(), this->height()));
    generator.setViewBox(QRect(0, 0, this->width(), this-
>height()));
    generator.setTitle("SVG Example");
    generator.setDescription("This SVG file is generated by
Qt.");
    paintAll(&generator);
}
```

13. Now, compile and run the program and you should be able to export the graphics by going to **File | Save as SVG**:

Figure 4.5 – Comparing the results between our program and the SVG file on a web browser

How it works...

By default, QPainter will use the paint engine from its parent object to draw the graphics assigned to it. If you don't assign any parent to QPainter, you can manually assign a paint engine to it, which is what we have done in this example.

The reason why we placed the code into paintAll() is that we want to reuse the same code for two different purposes: for displaying the graphics on the window and exporting the graphics to an SVG file. You can see that the default value of the generator variable in the paintAll() function is set to 0, which means no QSvgGenerator object is required to run the function unless specified. Later on, in the paintAll() function, we check whether the generator object exists. If it does exist, use it as the paint engine for the painter, as shown in the following code:

```
if (engine)
    painter.begin(engine);
else
    painter.begin(this);
```

Otherwise, pass the main window to the begin() function (since we're writing the code in the mainwindow.cpp file, we can directly use this to refer to the main window's pointer) so that it will use the paint engine of the main window itself, which means the graphics will be drawn onto the surface of the main window. In this example, it's required to use a single QPainter object to save the graphics into the SVG file. If you use multiple `QPainter` objects, the resulting SVG file will contain multiple XML header definitions, and thus the file will be deemed to be invalid by any graphics editor software out there.

`QFileDialog::getSaveFileName()` will open up the native save file dialog for the user to choose the save directory and set a desired filename. Once the user is done with that, the full path will be returned as a string, and we will be able to pass that information to the `QSvgGenerator` object to export the graphics.

Notice that in the previous screenshot, the penguin in the SVG file has been cropped. This is because the canvas size of the SVG was set to follow the size of the main window. To help the poor penguin get its body back, scale the window bigger before exporting the SVG file.

There's more...

SVG defines the graphics in XML format. Since it is a form of vector graphics, SVG files do not lose any quality if they are zoomed in on or resized. The SVG format not only allows you to store vector graphics in the working file, but it also allows you to store raster graphics and text, which is more or less similar to Adobe Illustrator's format. The SVG also allows you to group, style, transform, and composite graphical objects into previously rendered objects.

> **Note**
>
> You can check out the full specification of SVG graphics at `https://www.w3.org/TR/SVG`.

Coordinate transformation

In this example, we will learn how to use coordinate transformation and a timer to create a real-time clock display.

How to do it...

To create our first graphical clock display, let's follow these steps:

1. First, create a new **Qt Widgets Application** project. Then, open up `mainwindow.ui` and remove the `menuBar`, `mainToolBar`, and `statusBar` as we did before.

2. After that, open up the `mainwindow.h` file and include the following headers:

```
#include <QTime>
#include <QTimer>
#include <QPainter>
```

3. Then, declare the `paintEvent()` function, like so:

```
public:
    explicit MainWindow(QWidget *parent = 0);
    ~MainWindow();
    virtual void paintEvent(QPaintEvent *event);
```

4. In the `mainwindow.cpp` file, create three arrays to store the shapes of the hour hand, minute hand, and second hand, where each of the arrays contains three sets of coordinates:

```
void MainWindow::paintEvent(QPaintEvent *event) {
    static const QPoint hourHand[3] = {
        QPoint(4, 4),
        QPoint(-4, 4),
        QPoint(0, -40)
    };
    static const QPoint minuteHand[3] = {
        QPoint(4, 4),
        QPoint(-4, 4),
        QPoint(0, -70)
    };
    static const QPoint secondHand[3] = {
        QPoint(2, 2),
        QPoint(-2, 2),
        QPoint(0, -90)
    };
}
```

5. After that, add the following code below the arrays to create the painter and move it to the center of the main window. Also, we adjust the size of the painter so that it fits nicely in the main window, even when the window is being resized:

```
int side = qMin(width(), height());
QPainter painter(this);
painter.setRenderHint(QPainter::Antialiasing);
painter.translate(width() / 2, height() / 2);
painter.scale(side / 250.0, side / 250.0);
```

6. Once you are done with that, we will start drawing the dials by using a for loop. Each dial is rotated by an increment of 6 degrees, so 60 dials would complete a full circle. Also, the dial will look slightly longer at every five minutes:

```
for (int i = 0; i < 60; ++i) {
    if ((i % 5) != 0)
        painter.drawLine(92, 0, 96, 0);
    else
```

```
                    painter.drawLine(86, 0, 96, 0);
                painter.rotate(6.0);
        }
```

7. Then, we proceed with drawing the hands of the clock. Each hand's rotation is calculated according to the current time and its respective equivalent location over 360 degrees:

```
QTime time = QTime::currentTime();
// Draw hour hand
painter.save();
painter.rotate((time.hour() * 360) / 12);
painter.setPen(Qt::NoPen);
painter.setBrush(Qt::black);
painter.drawConvexPolygon(hourHand, 3);
painter.restore();
```

8. Let's draw the minute hand of the clock:

```
// Draw minute hand
painter.save();
painter.rotate((time.minute() * 360) / 60);
painter.setPen(Qt::NoPen);
painter.setBrush(Qt::black);
painter.drawConvexPolygon(minuteHand, 3);
painter.restore();
```

9. Then, we also draw the hand for seconds:

```
// Draw second hand
painter.save();
painter.rotate((time.second() * 360) / 60);
painter.setPen(Qt::NoPen);
painter.setBrush(Qt::black);
painter.drawConvexPolygon(secondHand, 3);
painter.restore();
```

10. Last, but not least, create a timer to refresh the graphics every second so that the program will work like a real clock:

```
MainWindow::MainWindow(QWidget *parent) : QMainWindow(parent),
ui(new Ui::MainWindow) {
    ui->setupUi(this);
    QTimer* timer = new QTimer(this);
    timer->start(1000);
    connect(timer, QTimer::timeout, this, MainWindow::update);
}
```

11. Compile and run the program now, and you should see something like this:

Figure 4.6 – A real-time analog clock displayed on the Qt application

How it works...

Each of the arrays contains three `QPoint` data instances, which form the shape of an elongated triangle. The arrays are then passed to the painter and rendered as a convex polygon using the `drawConvexPolygon()` function. Before drawing each of the clock hands, we use `painter.save()` to save the state of the `QPainter` object and then proceed with drawing the hand using coordinate transformation.

Once we're done with the drawing, we restore the painter to its previous state by calling `painter.restore()`. This function will undo all the transformations before `painter.restore()` so that the next clock hand will not inherit the transformations of the previous one. Without using `painter.save()` and `painter.restore()`, we will have to manually change the position, rotation, and scale before drawing the next hand.

A good example of not using `painter.save()` and `painter.restore()` is when drawing the dials. Since each dial's rotation is an increment of six degrees from the previous one, we don't need to save the painter's state at all. We just have to call `painter.rotate(6.0)` in a loop and each dial will inherit the previous dial's rotation. We also use a modulus operator (`%`) to check whether the unit represented by the dial can be divided by five. If it can, then we draw it slightly longer.

Without using a timer to constantly call the `update()` slot, the clock will not function properly. This is because `paintEvent()` will not be called by Qt when there is no change to the state of the parent widget, which in this case is the main window. Therefore, we need to manually tell Qt that we need to refresh the graphics by calling `update()` every second.

We used the `painter.setRenderHint(QPainter::Antialiasing)` function to enable anti-aliasing when rendering the clock. Without anti-aliasing, the graphics will look very jagged and pixelated:

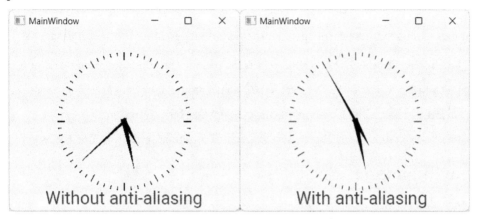

Figure 4.7 – Anti-aliasing produces a smoother result

There's more...

The `QPainter` class uses the coordinate system to determine the position and size of the graphics before rendering them on screen. This information can be altered to make the graphics appear at a different position, rotation, and size. This process of altering the coordinate information of a graphic is what we call coordinate transformation. There are several types of transformation: among them are **translation**, **rotation**, **scaling**, and **shearing**:

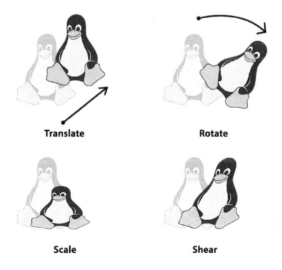

Figure 4.8 – Different types of transformations

Qt uses a coordinate system that has its origin at the top-left corner, meaning the x values increase to the right and the y values increase downward. This coordinate system might be different from the coordinate system used by the physical device, such as a computer screen. Qt handles this automatically by using the QPaintDevice class, which maps Qt's logical coordinates to the physical coordinates.

QPainter provides four transform operations to perform different types of transformation:

- QPainter::translate(): This offsets the graphic's position by a given set of units
- QPainter::rotate(): This rotates the graphics around the origin in a clockwise direction
- QPainter::scale(): This offsets the graphic's size by a given factor
- QPainter::shear(): This twists the graphic's coordinate system around the origin

Displaying images on screen

Qt not only allows us to draw shapes and images on screen, but it also allows us to overlay multiple images on top of each other and combine the pixel information from all the layers using different types of algorithms to create very interesting results. In this example, we will learn how to overlay images on top of each other and apply different composition effects to them.

How to do it...

Let's create a simple demo that shows the effect of different image compositions by following these steps:

1. First, set up a new **Qt Widgets Application** project and remove the menuBar, mainToolBar, and statusBar, as we did in the first recipe.

2. Next, add the QPainter class header to the mainwindow.h file:

   ```
   #include <QPainter>
   ```

3. After that, declare the paintEvent() virtual function, like so:

   ```
   virtual void paintEvent(QPaintEvent* event);
   ```

4. In mainwindow.cpp, we will first load several image files using the QImage class:

   ```
   void MainWindow::paintEvent(QPaintEvent* event) {
       QImage image;
       image.load("checker.png");
       QImage image2;
       image2.load("tux.png");
       QImage image3;
       image3.load("butterfly.png");
   }
   ```

5. Then, create a QPainter object and use it to draw two pairs of images, where one image is on top of the other:

```
QPainter painter(this);
painter.drawImage(QPoint(10, 10), image);
painter.drawImage(QPoint(10, 10), image2);
painter.drawImage(QPoint(300, 10), image);
painter.drawImage(QPoint(300, 40), image3);
```

6. Now, compile and run the program and you should see something like this:

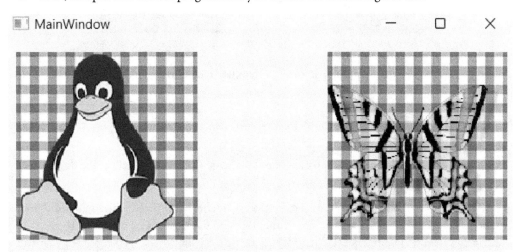

Figure 4.9 – Displaying images normally

7. Next, we will set the composition mode before drawing each image on screen:

```
QPainter painter(this);
painter.setCompositionMode(QPainter::CompositionMode_
Difference);
painter.drawImage(QPoint(10, 10), image);
painter.setCompositionMode(QPainter::CompositionMode_Multiply);
painter.drawImage(QPoint(10, 10), image2);
painter.setCompositionMode(QPainter::CompositionMode_Xor);
painter.drawImage(QPoint(300, 10), image);
painter.setCompositionMode(QPainter::CompositionMode_SoftLight);
painter.drawImage(QPoint(300, 40), image3);
```

8.   Compile and run the program again and you will now see something like this:

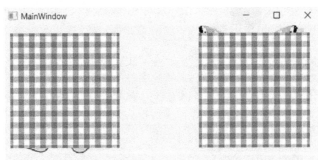

Figure 4.10 – Applying different composition modes to the images

How it works...

When drawing images with Qt, the sequence of calling the drawImage() function will determine which image is being rendered first and which one is rendered later. This will affect the depth order of the images and yield different outcomes.

In the previous example, we called the drawImage() function four times to draw four different images on screen. The first drawImage() function renders checker.png, and the second drawImage() function renders tux.png (the penguin). The image that gets rendered later will always appear in front of the others, which is why the penguin is showing in front of the checkered pattern. The same goes for the butterfly and the checkered pattern on the right. The reason why you can still see the checkered pattern even though the butterfly is rendered in front of it is because the butterfly image is not fully opaque.

Now, let's invert the render sequence and see what happens. We will try to render the penguin first, followed by the checkered box. The same goes for the other pair of images on the right: the butterfly gets rendered first, followed by the checkered box:

Figure 4.11 – Both the penguin and butterfly are covered by the checkered boxes

To apply a composition effect to the image, we'll have to set the painter's composition mode before drawing the image, by calling the `painter.setCompositionMode()` function. You can pick a desired composition mode from the auto-complete menu by typing `QPainter::CompositionMode`.

In the previous example, we applied `QPainter::CompositionMode_Difference` to the checkered box on the left, which inverted its color. Next, we applied `QPainter::CompositionMode_Overlay` to the penguin, which makes it blend with the checkered pattern, and were able to see both images overlaying each other. On the right-hand side, we applied `QPainter::CompositionMode_Xor` to the checkered box, where, if differences exist between the source and destination, colors are shown; otherwise, it will be rendered black.

Since it's comparing differences with the white background, the non-transparent part of the checkered box becomes completely black. We also applied `QPainter::CompositionMode_SoftLight` to the butterfly image. This blends the pixels with the background with reduced contrast. If you want to disable the composition mode that you've just set for the previous rendering before proceeding to the next, simply set it back to the default mode, which is `QPainter::CompositionMode_SourceOver`.

There's more...

For example, we can overlay multiple images on top of each other and use Qt's **Image Composition** feature to merge them together and calculate the resulting pixels on screen, based on the composition mode we used. This is often used in image editing software such as Photoshop and GIMP to composite image layers.

There are more than 30 types of composition modes available in Qt. Some of the most commonly used modes are as follows:

- `Clear`: The pixels in the destination are set to fully transparent, independent of the source.

- `Source`: The output is the source pixel. This mode is the inverse of `CompositionMode_Destination`.

- `Destination`: The output is the destination pixel. This means that the blending has no effect. This mode is the inverse of `CompositionMode_Source`.

- `Source Over`: This is often referred to as **alpha blending**. The alpha of the source is used to blend the pixel on top of the destination. This is the default mode used by `QPainter`.

- `Destination Over`: The output is the blend between the alpha of the destination on top of the source pixels. The opposite of this mode is `CompositionMode_SourceOver`.

- `Source In`: The output is the source, where the alpha is reduced by that of the destination.

- `Destination In`: The output is the destination, where the alpha is reduced by that of the source. This mode is the inverse of `CompositionMode_SourceIn`.

- Source Out: The output is the source, where the alpha is reduced by the inverse of the destination.

- Destination Out: The output is the destination, where the alpha is reduced by the inverse of the source. This mode is the inverse of CompositionMode_SourceOut.

- Source Atop: The source pixel is blended on top of the destination, with the alpha of the source pixel reduced by the alpha of the destination pixel.

- Destination Atop: The destination pixel is blended on top of the source, with the alpha of the source pixel reduced by the alpha of the destination pixel. This mode is the inverse of CompositionMode_SourceAtop.

- Xor: This is short for Exclusive OR, which is an advanced blending mode that is primarily used for image analysis. Using this is much more complicated with this composition mode. First, the alpha of the source is reduced by the inverse of the destination alpha. Then, the alpha of the destination is reduced by the inverse of the source alpha. Finally, both the source and destination are then merged to produce the output.

> **Note**
> For more information, you can visit this link: https://pyside.github.io.

The following figure shows the outcome of overlaying two images with different composition modes:

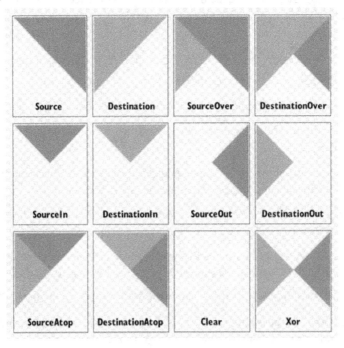

Figure 4.12 – Different types of composition modes

Applying image effects to graphics

Qt provides an easy way to add image effects to any graphics drawn using the `QPainter` class. In this example, we will learn how to apply different image effects, such as drop shadow, blur, colorize, and opacity effects, to a graphic before displaying it on screen.

How to do it...

Let's learn how to apply image effects to text and graphics by following these steps:

1. Create a new **Qt Widgets Application** project and remove the `menuBar`, `mainToolBar`, and `StatusBar`.

2. Create a new resource file by going to **File | New File or Project** and add all the images required by the project:

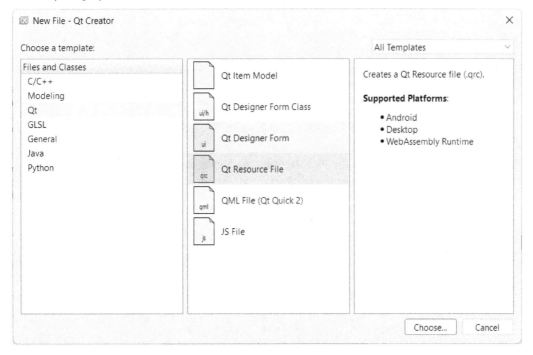

Figure 4.13 – Creating a new Qt resource file

3. Next, open up `mainwindow.ui` and add four labels to the window. Two of the labels will be text, and the two others we will load with the images we have just added to the resource file:

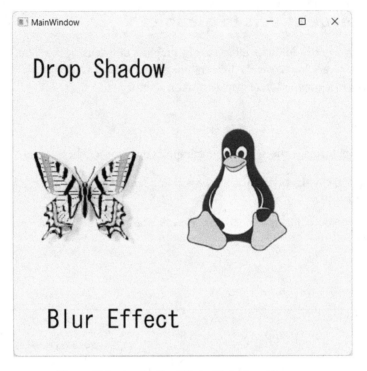

Figure 4.14 – Application filled with text and images

4. You may already notice that the font sizes are way bigger than the default size. That can be achieved by adding a style sheet to the label widget, for example, as follows:

```
font: 26pt "MS Gothic";
```

5. After that, open up mainwindow.cpp and include the following headers at the top of the source code:

```
#include <QGraphicsBlurEffect>
#include <QGraphicsDropShadowEffect>
#include <QGraphicsColorizeEffect>
#include <QGraphicsOpacityEffect>
```

6. Then, within the constructor of the MainWindow class, add the following code to create a DropShadowEffect, and apply it to one of the labels:

```
MainWindow::MainWindow(QWidget *parent) : QMainWindow(parent),
ui(new Ui::MainWindow) {
ui->setupUi(this);
QGraphicsDropShadowEffect* shadow = new
QGraphicsDropShadowEffect();
shadow->setXOffset(4);
```

```
shadow->setYOffset(4);
ui->label->setGraphicsEffect(shadow);
}
```

7. Next, we will create `ColorizedEffect` and apply it to one of the images, in this case, the butterfly. We also set the effect color to red:

```
QGraphicsColorizeEffect* colorize = new
QGraphicsColorizeEffect();
colorize->setColor(QColor(255, 0, 0));
ui->butterfly->setGraphicsEffect(colorize);
```

8. Once we're done with that, create `BlurEffect` and set its radius to 12. Then, apply the graphics effect to the other label:

```
QGraphicsBlurEffect* blur = new QGraphicsBlurEffect();
blur->setBlurRadius(12);
ui->label2->setGraphicsEffect(blur);
```

9. Lastly, create an alpha effect and apply it to the penguin image. We set the opacity value to 0.2, which means 20% opacity:

```
QGraphicsOpacityEffect* alpha = new QGraphicsOpacityEffect();
alpha->setOpacity(0.2);
ui->penguin->setGraphicsEffect(alpha);
```

10. Now, compile and run the program and you should be able to see something like this:

Figure 4.15 – Different types of graphics effects being applied to the texts and images

How it works...

Each of the graphic effects is a class of its own that inherits the QGraphicsEffect parent class. You can create your own custom effect by creating a new class that inherits QGraphicsEffect and re-implementing some of the functions in it.

Each effect has its own set of variables that are specifically created for it. For example, you can set the color of the colorized effect, but there is no such variable in the blur effect. This is because each effect is vastly different from the others, which is also why it needs to be a class of its own rather than using the same class for all the different effects.

It's only possible to add a single graphics effect to a widget at a time. If you add more than one effect, only the last one will be applied to the widget, as it replaces the previous one. Other than that, be aware that if you create a graphics effect, for example, the drop shadow effect, you can't assign it to two different widgets, as it will only get assigned to the last widget you applied it to. If you need to apply the same type of effect to several different widgets, create a few graphics effects of the same type and apply each of them to their respective widgets.

There's more...

Currently, Qt supports blur, drop shadow, colorize, and opacity effects. These effects can be used by calling the following classes: QGraphicsBlurEffect, QGraphicsDropShadowEffect, QGraphicsColorizeEffect, and QGraphicsOpacityEffect. All these classes are inherited from the QGraphicsEffect class. You can also create your own custom image effect by creating a subclass of QGrapicsEffect (or any other existing effects) and re-implementing the draw() function.

The graphics effect changes only the bounding rectangle of the source. If you want to increase the margin of the bounding rectangle, re-implement the virtual boundingRectFor() function, and call updateBoundingRect() to notify the framework whenever this rectangle changes.

Creating a basic paint program

Since we have learned so much about the QPainter class and how to use it to display graphics on screen, I guess it's time for us to do something fun where we can put our knowledge into practice.

In this recipe, we will learn how to make a basic paint program that allows us to draw lines on a canvas with different brush sizes and colors. We will also learn how to use the QImage class and mouse events in order to construct the paint program.

How to do it...

Let's start our fun project with the following steps:

1. Again, we start by creating a new **Qt Widgets Application** project and removing the toolbar and status bar. We will keep the menu bar this time.

2. After that, set up the menu bar like so:

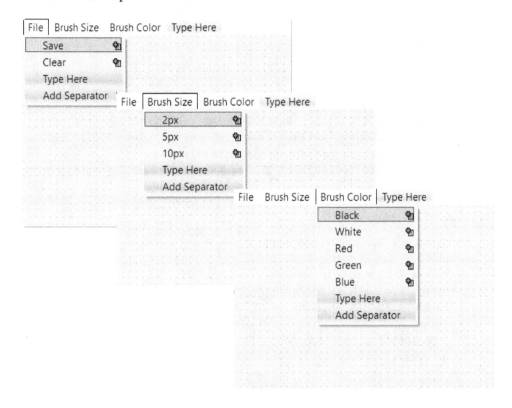

Figure 4.16 – Setting up the menu bar

3. We will leave the menu bar as it is for the moment, so let's proceed to the `mainwindow.h` file. First, include the following header files, as they are required for the project:

```
#include <QPainter>
#include <QMouseEvent>
#include <QFileDialog>
```

4. Next, declare the variables that we'll be using for this project, like so:

```
private:
    Ui::MainWindow *ui;
    QImage image;
    bool drawing;
    QPoint lastPoint;
    int brushSize;
    QColor brushColor;
```

5. Then, declare the event callback functions, which are inherited from the QWidget class. These functions will be triggered by Qt when the respective event happens. We will override these functions and tell Qt what to do when these events get called:

```
public:
    explicit MainWindow(QWidget *parent = 0);
    ~MainWindow();
    virtual void mousePressEvent(QMouseEvent *event);
    virtual void mouseMoveEvent(QMouseEvent *event);
    virtual void mouseReleaseEvent(QMouseEvent *event);
    virtual void paintEvent(QPaintEvent *event);
    virtual void resizeEvent(QResizeEvent *event);
```

6. After that, go to the mainwindow.cpp file and add the following code to the class constructor to set up some of the variables:

```
MainWindow::MainWindow(QWidget *parent) : QMainWindow(parent),
ui(new Ui::MainWindow) {
    ui->setupUi(this);
    image = QImage(this->size(), QImage::Format_RGB32);
    image.fill(Qt::white);
    drawing = false;
    brushColor = Qt::black;
    brushSize = 2;
}
```

7. Next, we will construct the mousePressEvent() event and tell Qt what to do when the left mouse button is pressed:

```
void MainWindow::mousePressEvent(QMouseEvent *event) {
    if (event->button() == Qt::LeftButton) {
        drawing = true;
        lastPoint = event->pos();
    }
}
```

8. Then, we will construct the mouseMoveEvent() event and tell Qt what to do when the mouse is moving. In this case, we want to draw the lines on the canvas if the left mouse button is being held:

```
void MainWindow::mouseMoveEvent(QMouseEvent *event) {
    if ((event->buttons() & Qt::LeftButton) && drawing) {
        QPainter painter(&image);
        painter.setPen(QPen(brushColor, brushSize,
Qt::SolidLine, Qt::RoundCap, Qt::RoundJoin));
        painter.drawLine(lastPoint, event->pos());
```

```
lastPoint = event->pos();
        this->update();
    }
}
```

9. After that, we will also construct the `mouseReleaseEvent()` event, which will be triggered when the mouse button is released:

```
void MainWindow::mouseReleaseEvent(QMouseEvent *event) {
    if (event->button() == Qt::LeftButton) {
        drawing = false;
    }
}
```

10. Once you're done with that, we will proceed to the `paintEvent()` event, which is surprisingly simple compared to the other examples we have seen in previous sections:

```
void MainWindow::paintEvent(QPaintEvent *event) {
    QPainter canvasPainter(this);
    canvasPainter.drawImage(this->rect(), image, image.rect());
}
```

11. Remember how we have a menu bar sitting around doing nothing? Let's right-click on each of the actions below the GUI editor and select **Go to slot...** in the pop-up menu. We want to tell Qt what to do when each of these options on the menu bar is selected:

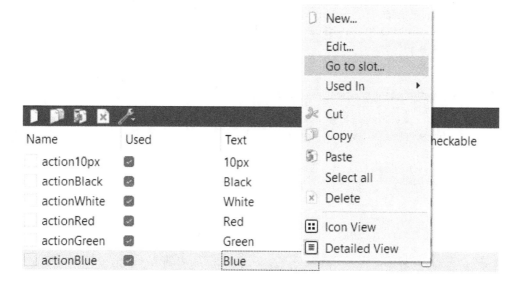

Figure 4.17 – Creating slot function for each of the menu actions

12. Then, select the default slot called `triggered()` and press the **OK** button. Qt will automatically generate a new slot function in both your `mainwindow.h` and `mainwindow.cpp` files. Once you are done with all the actions, you should see something like this in your `mainwindow.h` file:

```
private slots:
    void on_actionSave_triggered();
    void on_actionClear_triggered();
    void on_action2px_triggered();
    void on_action5px_triggered();
    void on_action10px_triggered();
    void on_actionBlack_triggered();
    void on_actionWhite_triggered();
    void on_actionRed_triggered();
    void on_actionGreen_triggered();
    void on_actionBlue_triggered();
```

13. Next, we will tell Qt what to do when each of these slots is triggered:

```
void MainWindow::on_actionSave_triggered() {
    QString filePath = QFileDialog::getSaveFileName(this, «Save
Image», «», «PNG (*.png);;JPEG (*.jpg *.jpeg);;All files
(*.*)»);
    if (filePath == "")
        return;
    image.save(filePath);
}
void MainWindow::on_actionClear_triggered() {
    image.fill(Qt::white);
    this->update();
}
```

14. Then, we continue to implement the other slots:

```
void MainWindow::on_action2px_triggered() {
    brushSize = 2;
}
void MainWindow::on_action5px_triggered() {
    brushSize = 5;
}
void MainWindow::on_action10px_triggered() {
    brushSize = 10;
}
void MainWindow::on_actionBlack_triggered() {
    brushColor = Qt::black;
}
```

15. Finally, we implement the rest of the slot functions:

```
void MainWindow::on_actionWhite_triggered() {
    brushColor = Qt::white;
}
void MainWindow::on_actionRed_triggered() {
    brushColor = Qt::red;
}
void MainWindow::on_actionGreen_triggered() {
    brushColor = Qt::green;
}
void MainWindow::on_actionBlue_triggered() {
    brushColor = Qt::blue;
}
```

16. If we compile and run the program now, we will get a simple but usable paint program:

Figure 4.18 – Our lovely paint program in action!

How it works...

In this example, we created a QImage widget when the program started. This widget acts as the canvas and will follow the size of the window whenever the window gets resized. In order to draw something on the canvas, we will need to use the mouse events provided by Qt. These events will tell us the position of the cursor, and we will be able to use this information to change the pixels on the canvas.

We use a Boolean variable called `drawing` to let the program know whether it should start drawing when a mouse button is pressed. In this case, when the left mouse button is pressed, the `drawing` variable will be set to `true`. We also save the current cursor position to the `lastPoint` variable when the left mouse button is pressed, so that Qt will know where it should start drawing. When the mouse moves, the `mouseMoveEvent()` event will be triggered by Qt. This is where we need to check whether the `drawing` variable is set to `true`. If it is, then `QPainter` can start drawing the lines onto the `QImage` widget based on the brush settings that we provide. The brush settings consist of `brushColor` and `brushSize`. These settings are saved as variables and can be altered by selecting a different setting from the menu bar.

Please remember to call the `update()` function when the user is drawing on the canvas. Otherwise, the canvas will remain empty even though we have changed the pixel information of the canvas. We also have to call the `update()` function when we select **File** | **Clear** from the menu bar to reset our canvas.

In this example, we use `QImage::save()` to save the image file, which is very straightforward. We use the file dialog to let the user decide where to save the image and its desired filename. Then, we pass the information to `QImage`, and it will do the rest by itself. If we don't specify the file format to the `QImage::save()` function, `QImage` will try to figure it out by looking at the extension of the desired filename.

Rendering a 2D canvas in QML

In all the previous examples of this chapter, we have discussed the methods and techniques used to render 2D graphics with Qt's C++ API. However, we have yet to learn how to achieve similar results using the powerful QML script.

How to do it...

In this project, we'll be doing something quite different:

1. As usual, the first step is to create a new project by going to **File** | **New File or Project** and selecting **Qt Quick Application** as the project template:

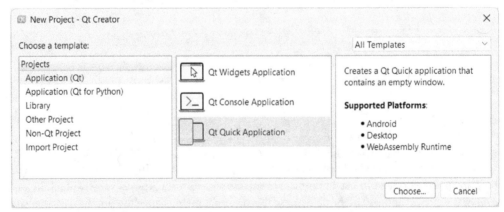

Figure 4.19 – Creating a new Qt Quick Application project

2. Once you are done creating the new project, open up `main.qml`, which is listed under `qml.qrc` in the project pane. After that, set an ID for the window and adjust its `width` and `height` values to larger values, like so:

```
import QtQuick
import QtQuick.Window
Window {
    id: myWindow
    visible: true
    width: 640
    height: 480
    title: qsTr("Hello World")
}
```

3. Then, add a `Canvas` object under `myWindow` and call it `myCanvas`. After that, we make its `width` and `height` values the same as `myWindow`:

```
Window {
    id: myWindow
    visible: true
    width: 640
    height: 480
    Canvas {
        id: myCanvas
        width: myWindow.width
        height: myWindow.height
    }
}
```

4. Next, we define what will happen when the `onPaint` event is triggered; in this case, we will draw a cross on the window:

```
Canvas {
    id: myCanvas
    width: myWindow.width
    height: myWindow.height
    onPaint: {
        var context = getContext('2d')
        context.fillStyle = 'white'
        context.fillRect(0, 0, width, height)
        context.lineWidth = 2
        context.strokeStyle = 'black'
```

5. Let's continue to write the code, like so:

```
// Draw cross
context.beginPath()
context.moveTo(50, 50)
context.lineTo(100, 100)
context.closePath()
context.stroke()
context.beginPath()
context.moveTo(100, 50)
context.lineTo(50, 100)
context.closePath()
context.stroke()
    }
}
```

6. After that, we add the following code to draw a tick beside the cross:

```
// Draw tick
context.beginPath()
context.moveTo(150, 90)
context.lineTo(158, 100)
context.closePath()
context.stroke()
context.beginPath()
context.moveTo(180, 100)
context.lineTo(210, 50)
context.closePath()
context.stroke()
```

7. Then, draw a triangle shape by adding the following code:

```
// Draw triangle
context.lineWidth = 4
context.strokeStyle = "red"
context.fillStyle = "salmon"
context.beginPath()
context.moveTo(50,150)
context.lineTo(150,150)
context.lineTo(50,250)
context.closePath()
context.fill()
context.stroke()
```

8. After that, draw a half circle and a full circle with the following code:

```
// Draw circle
context.lineWidth = 4
context.strokeStyle = "blue"
context.fillStyle = "steelblue"
var pi = 3.141592653589793
context.beginPath()
context.arc(220, 200, 60, 0, pi, true)
context.closePath()
context.fill()
context.stroke()
```

9. Then, we draw an arc:

```
context.beginPath()
context.arc(220, 280, 60, 0, 2 * pi, true)
context.closePath()
context.fill()
context.stroke()
```

10. Finally, we draw a 2D image from a file:

```
// Draw image
context.drawImage("tux.png", 280, 10, 150, 174)
```

11. However, the preceding code alone will not successfully render an image on screen because you must also load the image file beforehand. Add the following code within the `Canvas` object to ask QML to load the image file when the program is started, then call the `requestPaint()` signal when the image is loaded so that the `onPaint()` event slot will be triggered:

```
onImageLoaded: requestPaint();
onPaint: {
    // The code we added previously
}
```

12. Then, open up `qml.qrc` by right-clicking it in the project panel and select **Open in Editor**. After that, add the `tux.png` image file to our project resource:

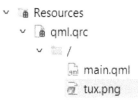

Figure 4.20 – The tux.png image file is now listed under qml.qrc

13. Now, build and run the program and you should get the following:

Figure 4.21 – Tux the penguin is amused by the geometrical shapes

In the preceding example, we learned how to draw simple vector shapes on our screen using the Canvas element. Qt's built-in modules make the complex rendering process more straightforward for programmers.

5

OpenGL Implementation

In this chapter, we will learn how to use **Open Graphics Library** (**OpenGL**), a powerful rendering **application program interface** (**API**), and combine it with **Qt**. OpenGL is a cross-language, cross-platform API for drawing 2D and 3D graphics on screen through the **graphics processing unit** (**GPU**) within our computer's graphics chip. In this chapter, we will be learning about OpenGL 3 instead of 2 because, even though the fixed-function pipeline is easier for beginners to grasp compared to the newer programmable pipeline, it is considered legacy code and has been deprecated by most modern 3D rendering software. Qt 6 supports both versions, so there should be no problem switching over to OpenGL 2 if you need backward compatibility for your software.

In this chapter, we're going to cover the following main topics:

- Setting up OpenGL in Qt
- Hello World!
- Rendering 2D shapes
- Rendering 3D shapes
- Texturing in OpenGL
- Basic lighting in OpenGL
- Moving an object using keyboard controls
- Qt Quick 3D in QML

Technical requirements

The technical requirements for this chapter include Qt 6.6.1 MinGW 64-bit and Qt Creator 12.0.2. All the code used in this chapter can be downloaded from the following GitHub repository: `https://github.com/PacktPublishing/QT6-C-GUI-Programming-Cookbook---Third-Edition-/tree/main/Chapter05`.

Setting up OpenGL in Qt

In this recipe, we will learn how to set up OpenGL in Qt 6.

How to do it...

Follow these steps to learn how to set up OpenGL in Qt:

1. Create a new **Qt Widgets Application** by going to **File | New Project**. Uncheck the **Generate form** option to avoid generating the mainwindow.ui, mainwindow.h, and mainwindow. cpp files.

2. Open up your project file (.pro) and add the OpenGL module to your project by adding an opengl keyword behind QT +=; after that, run qmake to reload the project modules:

   ```
   QT += core gui opengl
   ```

3. You also need to add another line in your project file so that it will load both the OpenGL and **OpenGL Utilities (GLU)** libraries during startup. Without these two libraries, your program will not be able to run:

   ```
   LIBS += -lopengl32 -lglu32
   ```

4. Open up main.cpp and replace mainwindow.h with the QtOpenGL header:

   ```
   #include <QtOpenGL>
   ```

5. Remove all of the code related to the MainWindow class from your main.cpp file and replace it with the code that's highlighted in the following snippet:

   ```
   #include <QApplication>
   #include <QtOpenGL>
   int main(int argc, char *argv[])
   {
       QApplication app(argc, argv);
       QOpenGLWindow window;
       window.setTitle("Hello World!");
       window.resize(640, 480);
       window.show();
       return app.exec();
   }
   ```

6. If you compile and run the project now, you will see an empty window with a black background. Don't worry about it—your program is now running on OpenGL:

Figure 5.1 - An empty OpenGL window

How it works...

The OpenGL module must be added to the project file (.pro) in order to access header files that are related to OpenGL, such as QtOpenGL and QOpenGLFunctions. We used the QOpenGLWindow class instead of QMainWindow for the main window because it is designed to easily create windows that perform OpenGL rendering, and it offers better performance compared to QOpenGLWidget due to the fact that it has no dependencies in its widget module.

We must call setSurfaceType(QWindow::OpenGLSurface) to tell Qt we would prefer to use OpenGL to render the images to screen instead of QPainter. The QOpenGLWindow class provides several virtual functions (initializeGL(), resizeGL(), paintGL(), and so on) for us to conveniently set up OpenGL and perform graphics rendering. We will be learning how to use these functions in the following example.

There's more...

OpenGL is a cross-language, cross-platform API for drawing 2D and 3D graphics on screen through the GPU within our computer's graphics chip. Computer graphics technology has been evolving rapidly over the years—so rapidly that the software industry can hardly keep up with its pace.

In 2008, the Khronos Group, the company that maintains and develops OpenGL, announced the release of the OpenGL 3.0 specification, which created a huge uproar and controversy throughout the industry. That was mainly because OpenGL 3.0 was supposed to deprecate the entire fixed-function pipeline from the OpenGL API, and it was simply an impossible task for the big players to make the sudden switch overnight from a fixed-function pipeline to a programmable pipeline. This resulted in two different major versions of OpenGL being maintained.

In this chapter, we will use the newer OpenGL 3 instead of the older, deprecated OpenGL 2. The coding style and syntax are very different between these two versions, which makes the switchover very troublesome. However, the performance improvement will make it worth the time it takes to switch over to OpenGL 3.

Hello World!

In this chapter, we will learn how to use OpenGL 3 with Qt 6. Common OpenGL functions such as `glBegin`, `glVertex2f`, `glColor3f`, `glMatrixMode`, and `glLoadIdentity` have all been removed from OpenGL 3. OpenGL 3 uses **vertex buffer objects** (**VBOs**) to send data to the GPU in batches instead of sending them one by one through functions such as `glVertex2f()`, which slows down the rendering while waiting for the CPU to submit the data one by one. Therefore, we will pack all of the data into VBOs and send it all in one huge package to the GPU and instruct the GPU to calculate the resulting pixels through shader programming. We will also be learning how to create simple **shader programs** through a C-like programming language called **OpenGL Shading Language (GLSL)**.

How to do it...

Let's get started by following these steps:

1. We will create a new class called `RenderWindow`, which inherits from the `QOpenGLWindow` class. Go to **File | New File**, then select **C++ Class** under the **Files and Classes** category. Name the class `RenderWindow` and set its base class as `QOpenGLWindow`. Then, proceed to create the C++ class:

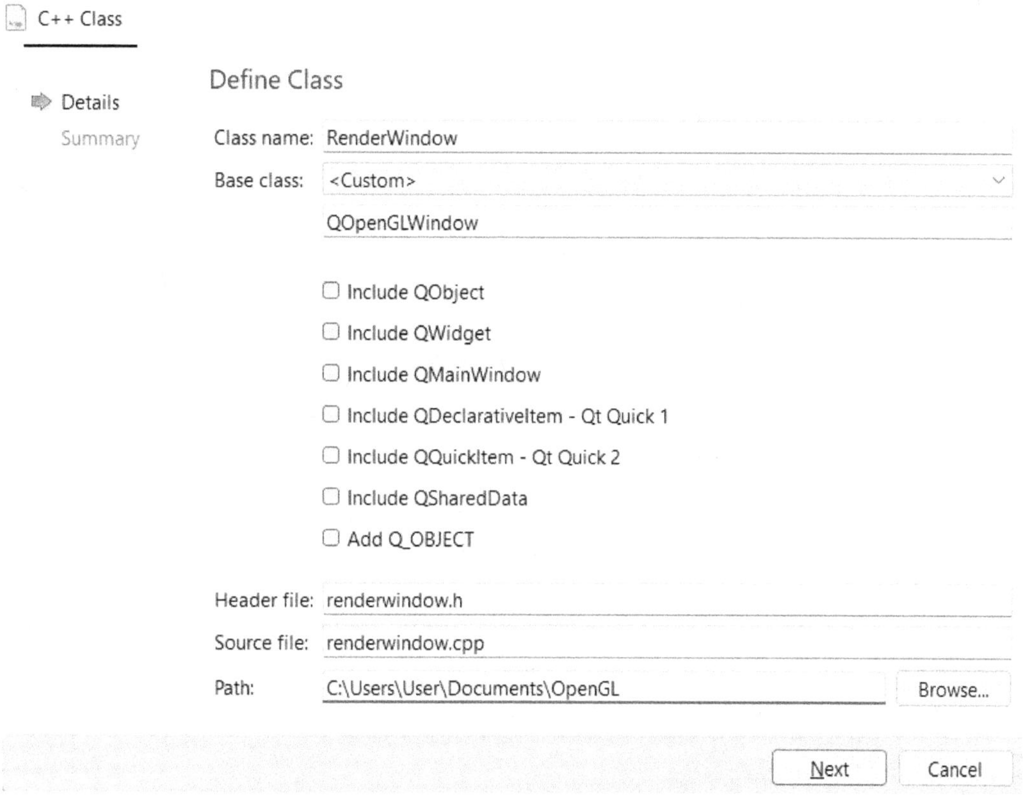

Figure 5.2 – Defining your custom render window class

2. Go to the `renderwindow.h` file we just created and add the following headers at the top of the source code:

```
#include <GL/glu.h>
#include <QtOpenGL>
#include <QSurfaceFormat>
#include <QOpenGLFunctions>
#include <QOpenGLWindow>
#include <QOpenGLBuffer>
#include <QOpenGLVertexArrayObject>
#include <QOpenGLShader>
#include <QOpenGLShaderProgram>
```

3. We need to create several functions and variables that look like this:

```
class RenderWindow : public QOpenGLWindow {
public:
```

```
        RenderWindow();
protected:
        void initializeGL();
        void paintGL();
        void paintEvent(QPaintEvent *event);
        void resizeEvent(QResizeEvent *event);
```

4. We will continue and add some private variables:

```
private:
        QOpenGLContext* openGLContext;
        QOpenGLFunctions* openGLFunctions;
        QOpenGLShaderProgram* shaderProgram;
        QOpenGLVertexArrayObject* vao;
        QOpenGLBuffer* vbo_vertices;
};
```

5. Open up renderwindow.cpp and define the class constructor as follows. We must tell the render window to use the OpenGL surface type; enable **core profile** (rather than **compatibility profile**) that runs version 3.2; create an OpenGL context; and, finally, apply the profile we just created into the context:

```
RenderWindow::RenderWindow() {
        setSurfaceType(QWindow::OpenGLSurface);
        QSurfaceFormat format;
        format.setProfile(QSurfaceFormat::CoreProfile);
        format.setVersion(3, 2);
        setFormat(format);
        openGLContext = new QOpenGLContext();
        openGLContext->setFormat(format);
        openGLContext->create();
        openGLContext->makeCurrent(this);
}
```

6. We need to define the initializeGL() function as follows. This function will be called before the rendering starts. First, we define the **vertex shader** and the **fragment shader**:

```
void RenderWindow::initializeGL() {
        openGLFunctions = openGLContext->functions();
        static const char *vertexShaderSource =
        "#version 330 core\n"
        "layout(location = 0) in vec2 posAttr;\n"
        "void main() {\n"
        "gl_Position = vec4(posAttr, 0.0, 1.0); }";
```

```
static const char *fragmentShaderSource =
"#version 330 core\n"
"out vec4 col;\n"
"void main() {\n"
"col = vec4(1.0, 0.0, 0.0, 1.0); }";
```

7. We initiate `shaderProgram` and declare a vertices array. Then, we also create a `QOpenGLVertexArrayObject` object:

```
shaderProgram = new QOpenGLShaderProgram(this);
shaderProgram->addShaderFromSourceCode(QOpenGLShader::Ver
tex, vertexShaderSource);
shaderProgram->addShaderFromSourceCode(QOpenGLShader::Fragm
ent, fragmentShaderSource);
shaderProgram->link();
// The vertex coordinates of our triangle
GLfloat vertices[] = {
-1.0f, -1.0f,
1.0f, -1.0f,
0.0f, 1.0f };
vao = new QOpenGLVertexArrayObject();
vao->create();
vao->bind();
```

8. Let's continue to write our code by defining `vbo_vertices`:

```
vbo_vertices = new
QOpenGLBuffer(QOpenGLBuffer::VertexBuffer);
vbo_vertices->create();
vbo_vertices->setUsagePattern(QOpenGLBuffer::StaticDraw);
vbo_vertices->bind();
vbo_vertices->allocate(vertices, sizeof(vertices) *
sizeof(GLfloat));
vao->release();
}
```

9. We will start by adding some code to the `paintEvent()` function:

```
void RenderWindow::paintEvent(QPaintEvent *event) {
Q_UNUSED(event);
glViewport(0, 0, width(), height());
// Clear our screen with corn flower blue color
glClearColor(0.39f, 0.58f, 0.93f, 1.f);
glClear(GL_COLOR_BUFFER_BIT);
```

10. We will then bind the VAO and shader program before calling `glDrawArrays()`:

```
vao->bind();
shaderProgram->bind();
shaderProgram->bindAttributeLocation("posAttr", 0);
shaderProgram->enableAttributeArray(0);
shaderProgram->setAttributeBuffer(0, GL_FLOAT, 0, 2);
glDrawArrays(GL_TRIANGLES, 0, 3);
shaderProgram->release();
vao->release();
}
```

11. You can refresh the viewport whenever the render window is being resized by adding the following code:

```
void RenderWindow::resizeEvent(QResizeEvent *event) {
    Q_UNUSED(event);
    glViewport(0, 0, this->width(), this->height());
    this->update();
}
```

12. If you compile and run the project now, you should be able to see a red rectangle being drawn in front of a blue background:

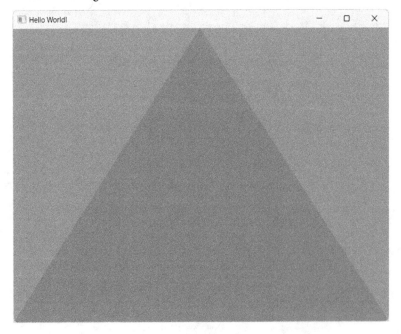

Figure 5.3 - Our first triangle rendered in OpenGL

How it works...

We must set the OpenGL version to 3.x and the surface format to the core profile so that we can access the newer shader pipeline, which is completely different from the older, deprecated compatibility profile. OpenGL 2.x still exists in the compatibility profile, solely for the sake of allowing OpenGL programs to run on old hardware. The profile that's created must be applied to the OpenGL context before it will work.

In OpenGL 3 and the later versions, most of the calculations are done in the GPU through shader programs, since all of the common fixed functions have now been completely deprecated. Therefore, we created a very simple vertex shader and fragment shader in the preceding example.

A shader program consists of three different parts: **geometry shader** (optional), vertex shader, and fragment shader. The geometry shader calculates the creation of geometry before passing the data to the vertex shader; the vertex shader handles the position and motion of the vertices before passing the data to the fragment shader; and finally, the fragment shader calculates and displays the resulting pixels on the screen.

In the preceding example, we only used vertex and fragment shaders and excluded the geometry shader since it is optional. You can save the GLSL code in a text file and load it into your Qt 6 program by calling `addShaderFromFile()`, but since our shaders are very simple and short, we just define it directly in our C++ source code.

After that, we use the VBO to store the vertex positions in bulk before sending it to the GPU. We can also use the VBO to store other information such as normals, texture coordinates, and vertex colors. You can send anything you want to the GPU as long as it matches the input inside your shader code. Then, we add the VBO into a **vertex array object** (**VAO**) and send the whole VAO to the GPU for processing. You can add many different VBOs into the VAO since the VAO is just like any ordinary C++ array.

Just like what we have learned in the previous chapters, all drawings happen within the `paintEvent()` function, and it will only be called by Qt when it thinks it is necessary to refresh the screen. To force Qt to update the screen, call `update()` manually. Also, we must update the viewport whenever the window screen has been resized by calling `glViewport(x, y ,width, height)`.

Rendering 2D shapes

Since we have already learned how to draw our first rectangle on screen, we will further enhance it in this section. We will take the previous example and continue from there.

How to do it...

Let's get started by following this example:

1. Open up `renderwindow.h` and add two more VBOs, one called `vbo_vertices2` and another called `vbo_colors`, as highlighted in the following code:

```
private:
    QOpenGLContext* openGLContext;
    QOpenGLFunctions* openGLFunctions;
    QOpenGLShaderProgram* shaderProgram;
    QOpenGLVertexArrayObject* vao;
    QOpenGLBuffer* vbo_vertices;
    QOpenGLBuffer* vbo_vertices2;
    QOpenGLBuffer* vbo_colors;
```

2. Open up `renderwindow.cpp` and add the following code to the shader code, as highlighted in the following snippet:

```
static const char *vertexShaderSource =
"#version 330 core\n"
"layout(location = 0) in vec2 posAttr;\n"
"layout(location = 1) in vec3 colAttr;\n"
"out vec3 fragCol;\n"
"void main() {\n"
"fragCol = colAttr;\n"
"gl_Position = vec4(posAttr, 1.0, 1.0); }";
```

3. Add the highlighted code to the fragment shader, which looks like this:

```
static const char *fragmentShaderSource =
"#version 330 core\n"
"in vec3 fragCol;\n"
"out vec4 col;\n"
"void main() {\n"
"col = vec4(fragCol, 1.0); }";
```

4. Change the vertices array to something like the following code. What we're doing here is creating three arrays that keep the vertices of two triangles and their colors so that we can pass them to the fragment shader at a later stage:

```
GLfloat vertices[] = {
-0.3f, -0.5f,
0.8f, -0.4f,
0.2f, 0.6f };
GLfloat vertices2[] = {
```

```
0.5f, 0.3f,
0.4f, -0.8f,
-0.6f, -0.2f };
GLfloat colors[] = {
1.0f, 0.0f, 0.0f,
0.0f, 1.0f, 0.0f,
0.0f, 0.0f, 1.0f };
```

5. Since we already initialized `vbo_vertices` in the previous example, this time, we only need to initialize two other VBOs, namely `vbo_vertices` and `vbo_colors`:

```
vbo_vertices2 = new
QOpenGLBuffer(QOpenGLBuffer::VertexBuffer);
vbo_vertices2->create();
vbo_vertices2->setUsagePattern(QOpenGLBuffer::StaticDraw);
vbo_vertices2->bind();
vbo_vertices2->allocate(vertices2, sizeof(vertices2) *
sizeof(GLfloat));

vbo_colors = new QOpenGLBuffer(QOpenGLBuffer::VertexBuffer);
vbo_colors->create();
vbo_colors->setUsagePattern(QOpenGLBuffer::StaticDraw);
vbo_colors->bind();
vbo_colors->allocate(colors, sizeof(colors) *
sizeof(GLfloat));
```

6. Before we start drawing the triangle using `glDrawArrays()`, we must also add the data of `vbo_colors` into our shader's `colAttr` attribute. Make sure you call `bind()` to set the VBO as the current active VBO, before sending the data to the shader. The location ID (in this case, 0 and 1) must match the location ID that's used in your shader:

```
vbo_vertices->bind();
shaderProgram->bindAttributeLocation("posAttr", 0);
shaderProgram->enableAttributeArray(0);
shaderProgram->setAttributeBuffer(0, GL_FLOAT, 0, 2);
vbo_colors->bind();
shaderProgram->bindAttributeLocation("colAttr", 1);
shaderProgram->enableAttributeArray(1);
shaderProgram->setAttributeBuffer(1, GL_FLOAT, 0, 3);
glDrawArrays(GL_TRIANGLES, 0, 3);
```

7. Right after the preceding code, we will send `vbo_vertices2` and `vbo_colors` to the shader attribute and call `glDrawArrays()` again to draw the second triangle:

```
vbo_vertices2->bind();
shaderProgram->bindAttributeLocation("posAttr", 0);
```

```
shaderProgram->enableAttributeArray(0);
shaderProgram->setAttributeBuffer(0, GL_FLOAT, 0, 2);
vbo_colors->bind();
shaderProgram->bindAttributeLocation("colAttr", 1);
shaderProgram->enableAttributeArray(1);
shaderProgram->setAttributeBuffer(1, GL_FLOAT, 0, 3);
glDrawArrays(GL_TRIANGLES, 0, 3);
```

8. If you build the program now, you should be able to see two triangles on screen, and one of the triangles sitting on top of the other:

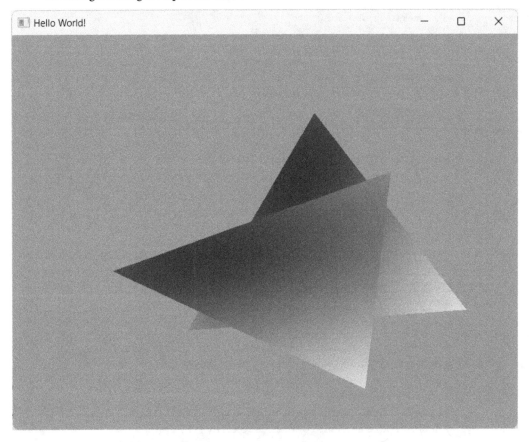

Figure 5.4 – Two colorful triangles overlapping each other

How it works...

The geometric primitive types supported by OpenGL are points, lines, line strips, line loops, polygons, quads, quad strips, triangles, triangle strips, and triangle fans. In this example, we drew two triangles, where each of the shapes is provided with a set of vertices and colors so that OpenGL knows how the shapes should be rendered.

The rainbow color effect is created by giving a different color to each of the vertices. OpenGL will automatically interpolate the colors between each vertex and display it on screen. Currently, the shape that gets rendered first will appear at the back of other shapes that get rendered later. This is because we are rendering the shapes in a 2D space and no depth information is involved to check which shape is located at the front and so on. We will learn how to do depth checking in the following example.

Rendering 3D shapes

We learned how to draw simple 2D shapes onscreen in the previous section. However, to fully utilize the OpenGL API, we also need to learn how to use it to render 3D images. In a nutshell, 3D images are simply illusions that are created using 2D shapes, stacked in such a way that it makes them look like they're 3D.

How to do it...

The main ingredient here is the depth value, which determines which shapes should appear in front of or behind the other shapes. The primitive shape that is positioned behind another surface (with a shallower depth than another shape) will not be rendered (or will be partially rendered). OpenGL provides a simple way to achieve this:

1. Let's continue our project from the previous 2D example. Enable depth testing by adding glEnable(GL_DEPTH_TEST) to the initializeGL() function in renderwindow. cpp:

    ```
    void RenderWindow::initializeGL() {
        openGLFunctions = openGLContext->functions();
        glEnable(GL_DEPTH_TEST);
    ```

2. Since we have enabled GL_DEPTH_TEST in the preceding step, we must also set the depth buffer size when setting the OpenGL profile:

    ```
    QSurfaceFormat format;
    format.setProfile(QSurfaceFormat::CoreProfile);
    format.setVersion(3, 2);
    format.setDepthBufferSize(16);
    ```

3. We will change our vertices array into something longer, which is the vertex information of a 3D cube shape. The vertex coordinates in the next code block are divided into three values per vertex coordinate, which eventually form a 3D cube. It's not realistic to hardcode the vertices of complex shapes, but achievable for simple shapes like this. We can remove the colors array for now since you are not supplying the color information to the shader this time. We can also remove the vbo_colors VBO for the same reason:

```
GLfloat vertices[] = {
  -1.0f,-1.0f,-1.0f,1.0f,-1.0f,-1.0f,-1.0f,-1.0f, 1.0f,
  1.0f,-1.0f,-1.0f,1.0f,-1.0f, 1.0f,-1.0f,-1.0f, 1.0f,
  -1.0f, 1.0f,-1.0f,-1.0f, 1.0f, 1.0f,1.0f, 1.0f,-1.0f,
  1.0f, 1.0f,-1.0f,-1.0f, 1.0f, 1.0f,1.0f, 1.0f, 1.0f,
  -1.0f,-1.0f, 1.0f,1.0f,-1.0f, 1.0f,-1.0f, 1.0f, 1.0f,
  1.0f,-1.0f, 1.0f,1.0f, 1.0f, 1.0f,-1.0f, 1.0f, 1.0f,
  -1.0f,-1.0f,-1.0f,-1.0f, 1.0f,-1.0f,1.0f,-1.0f,-1.0f,
  1.0f,-1.0f,-1.0f,-1.0f, 1.0f,-1.0f,1.0f, 1.0f,-1.0f,
  -1.0f,-1.0f, 1.0f,-1.0f, 1.0f,-1.0f,-1.0f,-1.0f,-1.0f,
  -1.0f,-1.0f, 1.0f,-1.0f, 1.0f, 1.0f,-1.0f, 1.0f,-1.0f,
  1.0f,-1.0f, 1.0f,1.0f,-1.0f,-1.0f,1.0f, 1.0f,-1.0f,
  1.0f,-1.0f, 1.0f,1.0f, 1.0f,-1.0f,1.0f, 1.0f, 1.0f
};
```

4. In the paintEvent() function, we must add GL_DEPTH_BUFFER_BIT to the glClear() function since we enabled depth checking in initializeGL() in the previous step:

```
glClear(GL_COLOR_BUFFER_BIT | GL_DEPTH_BUFFER_BIT);
```

5. After that, we need to send a piece of matrix information to the shader called **ModelView-Projection (MVP)** so that the GPU knows how to render the 3D shapes on a 2D screen. The MVP matrix is the result of multiplication between the projection matrix, view matrix, and model matrix. The multiplication order is very important so that you get the correct result:

```
QMatrix4x4 matrixMVP;
QMatrix4x4 model, view, projection;
model.translate(0, 1, 0);
model.rotate(45, 0, 1, 0);
view.lookAt(QVector3D(4, 4, 0), QVector3D(0, 0, 0),
QVector3D(0, 1, 0));
projection.perspective(60.0f,
  ((float)this->width()/(float)this->height()), 0.1f,
100.0f);
matrixMVP = projection * view * model;
shaderProgram->setUniformValue("matrix", matrixMVP);
```

6. Change the last value in `glDrawArrays()` to 36 since we now have 36 triangles in the cube shape:

```
glDrawArrays(GL_TRIANGLES, 0, 36);
```

7. We have to go back to our shader code and change some parts of it, as highlighted in the following code:

```
static const char *vertexShaderSource =
"#version 330 core\n"
"layout(location = 0) in vec3 posAttr;\n"
"uniform mat4 matrix;\n"
"out vec3 fragPos;\n"
"void main() {\n"
"fragPos = posAttr;\n"
"gl_Position = matrix * vec4(posAttr, 1.0); }";

static const char *fragmentShaderSource =
"#version 330 core\n"
"in vec3 fragPos;\n"
"out vec4 col;\n"
"void main() {\n"
"col = vec4(fragPos, 1.0); }";
```

8. If you build and run the project now, you should see a colorful cube appear on the screen. We use the same vertices array for the color, which gives this colorful result:

Figure 5.5 – Colorful 3D cube rendered with OpenGL

9. Even though the result looks pretty good, if we want to really show off the 3D effect, it would be by animating the cube. To do that, first, we need to open up `renderwindow.h` and include the following header to it:

    ```
    #include <QElapsedTimer>
    ```

10. Then, add the following variables to `renderwindow.h`. Note that you are allowed to initialize variables in the header file in modern C++ standard, which was not the case back in the older C++ standard:

    ```
    QElapsedTimer* time;
    int currentTime = 0;
    int oldTime = 0;
    float deltaTime = 0;
    float rotation = 0;
    ```

11. Open up `renderwindow.cpp` and add the following highlighted code to the class constructor:

    ```
    openGLContext = new QOpenGLContext();
    openGLContext->setFormat(format);
    openGLContext->create();
    openGLContext->makeCurrent(this);

    time = new QElapsedTimer();
    time->start();
    ```

12. After that, add the following highlighted code to the top of your `paintEvent()` function. `deltaTime` is the value of the elapsed time of each frame, which is used to make animation speed consistent, regardless of frame rate performance:

    ```
    void RenderWindow::paintEvent(QPaintEvent *event) {
        Q_UNUSED(event);

        // Delta time for each frame
        currentTime = time->elapsed();
        deltaTime = (float)(currentTime - oldTime) / 1000.0f;
        oldTime = currentTime;
    ```

13. Add the following highlighted code on top of your MVP matrix code and apply the `rotation` variable to the `rotate()` function, like so:

```
rotation += deltaTime * 50;

QMatrix4x4 matrixMVP;
QMatrix4x4 model, view, projection;
model.translate(0, 1, 0);
model.rotate(rotation, 0, 1, 0);
```

14. Call the `update()` function at the end of the `paintEvent()` function so that `paintEvent()` will be called again and again at the end of each draw call. Since we are changing the rotation value in the `paintEvent()` function, we can give the viewer the illusion of a rotating cube:

```
glDrawArrays(GL_TRIANGLES, 0, 36);
shaderProgram->release();
vao->release();

this->update();
}
```

15. If you compile and run the program now, you should see a spinning cube in your render window!

How it works...

In any 3D rendering, depth is very important and hence we need to enable the depth testing feature in OpenGL by calling `glEnable(GL_DEPTH_TEST)`. When we clear the buffer, we must also specify `GL_DEPH_BUFFER_BIT` so that the depth information is also being cleared, in order for the next image to be rendered correctly.

We use the MVP matrix in OpenGL so that the GPU knows how to render the 3D graphics correctly. In OpenGL 3 and later versions, OpenGL no longer handles this automatically through fixed functions. Programmers are given the freedom and flexibility to define their own matrices based on their use cases, and then simply supply it to the GPU through a shader for rendering the final image. The model matrix contains the transformation data of the 3D object, namely the position, rotation, and scale of the object. The view matrix, on the other hand, is the camera or view information. Lastly, the projection matrix tells the GPU which projection method to use when projecting the 3D world onto the 2D screen.

In our example, we used the perspective projection method, which gives a better perception of distance and depth. The opposite of perspective projection is **orthographic projection**, which makes everything look flat and parallel:

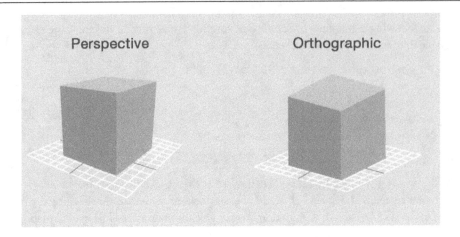

Figure 5.6 – Differences between perspective and orthographic views

In this example, we used a timer to increase the rotation value by 50 by multiplying it with the `deltaTime` value. The `deltaTime` value varies, depending on your rendering frame rate. However, it makes the resulting animation speed consistent across different hardware that renders at a different frame rate.

Remember to call `update()` manually so that the screen gets refreshed, otherwise the cube will not be animated.

Texturing in OpenGL

OpenGL allows us to map an image (also referred to as a **texture**) to a 3D shape or polygon. This process is also called texture mapping. Qt 6 appears to be the best combination with OpenGL in this case because it provides an easy way to load images that belong to one of the common formats (BMP, JPEG, PNG, TARGA, TIFF, and so on), and you do not have to implement it by yourself. We will use the previous example with a spinning cube and try to map it with a texture!

How to do it...

Let's follow these steps to learn how to use textures in OpenGL:

1. Open up `renderwindow.h` and add the variables that are highlighted in the following code block:

```
QOpenGLContext* openGLContext;
QOpenGLFunctions* openGLFunctions;
QOpenGLShaderProgram* shaderProgram;
QOpenGLVertexArrayObject* vao;
QOpenGLBuffer* vbo_vertices;
```

```
QOpenGLBuffer* vbo_uvs;
QOpenGLTexture* texture;
```

2. We must call glEnable(GL_TEXTURE_2D) in the initializeGL() function to enable the texture mapping feature:

```
void RenderWindow::initializeGL()
{
    openGLFunctions = openGLContext->functions();
    glEnable(GL_DEPTH_TEST);
    glEnable(GL_TEXTURE_2D);
```

3. We need to initialize our texture variable under the QOpenGLTexture class. We will load a texture called brick.jpg from our application folder and flip the image by calling mirrored(). OpenGL uses a different coordinate system, which is why we need to flip our texture before passing it to the shader. We will also set the min and max filters to Nearest and Linear accordingly, like so:

```
texture = new QOpenGLTexture(QImage(qApp-
>applicationDirPath() + "/brick.jpg").mirrored());
    texture->setMinificationFilter(QOpenGLTexture::Nearest);
    texture->setMagnificationFilter(QOpenGLTexture::Linear);
```

4. Add another array called uvs. This is where we save the texture coordinates for our cube object:

```
GLfloat uvs[] = {
 0.0f, 0.0f, 1.0f, 0.0f, 0.0f, 1.0f,
 1.0f, 0.0f, 1.0f, 1.0f, 0.0f, 1.0f,
 0.0f, 0.0f, 0.0f, 1.0f, 1.0f, 0.0f,
 1.0f, 0.0f, 0.0f, 1.0f, 1.0f, 1.0f,
 1.0f, 0.0f, 0.0f, 0.0f, 1.0f, 1.0f,
 0.0f, 0.0f, 0.0f, 1.0f, 1.0f, 1.0f,
 0.0f, 0.0f, 0.0f, 1.0f, 1.0f, 0.0f,
 1.0f, 0.0f, 0.0f, 1.0f, 1.0f, 1.0f,
 0.0f, 1.0f, 1.0f, 0.0f, 0.0f, 0.0f,
 0.0f, 1.0f, 1.0f, 1.0f, 1.0f, 0.0f,
 1.0f, 1.0f, 1.0f, 0.0f, 0.0f, 0.0f,
 1.0f, 1.0f, 0.0f, 0.0f, 0.0f, 1.0f
};
```

5. We have to amend our vertex shader so that it takes in the texture coordinates for calculating where the texture will be applied to the object's surface. Here, we simply pass the texture coordinate to the fragment shader without modifying:

```
static const char *vertexShaderSource =
"#version 330 core\n"
```

```
"layout (location = 0) in vec3 posAttr;\n"
"layout (location = 1) in vec2 uvAttr;\n"
"uniform mat4 matrix;\n"
"out vec3 fragPos;\n"
"out vec2 fragUV;\n"
"void main() {\n"
"fragPos = posAttr;\n"
"fragUV = uvAttr;\n"
"gl_Position = matrix * vec4(posAttr, 1.0); }";
```

6. In the fragment shader, we create a texture by calling the texture() function, which receives the texture coordinate information from fragUV and the image sampler from tex:

```
static const char *fragmentShaderSource =
"#version 330 core\n"
"in vec3 fragPos;\n"
"in vec2 fragUV;\n"
"uniform sampler2D tex;\n"
"out vec4 col;\n"
"void main() {\n"
"vec4 texCol = texture(tex, fragUV);\n"
"col = texCol; }";
```

7. We have to initialize the VBO for the texture coordinate as well:

```
vbo_uvs = new QOpenGLBuffer(QOpenGLBuffer::VertexBuffer);
vbo_uvs->create();
vbo_uvs->setUsagePattern(QOpenGLBuffer::StaticDraw);
vbo_uvs->bind();
vbo_uvs->allocate(uvs, sizeof(uvs) * sizeof(GLfloat));
```

8. In the paintEvent() function, we must send the texture coordinate information to the shader and then bind the texture before calling glDrawArrays():

```
vbo_uvs->bind();
shaderProgram->bindAttributeLocation("uvAttr", 1);
shaderProgram->enableAttributeArray(1);
shaderProgram->setAttributeBuffer(1, GL_FLOAT, 0, 2);
texture->bind();
glDrawArrays(GL_TRIANGLES, 0, 36);
```

9. If you compile and run the program now, you should see a brick cube rotating on the screen:

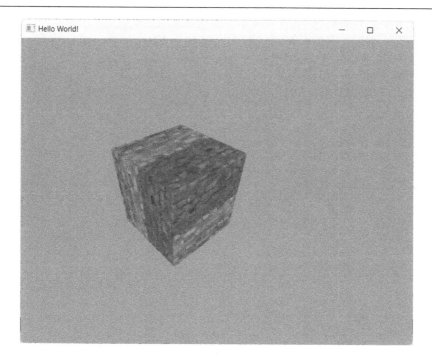

Figure 5.7 – Our 3D cube now looks like it was created from bricks

How it works...

Qt 6 makes loading textures a really easy job. All it takes is just a single line of code to load an image file, flip it, and convert it into an OpenGL-compatible texture. The texture coordinates are pieces of information that let OpenGL know how to stick the texture onto the object's surface before displaying it on screen.

The min and max filters are filters that make the texture look better when it is applied on a surface that is bigger than what its resolution can cover. The default setting for this is GL_NEAREST, which stands for **nearest neighbor filtering**. This filter tends to make textures look pixelated when viewed close up. Another common setting is GL_LINEAR, which stands for **bilinear filtering**. This filter takes two neighboring fragments and interpolates them to create an approximated color, which looks a lot better than GL_NEAREST:

GL_NEAREST

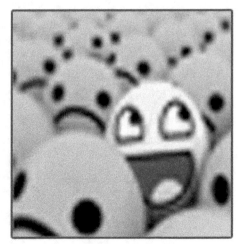
GL_LINEAR

Figure 5.8 - Differences between GL_NEAREST and GL_LINEAR

Basic lighting in OpenGL

In this example, we will learn how to add a simple point light to our 3D scene by using OpenGL and Qt 6.

How to do it...

Let's get started by following these steps:

1. Again, we will use the previous example and add a point light near the spinning cube. Open up `renderwindow.h` and add another variable called vbo_normals to the file:

```
QOpenGLBuffer* vbo_uvs;
QOpenGLBuffer* vbo_normals;
QOpenGLTexture* texture;
```

2. Open `renderwindow.cpp` and add another array called normals to the initializeGL() function:

```
GLfloat normals[] = {
    0.0f, -1.0f, 0.0f, 0.0f, -1.0f, 0.0f, 0.0f, -1.0f, 0.0f,
    0.0f, -1.0f, 0.0f, 0.0f, -1.0f, 0.0f, 0.0f, -1.0f, 0.0f,
    0.0f, 1.0f, 0.0f, 0.0f, 1.0f, 0.0f, 0.0f, 1.0f, 0.0f,
    0.0f, 1.0f, 0.0f, 0.0f, 1.0f, 0.0f, 0.0f, 1.0f, 0.0f,
    1.0f, 0.0f, 0.0f, 1.0f, 0.0f, 0.0f, 1.0f, 0.0f, 0.0f,
    1.0f, 0.0f, 0.0f, 1.0f, 0.0f, 0.0f, 1.0f, 0.0f, 0.0f,
```

```
        0.0f, 0.0f, 1.0f, 0.0f, 0.0f, 1.0f, 0.0f, 0.0f, 1.0f,
        0.0f, 0.0f, 1.0f, 0.0f, 0.0f, 1.0f, 0.0f, 0.0f, 1.0f,
        -1.0f, 0.0f, 0.0f, -1.0f, 0.0f, 0.0f, -1.0f, 0.0f, 0.0f,
        -1.0f, 0.0f, 0.0f, -1.0f, 0.0f, 0.0f, -1.0f, 0.0f, 0.0f,
        0.0f, 0.0f, -1.0f, 0.0f, 0.0f, -1.0f, 0.0f, 0.0f, -1.0f,
        0.0f, 0.0f, -1.0f, 0.0f, 0.0f, -1.0f, 0.0f, 0.0f, -1.0f
    };
```

3. Initialize the `vbo_normals` VBO in `initializeGL()` by adding the following code:

```
        vbo_normals = new
    QOpenGLBuffer(QOpenGLBuffer::VertexBuffer);
        vbo_normals->create();
        vbo_normals->setUsagePattern(QOpenGLBuffer::StaticDraw);
        vbo_normals->bind();
        vbo_normals->allocate(normals, sizeof(normals) *
    sizeof(GLfloat));
```

4. Since the shader we will be writing this time will be much longer than what we used in the previous examples, let's move the shader code over to text files and load them into the program by calling `addShaderFromSourceFile()`:

```
        shaderProgram = new QOpenGLShaderProgram(this);
        shaderProgram->addShaderFromSourceFile(QOpenGLShader::Ver
    tex,
        qApp->applicationDirPath() + "/vertex.txt");
        shaderProgram->addShaderFromSourceFile(QOpenGLShader::Fragm
    ent,
        qApp->applicationDirPath() + "/fragment.txt");
    shaderProgram->link();
```

5. Once you are done with that, add the following code to the `paintEvent()` function to pass the `normals` VBO over to the shader:

```
        vbo_normals->bind();
        shaderProgram->bindAttributeLocation("normalAttr", 2);
        shaderProgram->enableAttributeArray(2);
        shaderProgram->setAttributeBuffer(2, GL_FLOAT, 0, 3);
```

6. Let's open up the two text files we just created that contain the shader code. First, we need to make some changes to the vertex shader, like so:

```
        #version 330 core
        layout(location = 0) in vec3 posAttr;
        layout(location = 1) in vec2 uvAttr;
        layout(location = 2) in vec3 normalAttr;
        uniform mat4 matrix;
```

```
    out vec3 fragPos;
    out vec2 fragUV;
    out vec3 fragNormal;

void main() {
    fragPos = posAttr;
    fragUV = uvAttr;
    fragNormal = normalAttr;
    gl_Position = matrix * vec4(posAttr, 1.0);
}
```

7. We will also make some changes to the fragment shader. We will create a function called `calcPointLight()` in the shader code:

```
    #version 330 core
    in vec3 fragPos;
    in vec2 fragUV;
    in vec3 fragNormal;
    uniform sampler2D tex;
    out vec4 col;
    vec4 calcPointLight() {
    vec4 texCol = texture(tex, fragUV);
    vec3 lightPos = vec3(1.0, 2.0, 1.5);
    vec3 lightDir = normalize(lightPos - fragPos);
    vec4 lightColor = vec4(1.0, 1.0, 1.0, 1.0);
    float lightIntensity = 1.0;
```

8. Continuing from the preceding code, we calculated the lighting using `calcPointLight()` and output the resulting fragment to the `col` variable, as follows:

```
    // Diffuse
    float diffuseStrength = 1.0;
    float diff = clamp(dot(fragNormal, lightDir), 0.0, 1.0);
    vec4 diffuse = diffuseStrength * diff * texCol * lightColor
  * lightIntensity;
    return diffuse;
}

void main() {
    vec4 finalColor = calcPointLight();
    col = finalColor;
}
```

9.   If you compile and run the program now, you should see the lighting in action:

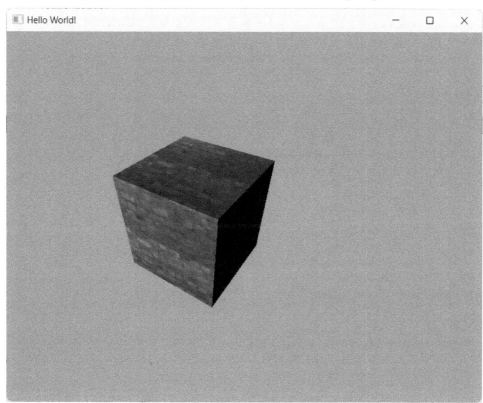

Figure 5.9 – Our 3D cube now has shading

How it works...

In OpenGL 3 and later versions, fixed-function lighting no longer exists. You can no longer call glEnable(GL_LIGHT1) to add light to your 3D scene. The new method for adding light is to calculate your own lighting in the shader. This gives you the flexibility of creating all types of lights, depending on your needs. The old method has a limitation of up to 16 lights in most hardware but, with the new programmable pipeline, you can have any number of lights in the scene; however, the lighting model will need to be coded entirely by you in the shaders, which is not an easy task.

Other than that, we also need to add a surface normal value to every surface of the cube. Surface normal indicates where the surface is facing and is used for lighting calculations. The preceding example is very simplified to let you understand how lighting works in OpenGL. In actual use cases, you may need to pass some variables such as light intensity, light color, and light position from C++ or load it from a material file instead of hardcoding it in the shader code.

Moving an object using keyboard controls

In this section, we will be looking at how to move an object in OpenGL using keyboard controls. Qt provides an easy way to detect keyboard events using virtual functions, namely `keyPressEvent()` and `keyReleaseEvent()`. We will be using the previous example and adding to it.

How to do it...

To move an object using keyboard controls, follow these steps:

1. Open up `renderwindow.h` and declare two floating-point numbers called `moveX` and `moveZ`. Then, declare a `QVector3D` variable called `movement`:

    ```cpp
    QElapsedTimer* time;
    int currentTime = 0;
    int oldTime = 0;
    float deltaTime = 0;
    float rotation = 0;
    float moveX = 0;
    float moveZ = 0;
    QVector3D movement = QVector3D(0, 0, 0);
    ```

2. We will also declare two functions called `keyPressEvent()` and `keyReleaseEvent()`:

    ```cpp
    protected:
        void initializeGL();
        void paintEvent(QPaintEvent *event);
        void resizeEvent(QResizeEvent *event);
        void keyPressEvent(QKeyEvent *event);
        void keyReleaseEvent(QKeyEvent *event);
    ```

3. We will implement the `keyPressEvent()` function in `renderwindow.cpp`:

    ```cpp
    void RenderWindow::keyPressEvent(QKeyEvent *event) {
        if (event->key() == Qt::Key_W) { moveZ = -10; }
        if (event->key() == Qt::Key_S) { moveZ = 10; }
        if (event->key() == Qt::Key_A) { moveX = -10; }
        if (event->key() == Qt::Key_D) { moveX = 10; }
    }
    ```

4. We will also implement the `keyReleaseEvent()` function:

    ```cpp
    void RenderWindow::keyReleaseEvent(QKeyEvent *event) {
        if (event->key() == Qt::Key_W) { moveZ = 0; }
        if (event->key() == Qt::Key_S) { moveZ = 0; }
        if (event->key() == Qt::Key_A) { moveX = 0; }
    ```

```
        if (event->key() == Qt::Key_D) { moveX = 0; }
    }
```

5. After that, we will comment out the rotation code in `paintEvent()` and add the movement code, as highlighted in the following snippet. We do not want to get distracted by the rotation and just want to focus on the movement:

```
//rotation += deltaTime * 50;
movement.setX(movement.x() + moveX * deltaTime);
movement.setZ(movement.z() + moveZ * deltaTime);

QMatrix4x4 matrixMVP;
QMatrix4x4 model, view, projection;
model.translate(movement.x(), 1, movement.z());
```

6. If you compile and run the program now, you should be able to move the cube around by pressing *W*, *A*, *S*, and *D*.

How it works...

What we did here was constantly add the `moveX` and `moveZ` values' movement vector's x and z values. When a key is pressed, `moveX` and `moveZ` will become a positive or negative number, depending on which button is pressed; otherwise, it will be zero. In the `keyPressEvent()` function, we checked whether the keyboard button that was pressed was *W*, *A*, *S*, or *D*; we then set the variables accordingly. To get the full list of key names that are used by Qt, visit `http://doc.qt.io/qt-6/qt.html#Key-enum`.

One way we can create movement input is by holding down the same key and not releasing it. Qt 6 will repeat the key press event after an interval, but it is not very fluid as modern operating systems limit the key press event to prevent double typing. The keyboard input interval varies between different operating systems. You can set the interval by calling `QApplication::setKeyboardInterval()`, but this may not work on every operating system. Therefore, we did not go for this method.

Instead, we only set `moveX` and `moveZ` once when the key was pressed or released, and then we constantly apply the value to the movement vector in our game loop so that it is moving continuously without being affected by the input interval.

Qt Quick 3D in QML

In this recipe, we will learn how to render 3D images using Qt 6.

How to do it...

Let's learn how to use a 3D canvas in QML by following this example:

1. Let's start this example by creating a new project in Qt Creator. This time around, we will go for **Qt Quick Application** and not the other options that we chose in the previous examples:

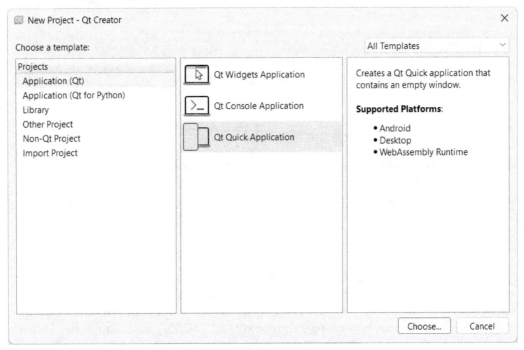

Figure 5.10 – Creating a new Qt Quick Application project

2. Once the project is created, you are required to create a resource file by going to **File** | **New File** and selecting **Qt** | **Qt Resource File** under **Files and Classes** and name it `resource.qrc`:

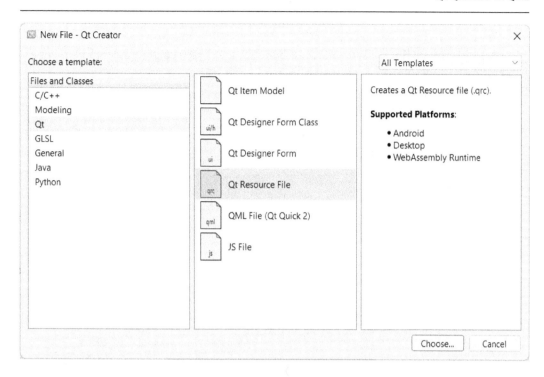

Figure 5.11 – Creating a Qt resource file

3. Add an image file to our project resources—we will be using it in this example. Open up
    resource.qrc with Qt Creator by right-clicking on it in the **Projects pane** and selecting
    Open in Editor. Once the resources file is opened by Qt Creator, click the **Add** button, followed
    by the **Add File** button, and then select the image file you want from your computer. In my case,
    I've added a brick.jpg image, which will be used as the surface texture for our 3D object:

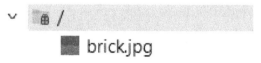

Figure 5.12 – Adding brick texture into the resource file

4. After that, open up `main.qml` using Qt Creator. You will see that there are already a few lines of code written in the file. What it does is basically open up an empty window and nothing else. Let's start adding our own code to the `Window` object.

5. First, import the `QtQuick3D` module to our project and create a `View3D` object under the `Window` object, which we will be using to render a 3D scene on it:

```
import QtQuick
import QtQuick3D

Window {
    width: 640
    height: 480
    visible: true
    title: qsTr("Hello World")

    View3D {
        id: view
        anchors.fill: parent
    }
}
```

6. After that, set the `environment` variable of the `View3D` object as a new `SceneEnvironment` object. We use this to set the background color of our 3D view to sky blue:

```
environment: SceneEnvironment {
    clearColor: "skyblue"
    backgroundMode: SceneEnvironment.Color
}
```

7. After that, we re-create the 3D cube from our previous OpenGL example by declaring a `Model` object inside our 3D view and setting its source as `Cube`. We then rotate it by `-30` units along the y-axis and apply a material to it. After that, we set the texture of the material as `brick.jpg`. The keyword `qrc:` here means we are taking the texture from the resource file we created earlier:

```
Model {
    position: Qt.vector3d(0, 0, 0)
    source: "#Cube"
    eulerRotation.y: -30
    materials: PrincipledMaterial {
        baseColorMap: Texture {
            source: "qrc:/brick.jpg"
        }
    }
}
```

```
    }
```

8. Before we're able to see our 3D cube clearly, we must create a light source as well as a camera, which helps to render our scene:

    ```
    PerspectiveCamera {
        position: Qt.vector3d(0, 200, 300)
        eulerRotation.x: -30
    }

    DirectionalLight {
        eulerRotation.x: -10
        eulerRotation.y: -20
    }
    ```

9. Once you are done, build and run the project. You should be able to see a 3D cube with a brick texture on the screen:

Figure 5.13 – Re-creating the 3D demo in QtQuick3D

10. To re-create the spinning animation, let's add `NumberAnimation` to our cube model:

```
Model {
    position: Qt.vector3d(0, 0, 0)
    source: "#Cube"
    eulerRotation.y: -30
    materials: PrincipledMaterial {
        baseColorMap: Texture {
            source: "qrc:/brick.jpg"
        }
    }
}

NumberAnimation on eulerRotation.y {
    duration: 3000
    to: 360
    from: 0
    easing.type:Easing.Linear
    loops: Animation.Infinite
}
}
```

How it works...

Originally, Qt 5 used something called **Qt Canvas 3D** to render 3D scenes in QML, which was based on the `three.js` library/API that used WebGL technology to display animated 3D computer graphics in a Qt Quick window. However, this feature has been completely deprecated in Qt 6 and has been since replaced by another module called **Qt Quick 3D**.

Qt Quick 3D works a lot better than Qt Canvas 3D as it uses native methods for rendering 3D scenes without depending on a third-party library such as `three.js`. It also produces better performance and integrates well with any existing Qt Quick components.

6

Transitioning from Qt 5 to Qt 6

In this chapter, we will learn about the changes that have been made in **Qt 6** and how you can upgrade your existing Qt 5 project to Qt 6. Unlike previous updates, Qt 6 is almost a complete rewrite of the entire Qt code base from the ground up, including all the underlying classes. Such major changes may break your existing Qt 5 project if you simply switch over to Qt 6.

In this chapter, we're going to cover the following main topics:

- Changes in C++ classes
- Using **Clazy checks** for Clang and C++
- Changes in QML types

Technical requirements

The technical requirements for this chapter include Qt 6.6.1 MinGW 64-bit, Qt 5.15.2 MinGW 64-bit, and Qt Creator 12.0.2. All the code used in this chapter can be downloaded from the following GitHub repository: `https://github.com/PacktPublishing/QT6-C-GUI-Programming-Cookbook---Third-Edition-/tree/main/Chapter06`.

Changes in C++ classes

In this recipe, we will learn what the changes in Qt6's C++ classes are.

How to do it...

Follow these steps to learn about C++ classes in Qt6:

1. Create a new **Qt Console Application** by going to **File | New Project**.

2. We will open up the main.cpp file and add the following headers:

```
#include <QCoreApplication>
#include <QDebug>

#include <QLinkedList>
#include <QRegExp>
#include <QStringView>
#include <QTextCodec>
#include <QTextEncoder>
#include <QTextDecoder>
```

3. After that, add the following code for demonstrating the QLinkedList class:

```
int main(int argc, char *argv[])
{
    QCoreApplication a(argc, argv);

    // QLinkedList
    QLinkedList<QString> list;
    list << "string1" << "string2" << "string3";
    QLinkedList<QString>::iterator it;
    for (it = list.begin(); it != list.end(); ++it)
    {
        qDebug() << "QLinkedList:" << *it;
    }
```

4. Then, we continue to add the following code to demonstrate how to extract numbers from a string by using the QRegExp class:

```
// QRegExp
QRegExp rx("\\d+");
QString text = "Jacky has 3 carrots, 15 apples, 9 oranges and 12 grapes.";
QStringList myList;
int pos = 0;
while ((pos = rx.indexIn(text, pos)) != -1)
{
    // Separate all numbers from the sentence
    myList << rx.cap(0);
```

```
        pos += rx.matchedLength();
    }
    qDebug() << "QRegExp:" << myList;
```

5. We then follow by adding the following code at the bottom of the preceding code to demonstrate the `QStringView` class:

```
// QStringView
QStringView x = QString("Good afternoon");
QStringView y = x.mid(5, 5);
QStringView z = x.mid(5);
qDebug() << "QStringView:" << y; // after
qDebug() << "QStringView:" << z; // afternoon
```

6. Not only that, but we are also adding the following code to demonstrate the `QTextCodec` class:

```
// QTextCodec
QByteArray data = "\xCE\xB1\xCE\xB2\xCE\xB3"; // Alpha, beta,
gamma symbols
QTextCodec *codec = QTextCodec::codecForName("UTF-8");
QString str = codec->toUnicode(data);
```

```
qDebug() << "QTextCodec:" << str;
```

7. Next, add the following code, which demonstrates how to convert hexadecimal code to a character using the `QTextEncoder` class:

```
// QTextEncoder
QString str2 = QChar(0x41); // Character "A"
QTextCodec *locale = QTextCodec::codecForLocale();
QTextEncoder *encoder = locale->makeEncoder();
QByteArray encoded = encoder->fromUnicode(str2);
qDebug() << "QTextEncoder:" << encoded.data();
```

8. Let's also add the following code to demonstrate how to convert a line of text from Shift JIS format to Unicode by using the `QTextDecoder` class:

```
// QTextDecoder
QByteArray data2 = "\x82\xB1\x82\xF1\x82\xC9\x82\xBF\x82\xCD\
x90\xA2\x8A\x45"; // "Hello world" in Japanese
QTextCodec *codec2 = QTextCodec::codecForName("Shift-JIS");
QTextDecoder *decoder = codec2->makeDecoder();
QString decoded = decoder->toUnicode(data2);
qDebug() << "QTextDecoder:" << decoded;
```

9. Now that we're done with the code, let's try and compile the project using Qt 5 for now and see what will happen. Your program should compile just fine and give you the following results in the output window:

```
QLinkedList: "string1"
QLinkedList: "string2"
QLinkedList: "string3"
QRegExp: ("3", "15", "9", "12")
QStringView: "after"
QStringView: "afternoon"
QTextCodec: "αβγ"
QTextEncoder: A
QTextDecoder: "こんにちは世界"
```

10. Now, let's change to Qt 6 and compile the project again, you should get errors like this:

```
QLinkedList: No such file or directory
fatal error: QLinkedList: No such file or directory
```

11. Open up your project file (.pro) and add the following code at the top:

```
QT += core5compat
```

12. Finally, compile the project again with Qt 6. You should be able to run it this time. core5compat is just a temporary solution for transitioning from Qt 5 to Qt 6. You may change to use std::list to replace QLinkedList since it will be deprecated in the future.

How it works...

We don't need any GUIs since we are just testing out some of the C++ classes, so the **Qt Console Application** is sufficient for this project. We needed the QDebug class to print out the results in the output window.

In the preceding example, we used some of the classes that have been deprecated in Qt 6, namely QLinkedList, QRegExp, QStringView, QTextCodec, QTextEncoder, and QTextDecoder. These are just some of the common classes that we will encounter when using Qt, which have been rewritten in Qt 6. If you are porting your project from Qt 5 to 6, the best way is to add the Core5Compat module to your project so that Qt 5 classes can continue to run under Qt 6. The Core5Compat module is a temporary measure for supporting Qt 5 classes under Qt 6 projects so that Qt programmers can safely move their projects to Qt 6 and take their time to slowly port their code over to Qt 6 classes.

The Core5Compat module will stop working when you move to Qt 7, so it's not recommended to keep using the deprecated classes for too long.

There's more...

In Qt 6, a lot of the core functionality has been rewritten from scratch to keep the library up to date with the modern computing architecture and workflow. Thus, Qt 6 is considered a transitional phase where some classes have been completed and some have not.

In order for it to work, Qt developers introduced the Core5Compat module to make it easier for Qt programmers to keep their projects going while slowly transitioning over to the new classes. You can check out what the replacements for these classes are from the official online documentation.

Lastly, Qt 6 is now leveraging on C++ 17. It's highly recommended for your project to adhere to C++ 17 standards so that your code can work nicely with Qt 6.

> **Note**
> There are many other C++ classes that have been deprecated or are being rewritten in Qt 6; please refer to this link to check the full list of C++ classes that have been changed or deprecated in Qt 6: https://doc.qt.io/qt-6/obsoleteclasses.html. You may also add the QT_DISABLE_DEPRECATED_UP_TO macro to your Qt project to disable the use of deprecated C++ APIs in your project. For example, adding DEFINES += QT_DISABLE_ DEPRECATED_UP_TO=0x050F00 to your profile will disable all C++ APIs deprecated in Qt 5.15.

Using Clazy checks for Clang and C++

In this chapter, we will learn how to use the Clazy checks from the Clang toolset to automatically display warnings when obsolete Qt 5 classes and functions are detected in your Qt project.

How to do it...

Let's get started by following these steps:

1. We will use the same project from the preceding example. Then, proceed to open up the preferences window by going to **Edit | Preferences…**.

2. After that, go to the **Analyzer** page and click on the button beside **Diagnostic configuration**:

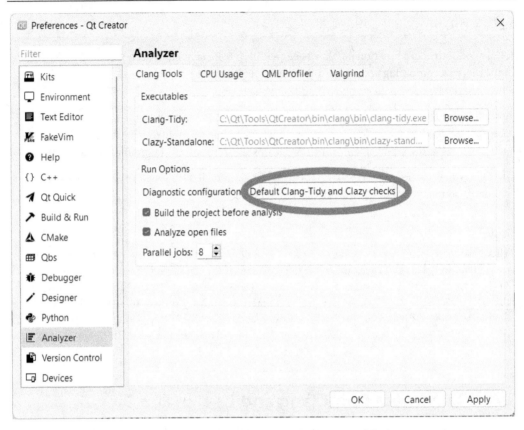

Figure 6.1 – Open up the Diagnostic configuration window

3. Select the **Default Clang-Tidy and Clazy checks** option at the top and click the **Copy...** button, as shown in *Figure 6.2*. Give it a name and click **OK**. The new option will now appear under the **Custom** category:

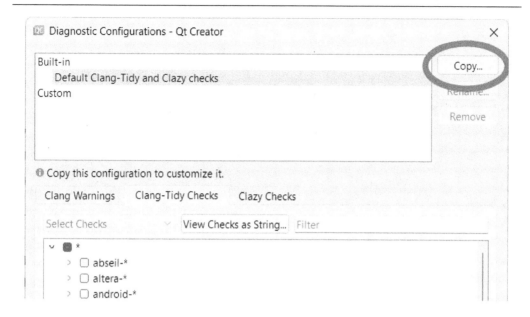

Figure 6.2 - Click on the Copy button

4. Then, open the **Clazy Checks** tab, enable the following options, and click **OK**:

    *   `qt6-deprecated-api-fixes`

    *   `qt6-header-fixes`

    *   `qt6-qhash-signature`

    *   `qt6-fwd-fixes`

    *   `missing-qobject-macro`

5. Once you're done, close the preference window and go to **Analyze | Clang-Tidy and Clazy....**
    The **Files to Analyze** window will pop up with all the source files being displayed on the
    window. We will just stick to the default option and proceed by clicking the **Analyze** button:

Figure 6.3 – Choose All Files and press the Analyze button

6. After the Clang-Tidy and Clazy tools finish analyzing the project, you should see the results displayed on a separate panel under the Qt Creator. It will show you the lines of code that have been deprecated in Qt 6 and give you suggestions on what to replace them with:

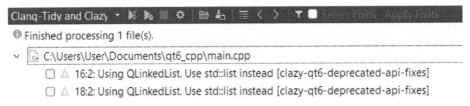

Figure 6.4 – Results from the analysis

How it works...

The Tidy and Clazy tool came with Clang packages so there is no need to install it separately. It is a powerful tool that can be used to check for many things, such as using deprecated functions in your code, placing a container inside a loop, marking a non-void slot as constant, registering QML type that starts with lowercase, and so on.

It's a tool that helps you to inspect and improve the quality of your code with ease. It should be widely promoted and used more frequently by Qt programmers.

Changes in QML types

In this chapter, we will learn what changes have been made in Qt 6 compared to Qt 5.

How to do it...

Let's get started by following these steps:

1. Create a new **Qt Quick Application** by going to **File | New Project**.

2. Select the **Qt 6.2** option for **Minimum required Qt version** when defining project details.

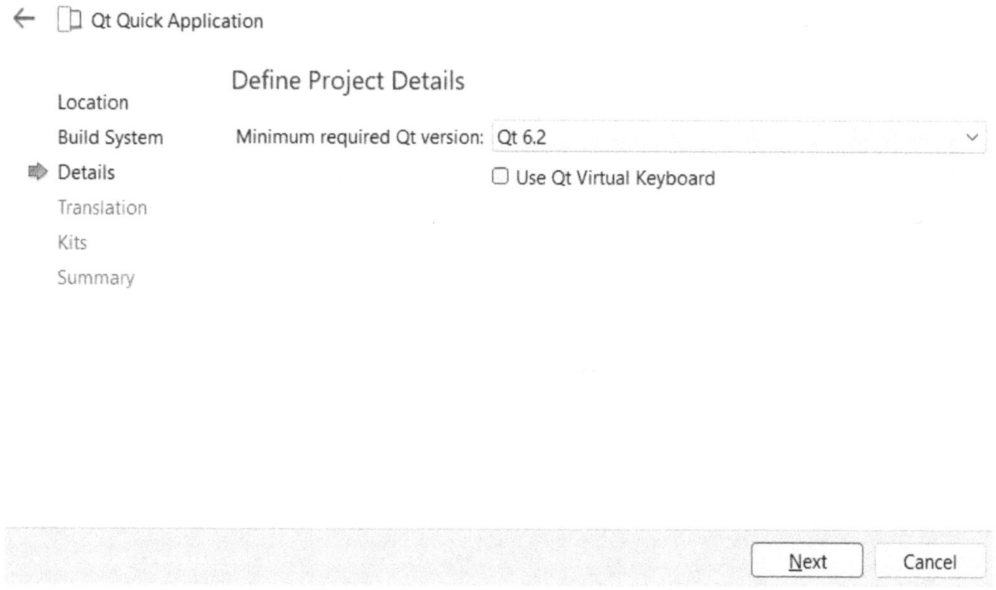

←   ▯ Qt Quick Application

Define Project Details

Location	
Build System	Minimum required Qt version: Qt 6.2 ⌄
➡ Details	☐ Use Qt Virtual Keyboard
Translation	
Kits	
Summary	

Next   Cancel

Figure 6.5 – Select Qt 6.2 as Minimum required Qt version

3. Once you have created the project, open up main.qml and add these properties to the file:

```
import QtQuick

Window {
    width: 640
    height: 480
    visible: true
    title: qsTr("Hello World")

    property variant myColor: "red"
    property url imageFolder: "/images"
```

4. Next, add a Rectangle object to main.qml, as shown in the following:

```
Rectangle {
    id: rect
    x: 100
    y: 100
    width: 100
    height: 100
    color: myColor
}
```

5. After that, we're going to add another Image object below the rectangle:

```
Image {
    id: img
    x: 300
    y: 100
    width: 150
    height: 180
    source: imageFolder + "/tux.png"
}
```

6. Next, we create a new resource file for our project by going to **File** | **New File...** and selecting **Qt Resource File** under the **Qt** template.

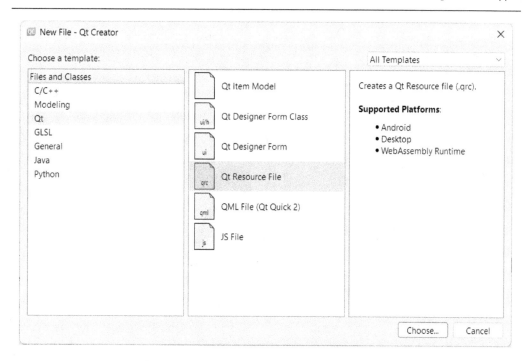

Figure 6.6 – Create a new Qt Resource File

7.   Then, create a folder called images in the resource file and add tux.png into the images folder.

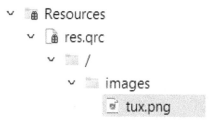

Figure 6.7 – Add tux.png to the images folder

8.   Build and run the project now, and you should similar results as follows:

Figure 6.8 – The Hello World demo in Qt Quick 6

How it works...

Qt 6 introduces many changes to Qt Quick as well but they are mostly underlying functions that do not affect much of the QML language and objects. Therefore, there are not many changes you need to make to your QML scripts when transitioning from Qt 5 to Qt 6. However, there are still some minor changes to how the project is structured and slight differences in the code.

One of the most obvious differences is that QML scripts are now listed under the QML category under the project structure instead of under Resources like how it used to be in Qt 5.

Figure 6.9 – QML files have their own category now

Hence, when we load the `main.qml` file in the `main.cpp` C++ source code, we will use the following:

```
const QUrl url(u"qrc:/qt6_qml_new/main.qml"_qs);
```

There are slight differences compared to how we did it in Qt 5:

```
const QUrl url(QStringLiteral("qrc:/main.qml"));
```

The u preceding the string creates a 16-bit string literal and the _qs after the string converts it to a QString. These operators are similar to the QStringLiteral macro used in Qt 5 but are easier to convert to the exact string format you want while complying with the C++ 17 coding style.

Another big difference in Qt 6 is that the **Qt Quick Controls 1** module is completely deleted from Qt Quick. Qt Quick now only supports **Qt Quick Controls** (formerly known as **Qt Quick Controls 2**) with some slight changes. Let's open up `main.qml` from the preceding example to see the differences:

```
import QtQuick
Window {
    width: 640
    height: 480
    visible: true
    title: qsTr("Hello World")
```

As you can see from the highlighted part in the preceding code block, the version number is now optional when importing a Qt Quick module. Qt will pick the latest version available by default.

Now, let's look at the properties we declared in the example:

```
property variant myColor: "red"
property url imageFolder: "/images"
```

Even though the preceding code will run fine, it's recommended to use Qt functions such as `Qt.color()` and `Qt.resolvedUrl()` to return properties with the correct types, instead of just passing a string:

```
property variant myColor: Qt.color("red")
property url imageFolder: Qt.resolvedUrl("/images")
```

Another small difference that you may or may not notice is the way Qt treats relative paths. Previously in Qt 5, we would write relative path as `./images`, which will return as `qrc:/images`. In Qt 6, however, `./images` will return as `qrc:/[project_name]/images/tux.png`, which is not correct. We must use `/images` without the preceding dot instead.

> **Note**
>
> For more information regarding the full changes of Qt Quick in Qt 6, please visit `https://doc.qt.io/qt-6/qtquickcontrols-changes-qt6.html`.

7

Using Network and Managing Large Documents

In this chapter, we will learn how to create a networking server program and a client program using Qt 6's networking module. We will also learn how to create a program that uses **File Transfer Protocol (FTP)** to upload and download files from the server. Lastly, we will learn how to send HTTP requests to a specific web service using Qt 6 and C++ language.

In this chapter, we're going to cover the following main topics:

- Creating a TCP server
- Creating a TCP client
- Uploading and downloading files using FTP

Technical requirements

The technical requirements for this chapter are Qt 6.6.1, Qt Creator 12.0.2, and FileZilla. All the code used in this chapter can be downloaded from the following GitHub repository: https://github.com/PacktPublishing/QT6-C-GUI-Programming-Cookbook---Third-Edition-/tree/main/Chapter07.

Creating a TCP server

In this recipe, we will learn how to create a **Transmission Control Protocol (TCP)** server in Qt 6. Before we're able to create a server that lets us upload and download files, let's scale it down a bit and learn how to create a networking server that receives and delivers texts.

How to do it...

Follow these steps to create a TCP server:

1. First, let's create a **Qt Console Application** project from **File | New File or Project**, as shown in the following screenshot:

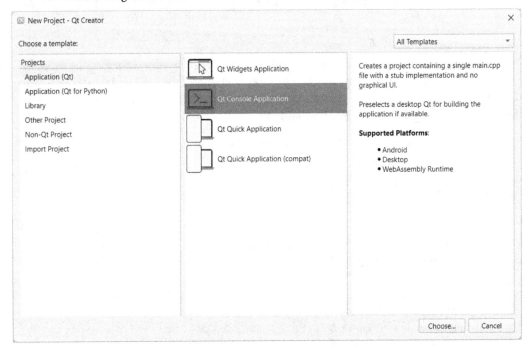

Figure 7.1 – Creating a new Qt Console Application project

2. After that, go to **File | New File or Project** again but this time, select **C++ Class** under the **C/ C++** category, as shown in the following screenshot:

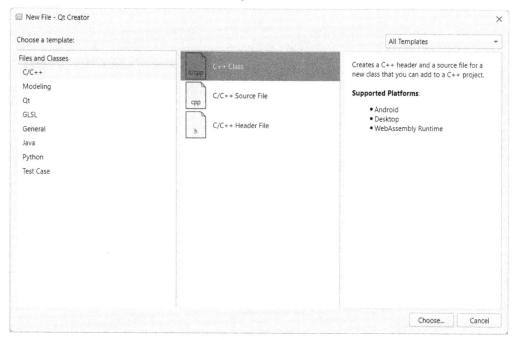

Figure 7.2 – Creating a new C++ class

3. Then, name your class `server`. Set its base class to **QObject** and make sure the **Include QObject** option is checked before clicking the **Next** button. Once the class has been created, two files will be created for you—`server.h` and `server.cpp`, as shown in the following screenshot:

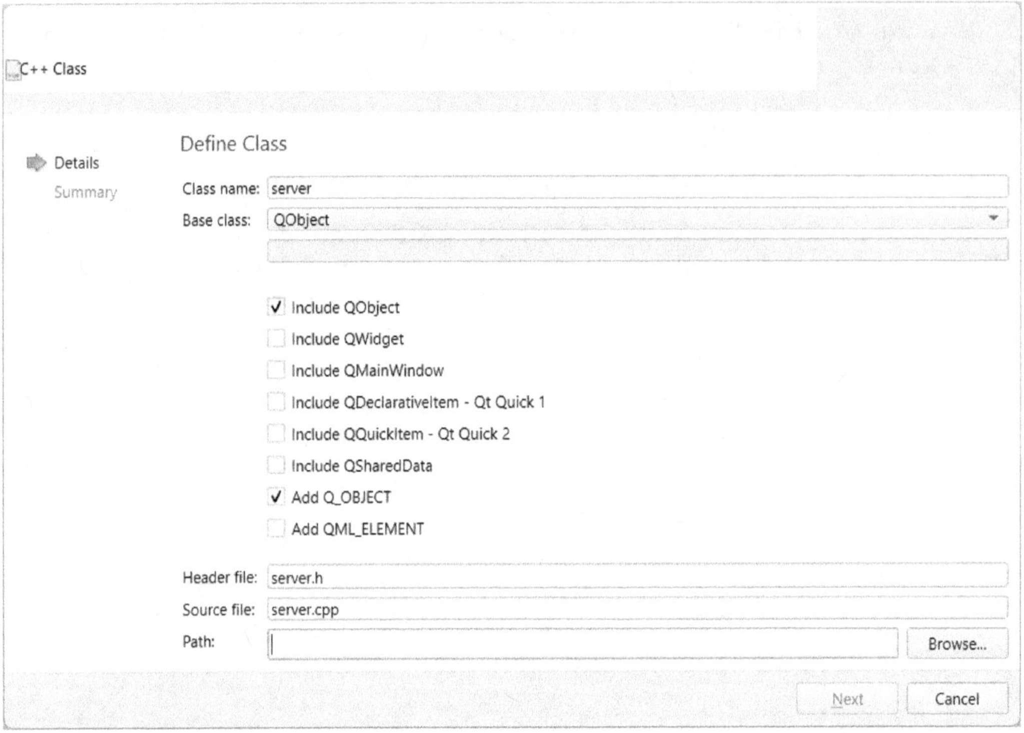

Figure 7.3 – Defining the server class

4. After that, open up your project file (.pro) and add the network module, as shown in the following code. Then, run qmake again to reload the modules:

```
QT += core network
```

5. Once you're done, open up server.h and add the following headers to it:

```
#include <QTcpServer>
#include <QTcpSocket>
#include <QVector>
#include <QDebug>
```

6. Right after that, declare the startServer() and sendMessageToClients() functions, as shown in the following code:

```
public:
        server(QObject *parent = nullptr);
        void startServer();
        void sendMessageToClients(QString message);
```

7. Then, declare the following slot functions for the `server` class:

```
public slots:
    void newClientConnection();
    void socketDisconnected();
    void socketReadReady();
    void socketStateChanged(QAbstractSocket::SocketState
state);
```

8. Finally, declare two private variables, as shown in the following code:

```
private:
    QTcpServer* chatServer;
    QVector<QTcpSocket*>* allClients;
```

9. Once you're done with the preceding step, open up `server.cpp` and define the `startServer()` function. Here, we create a `QVector` container to store all the clients that are connected to the server and use it to send out messages in later steps. This is shown in the following example:

```
void server::startServer() {
    allClients = new QVector<QTcpSocket*>;
    chatServer = new QTcpServer();
    chatServer->setMaxPendingConnections(10);
    connect(chatServer, &QTcpServer::newConnection,      this,
&server::newClientConnection);
    if (chatServer->listen(QHostAddress::Any, 8001))
        qDebug() << "Server has started. Listening to
port    8001.";
    else
        qDebug() << "Server failed to start. Error: "
+    chatServer->errorString();
}
```

10. Next, we implement the `sendMessageToClients()` function, where we iterate through the `allClients` container we just created in the previous step, and send the message to each client, as shown in the following example:

```
void server::sendMessageToClients(QString message) {
if (allClients->size() > 0) {
    for (int i = 0; i < allClients->size(); i++) {
        if (allClients->at(i)->isOpen() && allClients-    >at(i)-
>isWritable()) {
        allClients->at(i)->write(message.toUtf8());
}
}}}
```

11. After that, we will start implementing the slot functions. Let's start with the following code:

```cpp
void server::newClientConnection() {
    QTcpSocket* client = chatServer->nextPendingConnection();
    QString ipAddress = client->peerAddress().toString();
    int port = client->peerPort();
    connect(client, &QTcpSocket::disconnected, this,
&server::socketDisconnected);
    connect(client, &QTcpSocket::readyRead, this,
&server::socketReadReady);
    connect(client, &QTcpSocket::stateChanged, this,
&server::socketStateChanged);
    allClients->push_back(client);
    qDebug() << "Socket connected from " + ipAddress + ":" +
QString::number(port);
}
```

12. Then, we'll proceed with the `socketDisconnected()` function. This slot function will be called when a client has been disconnected from the server, as shown in the following example:

```cpp
void server::socketDisconnected() {
    QTcpSocket* client = qobject_
cast<QTcpSocket*>(QObject::sender());
    QString socketIpAddress = client->peerAddress().toString();
    int port = client->peerPort();
    qDebug() << "Socket disconnected from " + socketIpAddress +
":" + QString::number(port);
}
```

13. Next, we'll define the `socketReadReady()` function, which will be triggered when a client sends a text message to the server, as shown in the following example:

```cpp
void server::socketReadReady() {
    QTcpSocket* client = qobject_
cast<QTcpSocket*>(QObject::sender());
    QString socketIpAddress = client->peerAddress().toString();
    int port = client->peerPort();
    QString data = QString(client->readAll());
    qDebug() << "Message: " + data + " (" + socketIpAddress +
":" + QString::number(port) + ")";
    sendMessageToClients(data);
}
```

14. After that, let's implement the `socketStateChanged()` function, which will be called when the networking state of a client has changed, as shown in the following example:

```cpp
void server::socketStateChanged(QAbstractSocket::SocketState
state) {
    QTcpSocket* client = qobject_
cast<QTcpSocket*>(QObject::sender());
    QString socketIpAddress = client->peerAddress().toString();
    int port = client->peerPort();
    qDebug() << "Socket state changed (" + socketIpAddress +
":" + QString::number(port) + "): " + desc;
}
```

15. We also need to add the following code into `socketStateChanged()` to print out the status of the client:

```cpp
QString desc;
if (state == QAbstractSocket::UnconnectedState)
    desc = "The socket is not connected.";
else if (state == QAbstractSocket::HostLookupState)
    desc = "The socket is performing a host name
lookup.";
else if (state == QAbstractSocket::ConnectingState)
    desc = "The socket has started establishing a
connection.";
else if (state == QAbstractSocket::ConnectedState)
    desc = "A connection is established.";
else if (state == QAbstractSocket::BoundState)
    desc = "The socket is bound to an address and port.";
else if (state == QAbstractSocket::ClosingState)
    desc = "The socket is about to close (data may still
be waiting to be written).";
else if (state == QAbstractSocket::ListeningState)
    desc = "For internal use only.";
```

16. Lastly, let's open up `main.cpp` and add the highlighted code in the following example in order to initiate the server:

```cpp
#include <QCoreApplication>
#include "server.h"
    int main(int argc, char *argv[]) {
    QCoreApplication a(argc, argv);
    server* myServer = new server();
    myServer->startServer();
    return a.exec();
}
```

17. You can try and run the server program now but you won't be able to test it as we have not created the client program yet, as the following screenshot shows:

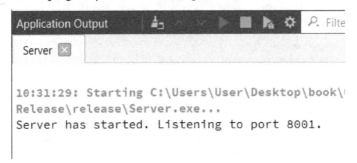

Figure 7.4 – Server is now listening to port 8001

18. Let's proceed to the next example project and learn how to create the client program. We will come back to test this program again later on.

How it works...

There are mainly two types of network connections—the TCP connection and the **User Datagram Protocol (UDP)** connection. TCP is a reliable networking connection, while UDP is unreliable.

These two connections are designed for very different purposes:

- TCP networking is usually for programs that require every single piece of data to be sent and received in order. It also makes sure that the client receives the data and that the server gets notified of that. Programs such as messaging software, web servers, and databases use TCP networking.

- UDP networking, on the other hand, does not require constant handholding between the server and client. Since the connection is unreliable, there is also no feedback on whether the data has been successfully received. The dropping of packets is tolerated, and data may not even come in the same order as it was sent. UDP connections are usually used by applications that stream huge amounts of data to their clients without strict requirements on its packet delivery, such as video games, video conferencing software, and domain name systems.

Creating networking software using Qt 6 is a lot easier through its signals and slots mechanism. All we need to do is connect the signals emitted by the QTcpServer class and QTcpSocket class to our slot functions. We will then implement these slot functions and define what to do within those functions.

> **Note**
>
> We used a `QVector` container to store the pointers to all the clients that have connected to the server so that we can use it to deliver the messages later on.

To keep this example project simple, we simply send text messages to all the clients, sort of like a group chat. You are free to explore other possibilities and make your own changes to improve the program.

Creating a TCP client

Since we created a TCP server in the previous recipe, we now need a client program to complete the project. Therefore, in this recipe, we will learn how to create a TCP client program using Qt 6 and its network module.

How to do it...

To create a TCP client in Qt 6, let's do the following:

1. First off, let's create a new **Qt Widgets Application** project from **Files | New File or Project**.

2. Once the project has been created, let's open up `mainwindow.ui` and set up the GUI as shown in the following diagram. Please note that the layout direction of the central widget has to be vertical:

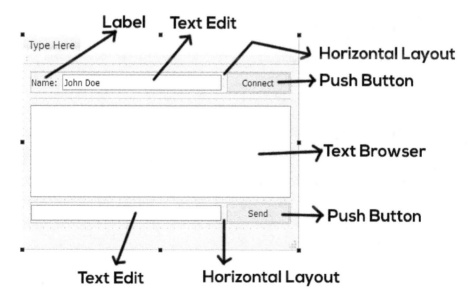

Figure 7.5 – The layout of our client program

3. Then, right-click on the push button that says **Connect** and create a `clicked()` slot function from the menu. Then, repeat the same step on the **Send** button as well. As a result, two slot functions will be created for you in the source code, which may or may not look like what we see in the following code, depending on your widget's name:

    ```
    void on_connectButton_clicked();
    void on_sendButton_clicked();
    ```

4. Next, open up `mainwindow.h` and add the following headers:

    ```
    #include <QDebug>
    #include <QTcpSocket>
    ```

5. Then, declare the `printMessage()` function and three slot functions: `socketConnected()`, `socketDisconnected()`, and `socketReadyRead()`, as shown in the following code:

    ```
    public:
        explicit MainWindow(QWidget *parent = 0);
        ~MainWindow();
        void printMessage(QString message);
    private slots:
        void on_connectButton_clicked();
        void on_sendButton_clicked();
        void socketConnected();
        void socketDisconnected();
        void socketReadyRead();
    ```

6. After that, declare the following variables as well:

    ```
    private:
        Ui::MainWindow *ui;
        bool connectedToHost;
        QTcpSocket* socket;
    ```

7. Once you're done with that, you can proceed to `mainwindow.cpp` and define the `printMessage()` function, as shown in the following example:

    ```
    void MainWindow::printMessage(QString message) {
        ui->chatDisplay->append(message);
    }
    ```

8. Then, we'll implement the `on_connectButton_clicked()` function, which will be triggered when the **Connect** button is clicked, as shown in the following code:

```
void MainWindow::on_connectButton_clicked() {
    if (!connectedToHost) {
        socket = new QTcpSocket();
        connect(socket, &QTcpSocket::connected, this,
&MainWindow::socketConnected);
        connect(socket, &QTcpSocket::disconnected, this,
&MainWindow::socketDisconnected);
        connect(socket, &QTcpSocket::readyRead, this,
&MainWindow::socketReadyRead);
        socket->connectToHost("127.0.0.1", 8001);
    }
    else {
        QString name = ui->nameInput->text();
        socket->write("<font color=\"Orange\">" + name.
toUtf8() + " has left the chat room.</font>");
        socket->disconnectFromHost();
    }
}
```

9. We also define the `on_sendButton_clicked()` function, which will be called when the **Send** button is clicked, as shown in the following example:

```
void MainWindow::on_sendButton_clicked() {
    QString name = ui->nameInput->text();
    QString message = ui->messageInput->text();
    socket->write("<font color=\"Blue\">" + name.toUtf8() + "</
font>: " + message.toUtf8());
    ui->messageInput->clear();
}
```

10. Right after that, we implement the `socketConnected()` function, which will be called when the client program has been successfully connected to the server, as shown in the following code:

```
void MainWindow::socketConnected() {
    qDebug() << "Connected to server.";
    printMessage("<font color=\"Green\">Connected to server.</
font>");
    QString name = ui->nameInput->text();
    socket->write("<font color=\"Purple\">" + name.toUtf8() + "
has joined the chat room.</font>");
    ui->connectButton->setText("Disconnect");
    connectedToHost = true;
}
```

11. We are not yet done at this point. We also need to implement the `socketDisconnected()` function, which will be triggered whenever the client has been disconnected from the server, as shown in the following code:

```
void MainWindow::socketDisconnected() {
    qDebug() << "Disconnected from server.";
    printMessage("<font color=\"Red\">Disconnected from
server.</font>");
    ui->connectButton->setText("Connect");
    connectedToHost = false;
}
```

12. Lastly, we also need to define the `socketReadyRead()` function, which prints out the message sent from the server, as shown in the following example:

```
void MainWindow::socketReadyRead() {
    printMessage(socket->readAll());
}
```

13. Before we run the client program, we must first turn on the server program that we created in the previous recipe. Then, build and run the client program. Once the program has been opened, go and click the **Connect** button. After you have successfully connected to the server, type something in the line edit widget located at the bottom and press the **Send** button. You should see something similar to the following screenshot:

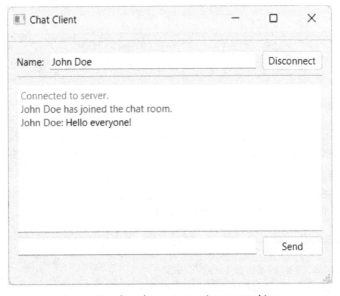

Figure 7.6 – Our chat program is now working

14. Let's go to the server program, shown in the following screenshot, and see whether there is anything printed on the terminal window:

```
Application Output                          🔍 Filter              + —

Server ☒

10:47:52: Starting C:\Users\User\Desktop\book\Qt5-CPP-GUI-Programming-Cookbook-Second-Edition\Chapter06
Release\release\Server.exe...
Server has started. Listening to port 8001.
"Socket connected from ::ffff:127.0.0.1:55227"
"Message: <font color=\"Purple\">John Doe has joined the chat room.</font> (::ffff:127.0.0.1:55227)"
"Message: <font color=\"Blue\">John Doe</font>: Hello everyone! (::ffff:127.0.0.1:55227)"
"Socket state changed (::ffff:127.0.0.1:55227): The socket is about to close (data may still be waiting
"Socket state changed (::ffff:127.0.0.1:55227): The socket is not connected."
"Socket disconnected from ::ffff:127.0.0.1:55227"
10:48:25: C:\Users\User\Desktop\book\Qt5-CPP-GUI-Programming-Cookbook-Second-Edition\Chapter06\build-Se
Release\release\Server.exe crashed
```

Figure 7.7 – Client activities are also shown on the server output

15. Congratulations, you have successfully created a program that looks a bit like an **Internet Relay Chat (IRC)** chat room!

How it works...

In order for this to work, we need two programs: a server program that connects all the clients and delivers their messages, and a client program used by the users to send and receive messages from other users.

Since the server program just sits behind the scenes and works out everything in silence, it doesn't need any user interface, and thus we only need it as a Qt Console application.

The client program, however, requires a visually pleasant yet easy-to-use GUI for the users to read and write their messages. Therefore, we created the client program as a Qt Widgets application instead.

The client program is relatively simple when compared to the server program. All it does is connect to the server, send out the message input by the user, and print out everything the server sends to it.

Uploading and downloading files using FTP

We have learned how to create simple chat software that distributes text messages among the users. Next, we will learn how to create a program that uploads and downloads files using FTP.

How to do it...

Let's get started by observing the following steps:

1. For this project, we need to install software called **FileZilla Server**, which we will use as the FTP server. FileZilla Server can be downloaded from `https://filezilla-project.org` by clicking on the **Download FileZilla Server** button, as shown in the following screenshot:

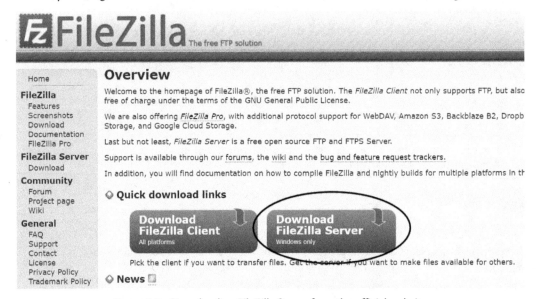

Figure 7.8 – Downloading FileZilla Server from the official website

2. Once you have downloaded the installer, run it and install **FileZilla Server** by agreeing to all the default options, as shown in the following screenshot:

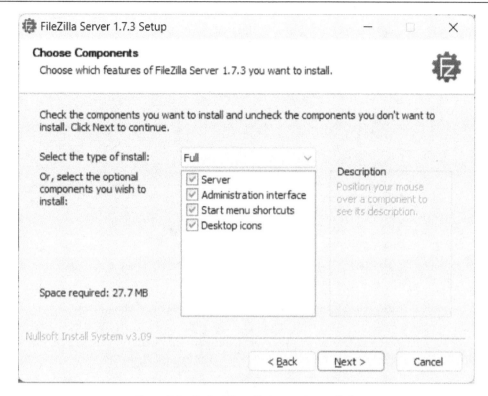

Figure 7.9 – Default installation options will do

3. When it has completed, open up **FileZilla Server** and press the **Connect to Server…** button, and the **Connection** window will pop up, as shown in the following screenshot:

Figure 7.10 – Setting the host, port, and password in the Connection window

4. After the server has been started, go to **Server** | **Configure…** from the top menu, as highlighted in the following screenshot:

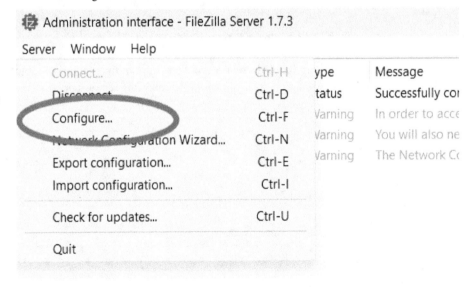

Figure 7.11 – Opening up the Settings window from the top menu

5. Once the **Settings** window has been opened, click on the **Add** button located under the **Available users** list to add a new user. Then, add a shared folder under the **Shared** folders list, where your users will be uploading and downloading files to and from, as shown in the following screenshot:

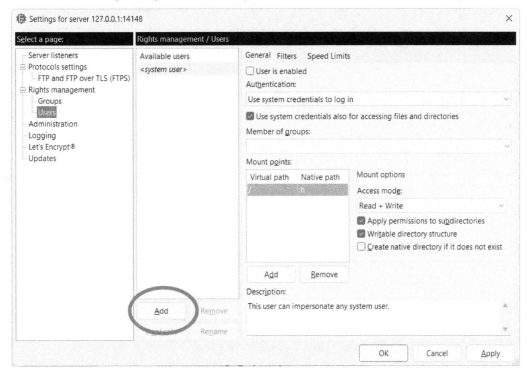

Figure 7.12 – Clicking the Add button to add a new user

6. We have now finished setting up FileZilla Server. Let's move on to Qt Creator and create a new **Qt Widgets Application** project. Then, open up `mainwindow.ui` and set up the GUI, as shown in the following diagram:

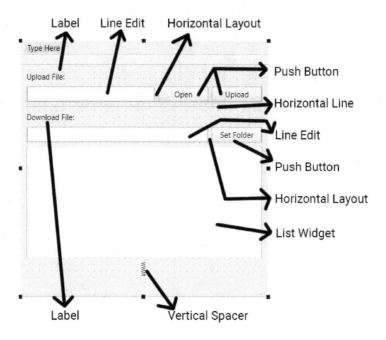

Figure 7.13 – Layout of our FPT program

7. Next, right-click on the **Open, Upload,** and **Set Folder** buttons and create their respective `clicked()` slot functions, as shown in the following code:

```
private slots:
        void on_openButton_clicked();
        void on_uploadButton_clicked();
        void on_setFolderButton_clicked();
```

8. After that, double-click on the list widget and select **Go to slot....** Then, select the `itemDoubleClicked(QListWidgetItem*)` option and click **OK**, as shown in the following screenshot:

Figure 7.14 – Selecting the itemDoubleClicked option

9. Then, declare additional slot functions such as `serverConnected()`, `serverReply()`, and `dataReceived()`, which we will implement later in this chapter:

```
private slots:
    void on_openButton_clicked();
    void on_uploadButton_clicked();
    void on_setFolderButton_clicked();
    void on_fileList_itemDoubleClicked(QListWidgetItem *item);
    void serverConnected(const QHostAddress &address, int
port);
    void serverReply(int code, const QString &parameters);
    void dataReceived(const QByteArray &data);
```

10. Once you have created the slot functions, go to **File** | **New File…** and create a new C++ class called `FtpDataChannel`.

11. Then, open up `ftpdatachannel.h` and add the following code to it:

```
#ifndef FTPDATACHANNEL_H
#define FTPDATACHANNEL_H
#include <QtCore/qobject.h>
#include <QtNetwork/qtcpserver.h>
#include <QtNetwork/qtcpsocket.h>
#include <memory>
class FtpDataChannel : public QObject{
    Q_OBJECT
public:
    explicit FtpDataChannel(QObject *parent = nullptr);
    void listen(const QHostAddress &address =
QHostAddress::Any);
    void sendData(const QByteArray &data);
    void close();
    QString portspec() const;
    QTcpServer m_server;
    std::unique_ptr<QTcpSocket> m_socket;
signals:
    void dataReceived(const QByteArray &data);
};
#endif
```

12. Right after that, open the `ftpdatachannel.cpp` source file and write the following code:

```
#include "ftpdatachannel.h"
FtpDataChannel::FtpDataChannel(QObject *parent) :
QObject(parent){
    connect(&m_server, &QTcpServer::newConnection, this, [this]
(){
        m_socket.reset(m_server.nextPendingConnection());
        connect(m_socket.get(), &QTcpSocket::readyRead, this,
[this](){
            emit dataReceived(m_socket->readAll());
        });

        connect(m_socket.get(), &QTcpSocket::bytesWritten, this,
[this](qint64 bytes){
            qDebug() << bytes;
            close();
        });
    });
}
```

13. Then, we continue to implement functions for the `FtpDataChannel` class, such as `listen()`, `sendData()`, and `close()`:

```cpp
void FtpDataChannel::listen(const QHostAddress &address){
    m_server.listen(address);
}
void FtpDataChannel::sendData(const QByteArray &data){
    if (m_socket)
        m_socket->write(QByteArray(data).replace("\n", "\r\n"));
}
void FtpDataChannel::close(){
    if (m_socket)
        m_socket->disconnectFromHost();
}
```

14. Lastly, we implement the `postspec()` function, which composes the FTP server's information in a special format that can be sent back to the FTP server for verification purposes:

```cpp
QString FtpDataChannel::portspec() const{
    QString portSpec;
    quint32 ipv4 = m_server.serverAddress().toIPv4Address();
    quint16 port = m_server.serverPort();
    portSpec += QString::number((ipv4 & 0xff000000) >> 24);
    portSpec += ',' + QString::number((ipv4 & 0x00ff0000) >>
16);
    portSpec += ',' + QString::number((ipv4 & 0x0000ff00) >> 8);
    portSpec += ',' + QString::number(ipv4 & 0x000000ff);
    portSpec += ',' + QString::number((port & 0xff00) >> 8);
    portSpec += ',' + QString::number(port &0x00ff);
    return portSpec;
}
```

15. Once we're done with the `FtpDataChannel` class, go to **File | New File...** again and create another new C++ class called `FtpControlChannel`.

16. Open up the newly created `ftpcontrolchannel.h` and add the following code to the header file:

```cpp
#ifndef FTPCONTROLCHANNEL_H
#define FTPCONTROLCHANNEL_H
#include <QtNetwork/qhostaddress.h>
#include <QtNetwork/qtcpsocket.h>
#include <QtCore/qobject.h>
class FtpControlChannel : public QObject{
    Q_OBJECT
public:
```

```
    explicit FtpControlChannel(QObject *parent = nullptr);
    void connectToServer(const QString &server);
    void command(const QByteArray &command, const QByteArray
&params);
public slots:
    void error(QAbstractSocket::SocketError);
signals:
    void opened(const QHostAddress &localAddress, int
localPort);
    void closed();
    void info(const QByteArray &info);
    void reply(int code, const QByteArray &parameters);
    void invalidReply(const QByteArray &reply);
private:
    void onReadyRead();
    QTcpSocket m_socket;
    QByteArray m_buffer;
};
#endif // FTPCONTROLCHANNEL_H
```

17. Then, let's open up `ftpcontrolchannel.cpp` and write the following code:

```
#include "ftpcontrolchannel.h"
#include <QtCore/qcoreapplication.h>
FtpControlChannel::FtpControlChannel(QObject *parent) :
QObject(parent){
    connect(&m_socket, &QIODevice::readyRead,
            this, &FtpControlChannel::onReadyRead);
    connect(&m_socket, &QAbstractSocket::disconnected,
            this, &FtpControlChannel::closed);
    connect(&m_socket, &QAbstractSocket::connected, this, [this]
() {
        emit opened(m_socket.localAddress(), m_socket.
localPort());
    });
    connect(&m_socket, &QAbstractSocket::errorOccurred,
            this, &FtpControlChannel::error);
}
```

18. Then, we continue to implement other functions of the class, such as `connectToServer()` and `command()`:

```
void FtpControlChannel::connectToServer(const QString &server){
    m_socket.connectToHost(server, 21);
}
void FtpControlChannel::command(const QByteArray &command, const
```

```
QByteArray &params) {
    QByteArray sendData = command;
    if (!params.isEmpty())
        sendData += " " + params;
    m_socket.write(sendData + "\r\n");
}
```

19. Right after that, we continue to write the code for its slot functions—namely, onReadyRead() and error():

```
void FtpControlChannel::onReadyRead() {
    m_buffer.append(m_socket.readAll());
    int rn = -1;
    while ((rn = m_buffer.indexOf("\r\n")) != -1) {
        QByteArray received = m_buffer.mid(0, rn);
        m_buffer = m_buffer.mid(rn + 2);
        int space = received.indexOf(' ');
        if (space != -1) {
            int code = received.mid(0, space).toInt();
            if (code == 0) {
                qDebug() << "Info received: " << received.
mid(space + 1);
                emit info(received.mid(space + 1));
            } else {
                qDebug() << "Reply received: " << received.
mid(space + 1);
                emit reply(code, received.mid(space + 1));
            }
        } else {
            emit invalidReply(received);
        }
    }
}
void FtpControlChannel::error(QAbstractSocket::SocketError
error) {
    qWarning() << "Socket error:" << error;
    QCoreApplication::exit();
}
```

20. After that, open up mainwindow.h and add the following headers:

```
#include <QDebug>
#include <QNetworkAccessManager>
#include <QNetworkRequest>
#include <QNetworkReply>
```

```
#include <QFile>
#include <QFileInfo>
#include <QFileDialog>
#include <QListWidgetItem>
#include <QMessageBox>
#include <QThread>
#include "ftpcontrolchannel.h"
#include "ftpdatachannel.h"
```

21. Then, declare the getFileList() function, as follows:

```
public:
    explicit MainWindow(QWidget *parent = 0);
    ~MainWindow();
    void getFileList();
```

22. Right after that, declare the following variables:

```
private:
    Ui::MainWindow *ui;
    FtpDataChannel* dataChannel;
    FtpControlChannel* controlChannel;
    QString ftpAddress;
    QString username;
    QString password;
    QStringList fileList;
    QString uploadFileName;
    QString downloadFileName;
```

23. Then, open up mainwindow.cpp and add the following code to the class constructor:

```
MainWindow::MainWindow(QWidget *parent) : QMainWindow(parent),
ui(new Ui::MainWindow) {
    ui->setupUi(this);
    dataChannel = new FtpDataChannel(this);
    connect(dataChannel, &FtpDataChannel::dataReceived, this,
&MainWindow::dataReceived);
    connect(controlChannel, &FtpControlChannel::reply, this,
&MainWindow::serverReply);
    connect(controlChannel, &FtpControlChannel::opened, this,
&MainWindow::serverConnected);
    controlChannel = new FtpControlChannel(this);
    ftpAddress = "127.0.0.1/";
    username = "myuser";
    password = "123456";
```

```
controlChannel->connectToServer(ftpAddress);
}
```

24. After that, implement the `getFileList()` function, as shown in the following code:

```
void MainWindow::getFileList() {
controlChannel->command("PORT", dataChannel->portspec().
toUtf8());
    controlChannel->command("MLSD", "");}
```

25. Then, define the `on_openButton_clicked()` slot function, which gets triggered when the **Open** button is clicked, as shown in the following code:

```
void MainWindow::on_openButton_clicked() {
    QString fileName = QFileDialog::getOpenFileName(this,
"Select File", qApp->applicationDirPath());
    ui->uploadFileInput->setText(fileName);
}
```

26. Once you're done with that, implement the slot function that gets called when the **Upload** button is clicked, as shown in the following example:

```
void MainWindow::on_uploadButton_clicked() {
    QFile* file = new QFile(ui->uploadFileInput->text());
    QFileInfo fileInfo(*file);
    uploadFileName = fileInfo.fileName();
    controlChannel->command("PORT", dataChannel->portspec().
toUtf8());
    controlChannel->command("STOR", uploadFileName.toUtf8());
}
```

27. The following code shows what the `on_setFolderButton_clicked()` slot function looks like:

```
void MainWindow::on_setFolderButton_clicked() {
    QString folder = QFileDialog::getExistingDirectory(this,
tr("Open Directory"), qApp->applicationDirPath(),
QFileDialog::ShowDirsOnly);
    ui->downloadPath->setText(folder);
}
```

28. Next, define the slot function that will be triggered when one of the list widget's items gets double-clicked, as shown in the following code:

```
void MainWindow::on_fileList_itemDoubleClicked(QListWidgetItem
*item) {
    downloadFileName = item->text();
    QString folder = ui->downloadPath->text();
```

```
        if (folder != "" && QDir(folder).exists()) {
            controlChannel->command("PORT", dataChannel-
>portspec().toUtf8());
                        controlChannel->command("RETR",
downloadFileName.toUtf8());
        }
        else {
            QMessageBox::warning(this, "Invalid Path", "Please
set the download path before download.");
    }}
```

29. We're not quite done yet. Next, we will implement the `serverConnected()` function, which will be called automatically when the program has successfully connected to the FTP server, as shown in the following code:

```
void MainWindow::serverConnected(const QHostAddress &address,
int port){
    qDebug() << "Listening to:" << address << port;
    dataChannel->listen(address);
    controlChannel->command("USER", username.toUtf8());
    controlChannel->command("PASS", password.toUtf8());
    getFileList();
}
```

30. We also need to implement the function that will be called when the FTP server replies to our request, as shown in the following example:

```
void MainWindow::serverReply(int code, const QString
&parameters){
    if (code == 150 && uploadFileName != ""){
        QFile* file = new QFile(ui->uploadFileInput->text());
        QFileInfo fileInfo(*file);
        uploadFileName = fileInfo.fileName();
        if (file->open(QIODevice::ReadOnly)){
            QThread::msleep(1000);
            QByteArray data = file->readAll();
            dataChannel->sendData(data + "\n\r");
            qDebug() << data;
        } else {
            QMessageBox::warning(this, "Invalid File", "Failed
to open file for upload.");
        }
    }
    if (code == 226 && uploadFileName != ""){
        uploadFileName = "";
```

```
            QMessageBox::warning(this, "Upload Success", "File
successfully uploaded.");
        }
    }
```

31. The `dataReceived()` function is used to obtain the data received from the FTP server, and it looks something like the following code:

```
void MainWindow::dataReceived(const QByteArray &data){
    if (data.startsWith("type=file")){
        ui->fileList->clear();
        QStringList fileList = QString(data).split("\r\n");
        if (fileList.length() > 0){
            for (int i = 0; i < fileList.length(); ++i){
                if (fileList.at(i) != ""){
                    QStringList fileInfo = fileList.at(i).
split(";");
                    QString fileName = fileInfo.at(4).
simplified();
                    ui->fileList->addItem(fileName);
                }
            }
        }
    } else {
        QString folder = ui->downloadPath->text();
        QFile file(folder + "/" + downloadFileName);
        file.open(QIODevice::WriteOnly);
        file.write((data));
        file.close();
        QMessageBox::information(this, "Success", "File
successfully downloaded.");
    }
}
```

32. Lastly, build and run the program. Try and upload some files to the FTP server. If it works, the file list should be updated and displayed on the **List** widget. Then, try and double-click on the filename on the list widget and download the file to your computer, as shown in the following screenshot:

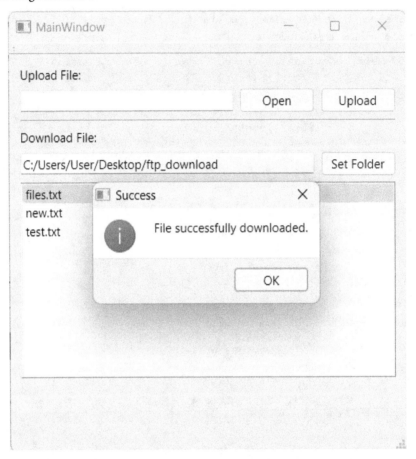

Figure 7.15 – Downloading a file from the FTP server by double-clicking on it

33. You can also try to upload a file by clicking on the **Open** button, selecting the desired file, and pressing the **Upload** button, as shown in the following screenshot:

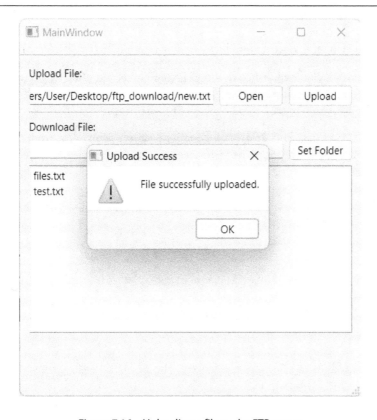

Figure 7.16 – Uploading a file to the FTP server

34. Congratulations, you have now successfully created a working FTP program!

> **Note**
>
> Do note that this example program is only meant to show you the most basic implementation of an FTP program and is not a fully featured program. It's not guaranteed to work if you try to upload/download files that are not in text format. It may also not upload correctly if a file already exists on the FTP server. You must implement these features by yourself if you wish to expand on top of this project.

How it works...

Although this project is much larger and with longer code, it is actually pretty similar to the TCP networking projects we have done in previous recipes. We have also made use of the signals and slots mechanism provided by Qt 6 to make our lives easier.

In the past, Qt used to support FTP in the `QNetworkAccessManager` class. However, FTP has since been deprecated in Qt 6 so we have to implement it on our own.

We must understand some of the most common FTP commands and utilize them in our program. For more information, check out `https://www.serv-u.com/resources/tutorial/appe-stor-stou-retr-list-mlsd-mlst-ftp-command`.

The `FtpControlChannel` and `FtpDataChannel` classes were taken from Qt's official Git repository with some tiny modifications: `https://code.qt.io/cgit/qt/qtscxml.git/tree/examples/scxml/ftpclient`.

8

Threading Basics – Asynchronous Programming

Most modern software runs its processes in parallel and offloads tasks to different threads to take advantage of modern CPU multicore architecture. This way, software can be more efficient by running multiple processes simultaneously without affecting performance. In this chapter, we will learn how to make use of **threads** to boost our Qt 6 application's performance and efficiency.

This chapter will cover the following recipes:

- Using threads
- QObject and QThread
- Data protection and sharing data between threads
- Working with QRunnable processes

Technical requirements

The technical requirements for this chapter include Qt 6.6.1 and Qt Creator 12.0.2. All the code used in this chapter can be downloaded from the following GitHub repository: https://github.com/PacktPublishing/QT6-C-GUI-Programming-Cookbook---Third-Edition-/tree/main/Chapter08.

Using threads

Qt 6 provides multiple methods to create and use threads. You can choose between high-level methods and low-level ones. High-level methods are much easier to get started but are limited in what you can do with them. Conversely, low-level methods are more flexible but not beginner-friendly. In this recipe, we will learn how to use one of the high-level methods to easily create a multithreading Qt 6 application.

How to do it...

Let's learn how to create multithreading applications by following these steps:

1. Create a **Qt widget application** and open up main.cpp. Then, add the following headers at the top of the file:

```
#include <QFuture>
#include <QtConcurrent/QtConcurrent>
#include <QFutureWatcher>
#include <QThread>
#include <QDebug>
```

2. Then, create a function called printText() before the main() function:

```
void printText(QString text, int count) {
    for (int i = 0; i < count; ++i)
        qDebug() << text << QThread::currentThreadId();
    qDebug() << text << "Done";
}
```

3. After that, add the following code to the main() function:

```
int main(int argc, char *argv[]) {
    QApplication a(argc, argv);
    MainWindow w;
    w.show();
    printText("A", 100);
    printText("B", 100);
    return a.exec();
}
```

4. If you build and run the program now, you should see that A gets printed first before B. Note that their thread IDs are all the same. This is because we are running the printText() functions in the main thread:

```
. . .
"A" 0x2b82c
"A" 0x2b82c
"A" 0x2b82c
"A" Done

. . .
"B" 0x2b82c
"B" 0x2b82c
"B" 0x2b82c
"B" Done
```

5. To separate them into different threads, let's use a high-level class provided by Qt 6 called QFuture. Comment out the two printText() functions in main() and use the following code instead:

```
    QFuture<void> f1 = QtConcurrent::run(printText,
QString("A"), 100);
    QFuture<void> f2 = QtConcurrent::run(printText,
QString("B"), 100);
    QFuture<void> f3 = QtConcurrent::run(printText,
QString("C"), 100);
    f1.waitForFinished();
    f2.waitForFinished();
    f3.waitForFinished();
```

6. If you build and run the program again, you should see something like the following being printed out on the debug window, which means that the three printText() functions now run in parallel:

```
...
"A" 0x271ec
"C" 0x26808
"B" 0x27a40
"A" 0x271ec
"C" Done
"B" 0x27a40
"A" Done
"B" Done
```

7. We can also use the QFutureWatcher class to notify a QObject class through a signals and slots mechanism. The QFutureWatcher class allows us to monitor QFuture using signals and slots:

```
    QFuture<void> f1 = QtConcurrent::run(printText,
QString("A"), 100);
    QFuture<void> f2 = QtConcurrent::run(printText,
QString("B"), 100);
    QFuture<void> f3 = QtConcurrent::run(printText,
QString("C"), 100);

    QFutureWatcher<void> futureWatcher;
    QObject::connect(&futureWatcher,
    QFutureWatcher<void>::finished, &w, MainWindow::mySlot);
    futureWatcher.setFuture(f1);

    f1.waitForFinished();
```

```
f2.waitForFinished();
f3.waitForFinished();
```

8. After that, open up `mainwindow.h` and declare the slot function:

```
public slots:
    void mySlot();
```

9. The `mySlot()` function looks like this in `mainwindow.cpp`:

```
void MainWindow::mySlot() {
    qDebug() << "Done!" << QThread::currentThreadId();
}
```

10. If you build and run the program again, this time, you will see results like this:

```
. . .
"A" 0x271ec
"C" 0x26808
"B" 0x27a40
"A" 0x271ec
"C" Done
"B" 0x27a40
"A" Done
"B" Done
Done! 0x27ac0
```

11. Even though `QFutureWatcher` is linked to `f1`, the `Done!` message only gets printed after all of the threads have finished executing. This is because `mySlot()` runs in the main thread, proven by the thread ID shown in the debug window alongside the `Done!` message.

How it works...

By default, there is a main thread (also known as a GUI thread) in any Qt 6 application. Other threads that you create are called the **worker threads**.

GUI-related classes, such as `QWidget` and `QPixmap`, can only exist in the main thread, so you must be extra careful when dealing with these classes.

`QFuture` is a high-level class that deals with **asynchronous computation**.

We use the `QFutureWatcher` class to let `QFuture` interact with signals and slots. You can even use this to display the progress of the operation on a progress bar.

QObject and QThread

Next, we want to explore some other methods so that we can use threads in Qt 6 applications. Qt 6 provides a class called QThread, which gives you more control over how you create and execute a thread. A QThread object begins to execute its event loops in a thread by calling the run() function. In this example, we will learn how to make the QObject class work together asynchronously through the Qthread class.

How to do it...

Let's get started by performing the following steps:

1. Create a new Qt widget application project. Then, go to **File | New File or Project...** and create a **C++ Class** file:

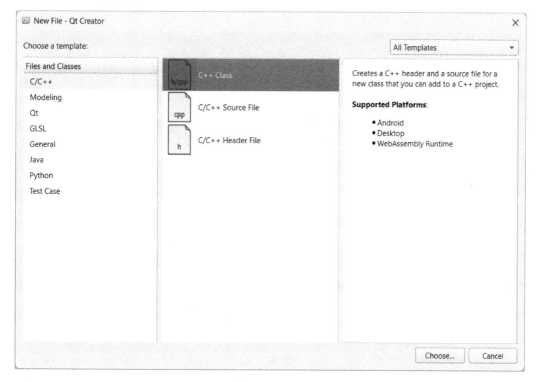

Figure 8.1 – Create a new C++ class

2. After that, name the new class MyWorker and make it inherit from the QObject class. Don't forget to include the QObject class by default as well:

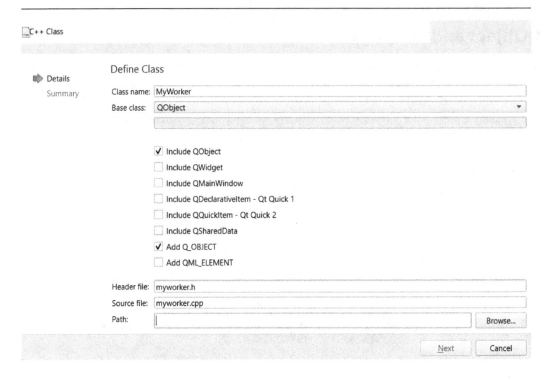

Figure 8.2 – Define the MyWorker C++ class

3. Once you have created the MyWorker class, open up myworker.h and add the following headers at the top:

```
#include <QObject>
#include <QDebug>
```

4. After that, add the following signals and slot functions to the file as well:

```
signals:
    void showResults(int res);
    void doneProcess();
public slots:
    void process();
```

5. Next, open up myworker.cpp and implement the process() function:

```
void MyWorker::process() {
    int result = 0;
    for (int i = 0; i < 2000000000; ++i) {
    result += 1;
    }
```

```
    emit showResults(result);
    emit doneProcess();
}
```

6. After that, open up `mainwindow.h` and add the following headers at the top:

```
#include <QDebug>
#include <QThread>
#include "myworker.h"
```

7. Then, declare a slot function, as shown in the following code:

```
public slots:
    void handleResults(int res);
```

8. Once you're done, open up `mainwindow.cpp` and implement the `handResults()` function:

```
void MainWindow::handleResults(int res) {
    qDebug() << "Handle results" << res;
}
```

9. Lastly, we will add the following code to the class constructor of the `MainWindow` class:

```
MainWindow::MainWindow(QWidget *parent)
    :    QMainWindow(parent), ui(new Ui::MainWindow) {
    ui->setupUi(this);
    QThread* workerThread = new QThread;
    MyWorker *workerObject = new MyWorker;
    workerObject->moveToThread(workerThread);
    connect(workerThread, &QThread::started,  workerObject,
&MyWorker::process);
    connect(workerObject, &MyWorker::doneProcess,  workerThread,
&QThread::quit);
    connect(workerObject, &MyWorker::doneProcess, workerObject,
&MyWorker::deleteLater);
    connect(workerObject, &MyWorker::showResults, this,
&MainWindow::handleResults);
    connect(workerThread, &QThread::finished, workerObject,
&MyWorker::deleteLater);
    workerThread->start();
}
```

10. Build and run the program now. You should see that the main window pops out and does nothing for a couple of seconds before a line of message is printed on the debug window:

```
Final result: 2000000000
```

11. The result was calculated in a separate thread, which is why the main window can display smoothly and can even be moved around by a mouse during the calculation. To see the difference when running the calculation on the main thread, let's comment out some of the code and call the process() function directly:

```
//QThread* workerThread = new QThread;
MyWorker *workerObject = new MyWorker;
//workerObject->moveToThread(workerThread);
//connect(workerThread, &QThread::started, workerObject,
&MyWorker::process);
//connect(workerObject, &MyWorker::doneProcess,
workerThread, &QThread::quit);
connect(workerObject, &MyWorker::doneProcess, workerObject,
&MyWorker::deleteLater);
connect(workerObject, &MyWorker::showResults, this,
&MainWindow::handleResults);
//connect(workerThread, &QThread::finished, workerObject,
&MyWorker::deleteLater);
//workerThread->start();
workerObject->process();
```

12. Build and run the project now. This time, the main window will only appear on the screen once the calculation has been done. This is because the calculation was blocking the main thread (or GUI thread) and prevented the main window from being displayed.

How it works...

QThread is an alternative method to run a process asynchronously, besides using the QFuture class. It gives us more control compared with QFuture, which we will demonstrate in the following recipe.

Do note that the QObject class that gets moved to the working thread cannot have any parent, as Qt is designed in such a way that an entire object tree must exist in the same thread. Therefore, all of the children of a QObject class will also be moved to the working thread when you call moveToThread().

Use a signals and slots mechanism if you want your working thread to communicate with the main thread. We use the started signal that's provided by the QThread class to inform our working object to start the calculation, since the working thread has already been created.

Then, when the calculation has been completed, we emit the showResult and doneProcess signals to inform the thread to quit, while passing the final result to the main thread for it to be printed.

Lastly, we also use the signals and slots mechanism to safely delete both the working thread and working object when everything is done.

Data protection and sharing data between threads

Even though multithreading makes processes run asynchronously, there will be times when threads must stop and wait for other threads. This usually happens when both threads modify the same variable simultaneously. It is common to force threads to wait for one another to protect shared resources, such as data. Qt 6 also provides both low-level methods and high-level mechanisms to synchronize threads.

How to do it...

We will continue to use the code from the previous example project, since we have already established a working program with multithreading:

1. Open up `myworker.h` and add the following header:

    ```
    #include <QObject>
    #include <QDebug>
    #include <QMutex>
    ```

2. Then, we will add two new variables and make some changes to the class constructor:

    ```
    public:
        explicit MyWorker(QMutex *mutex);
        int* myInputNumber;
        QMutex* myMutex;
    signals:
        void showResults(int res);
        void doneProcess();
    ```

3. After that, open up `myworker.cpp` and change the class constructor to look like the following code. We no longer require the parent input, since the object will not have a parent:

    ```
    MyWorker::MyWorker(QMutex *mutex) {
        myMutex = mutex;
    }
    ```

4. We will also change the `process()` function to look like this:

    ```
    void MyWorker::process() {
        myMutex->lock();
        for (int i = 1; i < 100000; ++i){
        *myInputNumber += i * i + 2 * i + 3 * i;
        }
    ```

```
        myMutex->unlock();
        emit showResults(*myInputNumber);
        emit doneProcess();
    }
```

5. Once you're done, open up `mainwindow.cpp` and make some changes to the code:

```
MainWindow::MainWindow(QWidget *parent) : QMainWindow(parent),
    ui(new Ui::MainWindow) {
    ui->setupUi(this);
    int myNumber = 5;
    QMutex* newMutex = new QMutex;
    QThread* workerThread = new QThread;
    QThread* workerThread2 = new QThread;
    QThread* workerThread3 = new QThread;
    MyWorker *workerObject = new MyWorker(newMutex);
    MyWorker *workerObject2 = new MyWorker(newMutex);
    MyWorker *workerObject3 = new MyWorker(newMutex);
```

6. After that, we will set the `myInputNumber` variable of the worker object to `myNumber`. Note that we are referencing its pointer instead of the value:

```
        workerObject->myInputNumber = &myNumber;
        workerObject->moveToThread(workerThread);
        connect(workerThread, &QThread::started, workerObject,
&MyWorker::process);
        connect(workerObject, &MyWorker::doneProcess, workerThread,
&QThread::quit);
        connect(workerObject, &MyWorker::doneProcess, workerObject,
&MyWorker::deleteLater);
        connect(workerObject, &MyWorker::showResults, this,
&MainWindow::handleResults);
        connect(workerThread, &QThread::finished, workerObject,
&MyWorker::deleteLater);
```

7. Repeat the previous step twice more to set `workerObject2`, `workerThread2`, `workerObject3`, and `workerThread3`:

```
        workerObject2->myInputNumber = &myNumber;
        workerObject2->moveToThread(workerThread2);
        connect(workerThread2, &QThread::started, workerObject2,
&MyWorker::process);
        connect(workerObject2, &MyWorker::doneProcess,
workerThread2, &QThread::quit);
        connect(workerObject2, &MyWorker::doneProcess,
workerObject2, &MyWorker::deleteLater);
        connect(workerObject2, &MyWorker::showResults, this,
```

```
&MainWindow::handleResults);
    connect(workerThread2, &QThread::finished, workerObject2,
&MyWorker::deleteLater);
    workerObject3->myInputNumber = &myNumber;
    workerObject3->moveToThread(workerThread3);
    connect(workerThread3, &QThread::started, workerObject3,
&MyWorker::process);
    connect(workerObject3, &MyWorker::doneProcess,
workerThread3, &QThread::quit);
    connect(workerObject3, &MyWorker::doneProcess,
workerObject3, &MyWorker::deleteLater);
    connect(workerObject3, &MyWorker::showResults, this,
&MainWindow::handleResults);
    connect(workerThread3, &QThread::finished, workerObject3,
&MyWorker::deleteLater);
```

8. Finally, we will start running those threads by calling `start()`:

```
workerThread->start();
workerThread2->start();
workerThread3->start();
```

9. If you build and run the program now, you should see a consistent result, no matter how many times you run it:

```
Final result: -553579035
Final result: -1107158075
Final result: -1660737115
```

10. We get results every time we run the program because the mutex lock ensures that only one of the threads can modify the data while other threads await their completion. To see the difference without mutex locking, let's comment out the code:

```
void MyWorker::process() {
    //myMutex->lock();
    for (int i = 1; i < 100000; ++i) {
        *myInputNumber += i * i + 2 * i + 3 * i;
        }
    //myMutex->unlock();
    emit showResults(*myInputNumber);
    emit doneProcess();
}
```

11. Build and run the program again. This time, you will get a very different result when you run the program. For example, I've obtained the following results when running it on three occasions:

```
1st time:
Final result: -589341102
Final result: 403417142
Final result: -978935318
2nd time:
Final result: 699389030
Final result: -175723048
Final result: 1293365532
3rd time:
Final result: 1072831160
Final result: 472989964
Final result: -534842088
```

12. This happens because the myNumber data is manipulated by all the threads simultaneously in a random order, due to the nature of parallel computation. By locking the mutex, we make sure that the data can only be modified by a single thread and, hence, eliminate this issue.

How it works...

Qt 6 provides two classes, namely QMutex and QReadWriteLock, for data protection when multiple threads access and modify the same data. We only used QMutex in the previous example, but both classes are very similar in nature. The only difference is that QReadWriteLock allows data to be read simultaneously by other threads while the data is written. Unlike QMutex, it separates the read and write states, but only one can occur at a time (either lock for read or lock for write), and not both. For complex functions and statements, use the high-level QMutexLocker class instead of QMutex for simplifying the code and easier debugging.

The downside of this method is that all of the other threads will stand idle while the data is modified by a single thread. It is best not to share data with multiple threads unless there is no other way to do so, as it will halt the other threads and defeat the object of parallel computation.

Working with QRunnable processes

In this recipe, we will learn how to use another type of high-level method to easily create a multithreading Qt 6 application. We will use the QRunnable and QThreadPool classes in this recipe.

How to do it...

1. Create a new Qt widget application project and then a new C++ class called `MyProcess`, which inherits the `QRunnable` class.

2. Next, open up `myprocess.h` and add the following headers:

```
#include <QRunnable>
#include <QDebug>
```

3. Then, declare the `run()` function, as follows:

```
class MyProcess : public QRunnable {
    public:
            MyProcess();
            void run();
};
```

4. After that, open up `myprocess.cpp` and define the `run()` function:

```
void MyProcess::run() {
    int myNumber = 0;
    for (int i = 0; i < 100000000; ++i) {
    myNumber += i;
    }
    qDebug() << myNumber;
}
```

5. Once you're done, add the following headers to `mainwindow.h`:

```
#include <QMainWindow>
#include <QThreadPool>
#include "myprocess.h"
```

6. After that, we will implement the class constructor by adding the following code:

```
MainWindow::MainWindow(QWidget *parent) : QMainWindow(parent),
    ui(new Ui::MainWindow) {
    ui->setupUi(this);
    MyProcess* process = new MyProcess;
    MyProcess* process2 = new MyProcess;
    MyProcess* process3 = new MyProcess;
    MyProcess* process4 = new MyProcess;
    QThreadPool::globalInstance()->start(process);
    QThreadPool::globalInstance()->start(process2);
    QThreadPool::globalInstance()->start(process3);
    QThreadPool::globalInstance()->start(process4);
```

```
        qDebug() <<
QThreadPool::globalInstance()-            >activeThreadCount();
    }
```

7. Now, build and run the project. You should see that the processes are successfully run in different threads where the active thread count is four.

8. The QThreadPool class automatically deactivates threads when its last process has been executed. Let's try and prove that by pausing the program for three seconds and printing out the active thread count again:

```
        qDebug() << QThreadPool::globalInstance()-
>activeThreadCount();
        this->thread()->sleep(3);
        qDebug() << QThreadPool::globalInstance()-
>activeThreadCount();
```

9. Build and run the program again. This time, you should see that the active thread count is four, and then, after three seconds, the active thread count becomes zero. This is because all of the processes have been executed.

How it works...

The QRunnable class works hand in hand with the QThreadPool class, which manages a collection of threads. The QThreadPool class automatically manages and recycles individual QThreads objects to avoid creating and destroying threads too frequently, which helps in reducing computing costs.

To use QThreadPool, you must sub-class the QRunnable object and implement the virtual function called run(). By default, QThreadPool will automatically delete the QRunnable object when the last thread exits the run function. You can change this behavior by calling setAutoDelete() to change the autoDelete variable to false.

By default, threads that are unused for more than 30 seconds will expire. You can change this duration by calling setExpiryTimeout() before the thread runs. Otherwise, there will be no effect on the timeout setting.

You can also set the maximum number of threads that can be used by calling setMaxThreadCount(). To get the total number of currently active threads, simply call activeThreadCount().

9

Building a Touch Screen Application with Qt 6

Qt is not only a cross-platform software development kit for PC platforms; it also supports mobile platforms, such as iOS and Android. The developers of Qt introduced **Qt Quick** back in 2010, which provides an easy way to build custom user interfaces that are highly dynamic, where users can easily create fluid transitions and effects with only minimal coding.

Qt Quick uses a declarative scripting language called **QML**, which is similar to the **JavaScript** language used in web development. Advanced users can also create custom functions in C++ and port them over to Qt Quick to enhance their functionality. At the moment, Qt Quick supports multiple platforms, such as Windows, Linux, macOS, iOS, and Android.

This chapter will cover the following recipes:

- Setting up Qt for mobile applications
- Designing a basic user interface with QML
- Touch events
- Animation in QML
- Displaying information using model/view
- Integrating QML and C++

Technical requirements

The technical requirements for this chapter include Qt 6.6.1, Qt Creator 12.0.2, Android **Software Development Kit (SDK)**, Android **Native Development Kit (NDK)**, **Java Development Kit (JDK)**, and Apache Ant. All the code used in this chapter can be downloaded from the following GitHub repository: `https://github.com/PacktPublishing/QT6-C-GUI-Programming-Cookbook---Third-Edition-/tree/main/Chapter09`.

Setting up Qt for mobile applications

In this example, we will learn how to set up our Qt project in Qt Quick and enable it to be built and exported to mobile devices.

How to do it...

Let's get started and learn how to create our first mobile application using Qt 6:

1. First of all, let's create a new project by going to **File | New Project…**. Then, a window will pop up for you to choose a project template. Select **Qt Quick Application** and click the **Choose…** button, as shown in the following screenshot:

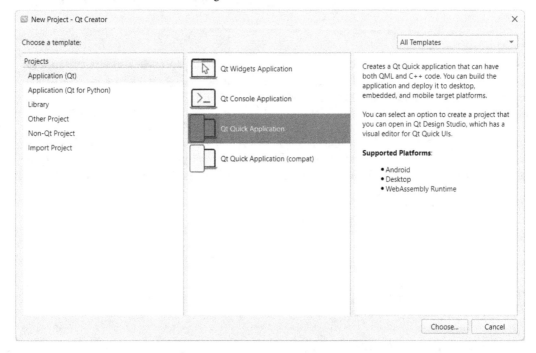

Figure 9.1 – Create a Qt Quick application project

2. After that, insert the project name and select the project location. Click the **Next** button, and it will ask you to select the minimum Qt version required for your project.

> **Important note**
> Please make sure that you select a version that exists on your computer. Otherwise, you won't be able to run it properly.

3. Once you have done that, proceed by clicking the **Next** button.

4. Then, Qt Creator will ask you which kit you want to use for your project. These **kits** are basically different compilers that you can use to compile your project for different platforms. Since we're making an application for a mobile platform, we will enable the Android kit (or the iOS kit if you're running a Mac) to build and export your app to your mobile device, as shown in the following screenshot. You can also enable one of the desktop kits so you can test your program on the desktop beforehand. Do note that you need to configure the Android kit if you're using it for the first time so that Qt can find the directory of the Android SDK. Click **Next** once you're done with it:

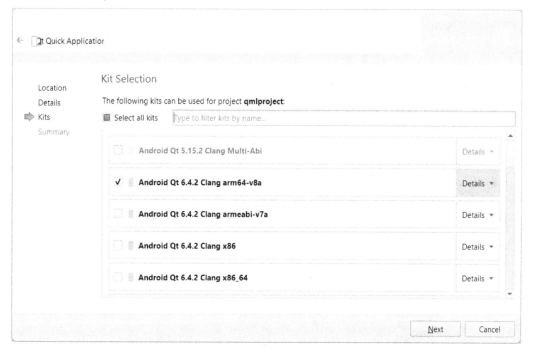

Figure 9.2 – Create an Android Kit for this project

5. Once the project has been created, Qt Creator will automatically open up a file from your project called Main.qml. You will see a different type of script, as shown in the following code, that is very different from your usual C/C++ projects:

```
import QtQuick
import QtQuick.Window
Window {
    visible: true
    width: 640
    height: 480
```

```
        title: qsTr("Hello World")
    }
```

6. Build and run the project now by clicking on the green arrow button located at the bottom-left corner of your Qt Creator, as shown in *Figure 9.3*. If you set the default kit to one of the desktop kits, an empty window will pop up once the project has been compiled:

Figure 9.3 – Press the triangle button to build and run

7. As shown in the next screenshot, We can switch between different kits by going to the Projects interface and selecting the kit you want your project to be built with. You can also manage all the kits available on your computer or add a new kit to your project from the **Projects** interface:

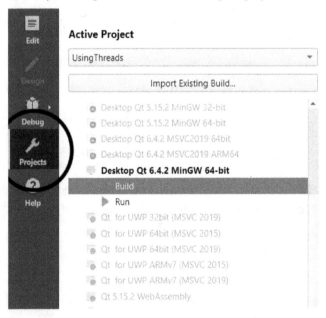

Figure 9.4 – Change to any kits in the Projects interface

8. If this is your first time building and running your project, you need to create a template for the Android kit under the **Build** settings. Once you have clicked the **Create Templates** button under the **Build Android APK** tab, as shown in *Figure 9.5*, Qt will generate all the files required to run your app on an Android device. If you don't plan to use Gradle in your project, disable the **Copy the Gradle files to Android directory** option. Otherwise, you may encounter problems when trying to compile and deploy your app to your mobile device:

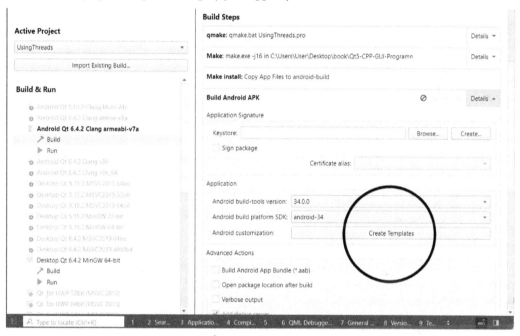

Figure 9.5 – Click the Create Templates button to create an Android template file

9. Once you click the **Create Templates** button, several files will be added to your project by Qt. These files are specifically for Android projects, including `AndroidManifest.xml`, Gradle-related files, and other resources that are required by the Android platform. Let's open up the `AndroidManifest.xml` file:

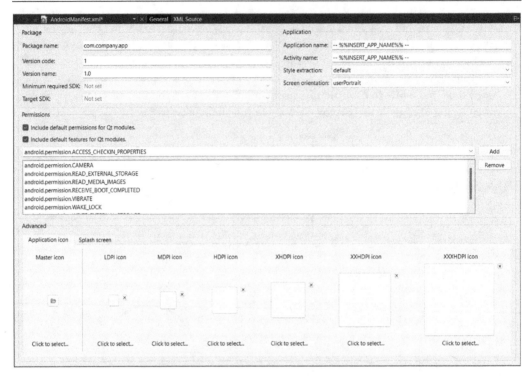

Figure 9.6 – Set your app's settings in AndroidManifest.xml

10. Once you have opened `AndroidManifest.xml`, you can set your app's package name, version code, app icon, and permissions before exporting the app. To build and test your Android app, click on the **Run** button on Qt Creator. You should now see the following window pop up, asking which device it should export to.

11. Select the device that is currently connected to your computer and press the **OK** button. Wait for a while for it to build the project, and you should be able to get a blank app running on your mobile device.

How it works...

A Qt Quick application project is quite different from a widget application project. You will be writing QML script most of the time instead of writing C/C++ code. **Android Software Development Kit (SDK)**, **Android Native Development Kit (NDK)**, **Java Development Kit (JDK)**, and **Apache Ant** are required to build and export your app to the Android platform.

Alternatively, you can also use Gradle instead of Apache Ant for your Android kit. All you need to do is enable the **Use Gradle** instead of Ant option and provide Qt with Gradle's installation path. Note that Android Studio is currently (at the time of authoring this book) not supported by Qt Creator:

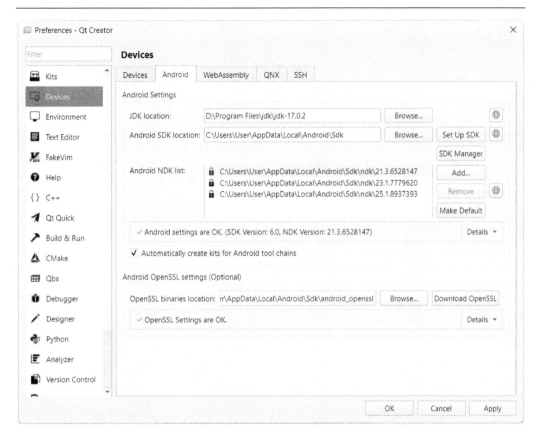

Figure 9.7 – Set up your Android settings in the Android tab in the Preferences window

If you're running the app on an Android device, make sure that you have **USB debugging mode** enabled. To enable USB debugging mode, you need to first enable the developer options on your Android device by going to **Settings | About Phone** and tapping **Build Number** seven times. After that, go to **Settings | Developer Options**, and you will see the **USB debugging** option in the menu. Enable that option, and you can now export your app to your device for testing.

To build for the iOS platform, you need to run Qt Creator on a Mac and make sure the latest **Xcode** is installed on your Mac as well. To test your app on an iOS device, you need to register a developer account with Apple, register your device at the developer portal, and install the provisioning to your **Xcode**, which is a lot trickier than Android. You will be given access to the developer portal once you have obtained a developer account from Apple.

Designing a basic user interface with QML

This example will teach us how to use Qt Design Studio to design our program's user interface.

How to do it...

Let's follow these steps to get started:

1. First of all, create a new **Qt Quick application** project, just like we did in the previous recipe. This time, however, make sure you check on the **Creates a project that you can open in Qt Design Studio** option as well:

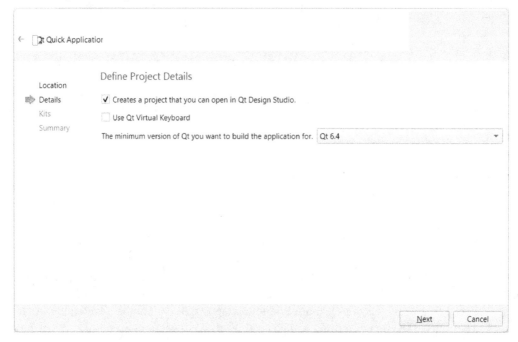

Figure 9.8 – Make sure your project can be opened by Qt Design Studio

2. You will see a QML file in your project resources called main.qml. This is where we implement the logic for our application, but we will also need another QML file where we define our user interface.

3. Before we proceed to design our program's user interface, let's download and install **Qt Design Studio** from Qt's official website: https://www.qt.io/product/ui-design-tools. This is a new editor created by Qt for UI/UX designers to design user interfaces for their Qt Quick projects.

4. Once you have installed **Qt Design Studio**, open up the editor and open the `.qmlproject` file in your project directory by pressing the **Open Project...** button:

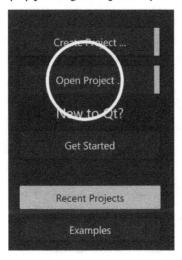

Figure 9.9 – Click the Open Project ... button

5. After that, a default QML UI file called `Sreen01.ui.qml` will be opened by **Qt Design Studio**. You will see an entirely different user interface editor compared to the one we used in previous chapters.

6. Since Qt 6, the Qt team released the **Qt Design Studio**, which is a new editor used specifically to design user interfaces for Qt Quick projects. The components of this editor are described as follows:

    *   **Components**: The **Components** window displays all the predefined QML types that you can add to your user interface canvas. You can also create custom Qt Quick components from the Create Component button and display them here.

    *   **Navigator**: The **Navigator** window displays the items in the current QML file in a tree structure.

    *   **Connections**: You can use the tools provided in the **Connections** window to connect objects to signals, specify dynamic properties for objects, and create bindings between the properties of two objects.

    *   **States**: The **States** window displays the different states of an item. You can add a new state for an item by clicking on the + button on the right of the **State** window.

    *   **2D/3D Canvas**: The canvas is where you design your program's user interface. You can drag and drop a **Qt Quick** component from the **Components** window onto the canvas and instantly see what it will look like in the program. You can create a 2D or 3D canvas for different types of applications.

    *   **Properties**: This is where you change the properties of a selected item.

7. You can also select pre-defined workspaces for your **Qt Design Studio** editor by selecting from the drop-down box in the top-right corner:

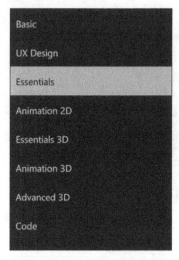

Figure 9.10 – Select a pre-defined workspace

8. We're about to make a simple login screen. First, delete the editing components from the 2D canvas. Then, from the **Components** window, drag two text widgets onto the canvas.

9. Set the **Text** properties of both the text widgets to Username: and Password::

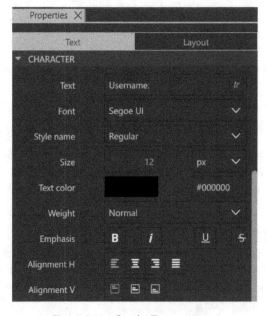

Figure 9.11 – Set the Text property

10. Drag two rectangles from the **Components** window to the canvas, then drag two text input widgets onto the canvas and parent each of them to the rectangles you just added to the canvas. Set the **Border** property of the rectangles to 1 and the **Radius** to 5. Then, set the echo mode of one of the text fields to **Password**.

11. Now, we're going to manually create a button widget by combining a mouse area widget with a rectangle and a text widget. Drag a mouse area widget onto the canvas, then drag a rectangle and a text widget onto the canvas and parent them both to the mouse area. Set the color of the rectangle to #bdbdbd, then set its **Border** property to 1 and its **Radius** to 5. Then, set the **text** to Login and make sure the size of the mouse area is the same as the rectangle.

12. After that, drag another rectangle onto the canvas to act as the container for the login form so that it will look neat. Set its **Border Color** to #5e5858 and its **Border** property to 2. Then, set its **Radius** property to 5 to make its corners look a little rounded.

13. Make sure the rectangle that we added in the previous step is positioned at the top of the hierarchy in the **Navigator** window so that it appears behind all the other widgets. You can arrange the widget positions within the hierarchy by pressing the arrow buttons located at the top of the **Navigator** window as follows:

Figure 9.12 – Click the Move up button

14. Next, we will export three widgets: mouse area and the two text input widgets as the alias properties of the root item so that later on, we can access these widgets from the App.qml file. The widgets can be exported by clicking on the small icon behind the widget name and making sure the icon changes to the **On** status.

15. By now, your user interface should look something like this:

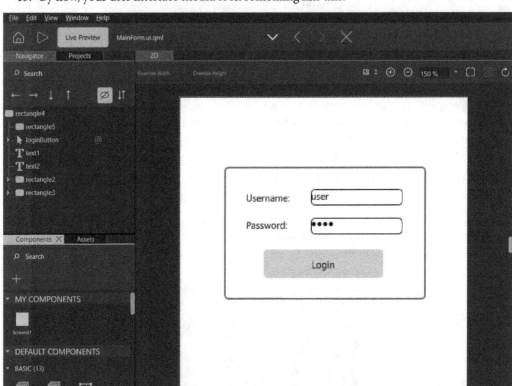

Figure 9.13 – A simple login screen

16. Now, let's open up `App.qml`. Qt Creator will not open this file in **Qt Design Studio** by default; instead, it will be opened with the script editor. This is because all the user interface design-related tasks were carried out in `Screen01.ui.qml`, and `App.qml` is only used for defining the logic and functions that will be applied to the UI. You can, however, open it with Qt Design Studio to preview the user interface by clicking on the **Design** button located in the sidebar on the left of the editor.

17. At the top of the script, add the third line to import the dialog module to `App.qml`, as shown in the following code:

```
import QtQuick
import QtQuick.Dialogs
import yourprojectname
```

18. After that, replace the following code with this:

```
Window {
    visible: true
    title: "Hello World"
    width: 360
    height: 360
    Screen01 {
        anchors.fill: parent
        loginButton.onClicked: {
        messageDialog.text = "Username is " +
        userInput.text + " and password is " + passInput.text
        messageDialog.visible = true
        }
    }
}
```

19. We continue to define messageDialog as follows:

```
MessageDialog {
    id: messageDialog
    title: "Fake login"
    text: ""
    onAccepted: {
    console.log("You have clicked the login button")
    Qt.quit()
    }
}
}
```

20. Build and run this program on your PC, and you should get a simple program that shows a message box when you click on the **Login** button:

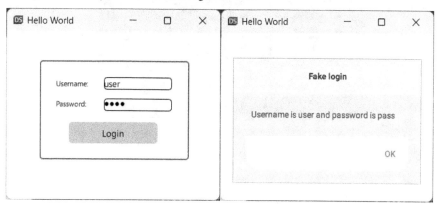

Figure 9.14 – A message box showing after clicking on the Login button

How it works...

Since Qt 5.4, a new file extension called `.ui.qml` has been introduced. The QML engine handles it like the normal `.qml` files but forbids any logic implementation from being written in it. It serves as the user interface definition template that can be reused in different `.qml` files. The separation of UI definition and logic implementation improves the maintainability of QML code and creates a better workflow.

Since Qt 6, `.ui.qml` files have no longer been handled by Qt Creator. Instead, Qt provides you with another program called Qt Design Studio to edit your Qt Quick UI. They intend to give programmers and designers their separate tools that fit their workflow.

All the widgets under **Basic** are the most basic widgets that we can use to mix and match and create a new type of widget, as follows:

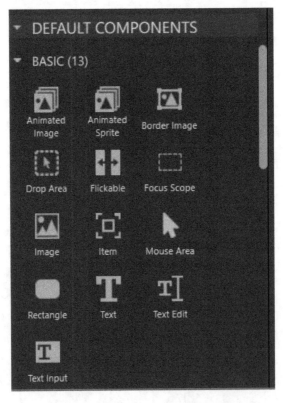

Figure 9.15 – Drag and drop widgets from here

In the previous example, we learned how to put three widgets together—a text, a mouse area, and a rectangle—to form a button widget. You can also create your custom component by clicking the **Create Component** button at the top right corner:

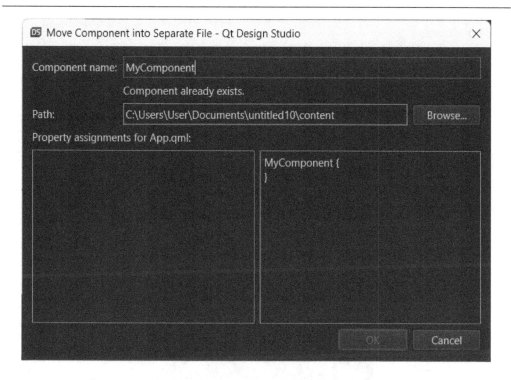

Figure 9.16 – You can also create your custom component

We imported the `QtQuick.Dialogs` module in `App.qml` and created a message box that displays the username and password filled in by the user when the **Login** button is pressed so that we can prove that the user interface function is working. If the widgets are not exported from `Screen01.ui.qml`, we will not be able to access their properties in `App.qml`.

At this point, we can export the program to iOS and Android, but the user interface may not look accurate on some of the devices that have a higher resolution or a higher **density-per-pixel** (**DPI**) unit. We will cover this issue later on in this chapter.

Touch events

In this section, we will learn how to develop a touch-driven application that runs on mobile devices using Qt Quick.

How to do it...

Let's get started by following this step-by-step guide:

1. Create a new **Qt Quick application** project.

2. In Qt Design Studio, click on the + button on the **Assets** Window. Then, select tux.png and add it to the project as follows:

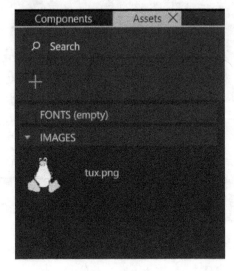

Figure 9.17 – Import tux.png into your project

3. Next, open up Screen01.ui.qml. Drag an image widget from the **Components** window to the canvas. Then, set the source of the image to tux.png and set its **fillMode** to **PreserveAspectFit**. After that, set its **width** to 200 and its **height** to 220.

4. Make sure that both the mouse area widget and the image widget are exported as the alias properties of the root item by clicking on the small icon beside their respective widget name.

5. After that, switch over to the script editor by clicking on the **Edit** button on the sidebar located on the left side of the editor. We need to change the mouse area widget to a multi-point touch area widget, as in the following code:

```
MultiPointTouchArea {
    id: touchArea
    anchors.fill: parent
    touchPoints: [
        TouchPoint { id: point1 },
        TouchPoint { id: point2 }
    ]
}
```

6. We also set the **Image** widget to be automatically placed at the center of the window by default, as follows:

```
Image {
    id: tux
    x: (window.width / 2) - (tux.width / 2)
    y: (window.height / 2) - (tux.height / 2)
    width: 200
    height: 220
    fillMode: Image.PreserveAspectFit
    source: "tux.png"
}
```

7. The final user interface should look something like this:

Figure 9.18 – Place the penguin in your application window

8. Once you're done with that, let's open up App.qml. First, clear everything within the **Screen01** object except anchors.fill: parent, as shown in the following code:

```
import QtQuick
import QtQuick.Window
Window {
    visible: true
    Screen01 {
        anchors.fill: parent
    }
}
```

9. After that, declare several variables within the **MainForm** object that will be used to rescale the image widget. If you want to know more about the property keyword used in the following code, check out the **There's more…** section at the end of this example:

```
property int prevPointX: 0
property int prevPointY: 0
property int curPointX: 0
property int curPointY: 0
property int prevDistX: 0
property int prevDistY: 0
property int curDistX: 0
property int curDistY: 0
property int tuxWidth: tux.width
property int tuxHeight: tux.height
```

10. Using the following code, we will define what will happen when our finger touches the multi-point area widget. In this case, we will save the positions of the first and second touch points if more than one finger touches the multi-point touch area. We also save the width and height of the image widget so that, later on, we can use these variables to calculate the scale of the image when the fingers start to move:

```
touchArea.onPressed: {
    if (touchArea.touchPoints[1].pressed) {
        if (touchArea.touchPoints[1].x < touchArea.
touchPoints[0].x)
            prevDistX = touchArea.touchPoints[1].x
-     touchArea.touchPoints[0].x
        else
            prevDistX = touchArea.touchPoints[0].x -
            touchArea.touchPoints[1].x
        if (touchArea.touchPoints[1].y < touchArea.
touchPoints[0].y)
            prevDistY = touchArea.touchPoints[1].y -
            touchArea.touchPoints[0].y
```

```
        else
                prevDistY = touchArea.touchPoints[0].y -
                touchArea.touchPoints[1].y
                tuxWidth = tux.width
                tuxHeight = tux.height
        }
    }
```

11. The following diagram shows the example of touch points being registered when two fingers are touching the screen within the touchArea boundary. The touchArea.touchPoints[0] is the first registered touch point, and touchArea.touchPoints[1] is the second. We then calculate the X and Y distance between the two touch points and save them as prevDistX and prevDistY, as follows:

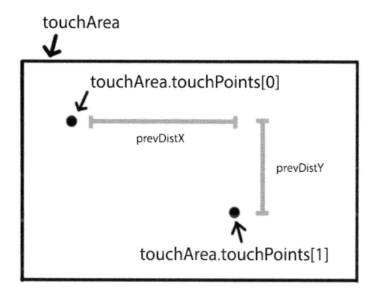

Figure 9.19 – Calculate the distances between two touch points

12. After that, we will define what will happen when our fingers move while remaining in contact with the screen and still within the boundary of the touch area using the following code. At this point, we will calculate the scale of the image by using the variables we saved in the previous step. At the same time, if we detect that only a single touch is found, then we will move the image instead of altering its scale:

```
            touchArea.onUpdated: {
                if (!touchArea.touchPoints[1].pressed) {
                    tux.x += touchArea.touchPoints[0].x -
                touchArea.touchPoints[0].previousX
```

```
                    tux.y += touchArea.touchPoints[0].y -
            touchArea.touchPoints[0].previousY
            }
         else {
            if (touchArea.touchPoints[1].x <
            touchArea.touchPoints[0].x)
                 curDistX = touchArea.touchPoints[1].x -
        touchArea.touchPoints[0].x
            else
                 curDistX = touchArea.touchPoints[0].x -
        touchArea.touchPoints[1].x
            if (touchArea.touchPoints[1].y <
            touchArea.touchPoints[0].y)
                 curDistY = touchArea.touchPoints[1].y -
        touchArea.touchPoints[0].y
            else
                 curDistY = touchArea.touchPoints[0].y -
        touchArea.touchPoints[1].y
            tux.width = tuxWidth + prevDistX - curDistX
            tux.height = tuxHeight + prevDistY - curDistY
         }
      }
```

13. The following diagram shows the example of moving touch points; `touchArea.touchPoints[0]` moved from point A to point B, and `touchArea.touchPoints[1]` moved from point C to point D. We can then determine how many units have the touch points moved by looking at the differences between the previous X, and Y variables with the current ones:

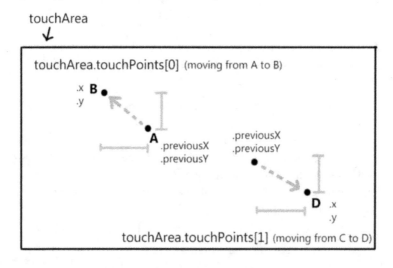

Figure 9.20 – Compare two sets of touch points to determine movement

14. You can now build and export the program to your mobile device. You will not be able to test this program on a platform that does not support multi-touch.

15. Once the program is running on the mobile device (or a desktop/laptop that supports multi-touch), try two things—put only one finger on the screen and move it around, and put two fingers on the screen and move them in opposite directions. What you should see is that the penguin will be moved to another place if you use only one finger, and it will be scaled up or down if you use two fingers, as shown in the following screenshot:

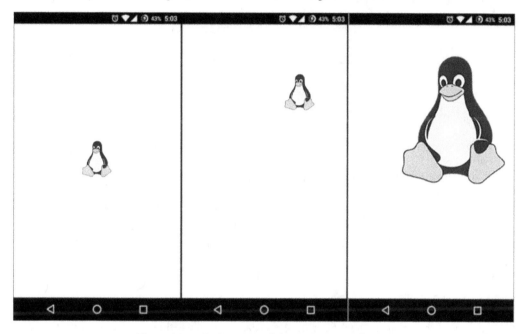

Figure 9.21 – Scaling up and down using your fingers

How it works...

When a finger touches the screen of the device, the multi-point touch area widget triggers the onPressed event and registers the position of each of the touch points in an internal array. We can get these data by telling Qt which touch point we want to get access to. The first touch will bear the index number of 0, the second touch will be 1, and so on. We will then save these data into variables so that we can retrieve them later to calculate the scaling of the penguin image. Other than onPressed, you can also use onReleased if you want the event to be triggered when the user releases his/her finger from the touch area.

When one or more fingers remain in contact with the screen while moving, a multi-point touch area will trigger the onUpdated event. We will then check how many touches there are; if only one touch is found, we will just move the penguin image based on how much our finger has moved. If there is more than one touch, we will compare the distance between the two touches and compare this with the previous variables we have saved to determine how much we should rescale the image.

The diagram shows tapping your finger on the screen will trigger the onPressed event, while swiping your finger on the screen will trigger the onUpdated event:

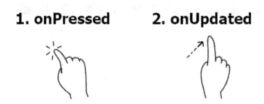

1. onPressed   2. onUpdated

Figure 9.22 – Difference between onPressed and onUpdated

We must also check whether the first touch is on the left side or if the second touch is on the right side. In this way, we can prevent the image from being scaled in the inverse direction of the finger movement and producing an inaccurate result. As for the movement of the penguin, we will just get the difference between the current touch position and the previous one and add that to the coordinate of the penguin; after this, it's done. A single touch event is usually a lot more straightforward than a multi-touch event.

There's more...

In Qt Quick, all its components have built-in properties, such as **width**, **height**, and **color**, that are attached to the components by default. However, Qt Quick also allows you to create your custom properties and attach them to the components you declared in your QML script. A custom property of an object type may be defined in an object declaration in a QML document by adding the property keyword before the type (int, float, and so on) keyword; here is an example:

```
property int myValue;
```

You can also bind the custom property to a value by using a colon (:) before the value, as shown in the following code:

```
property int myValue: 100;
```

> **Important note**
>
> To learn more about the property types supported by Qt Quick, check out this link: http://doc.qt.io/qt-6/qtqml-typesystem-basictypes.html.

Animation in QML

Qt allows us to easily animate a user interface component without writing a bunch of code. In this example, we will learn how to make our program's user interface more interesting by applying animations to it.

How to do it...

Let's learn how to add animation to our Qt Quick application by following these steps:

1. Once again, we will start everything from scratch. Therefore, create a new **Qt Quick application** project in Qt Creator and open the Screen01.ui.qml file.

2. Open up Screen01.ui.qml and go to the + button in the **Components** window and add a Qt Quick module called QtQuick.Controls to your project.

3. After that, you will see a new category appear in the **QML Types** tab called **QtQuick Controls**, which contains many new widgets that can be placed on the canvas.

4. Next, drag three button widgets to the canvas and set their **height** to 45. Then, go to the **Layout** tab on the **Properties** window and enable both the left and right anchors for all three button widgets. Make sure the target for the anchors is set to **Parent** and the margins remain as 0. This will make the buttons resize horizontally according to the width of the main window. After that, set the y value of the first button to 0, the second to 45, and the third to 90. The user interface should now look like this:

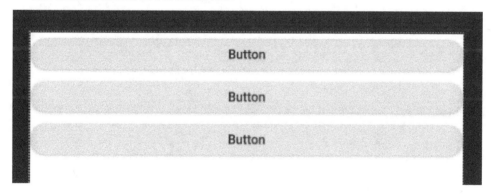

Figure 9.23 – Add three buttons to the layout

5. Now, open up the **Assets** window and add `fan.png` to the project, as follows:

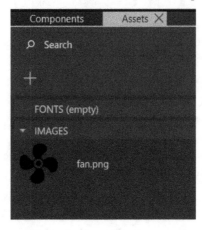

Figure 9.24 – Add fan.png to your project

6. Then, add two mouse area widgets to the canvas. After that, drag a **Rectangle** widget and an **Image** widget onto the canvas. Parent the rectangle and image to the mouse areas we have just added before this.

7. Set the **color** of the rectangle to `#0000ff` and apply `fan.png` to the image widget. Your user interface should now look like this:

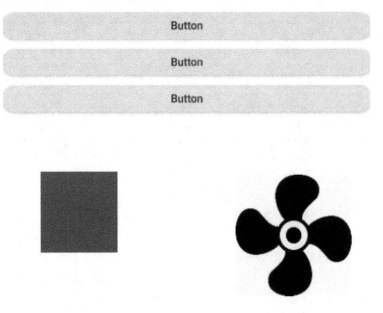

Figure 9.25 – Place a rectangle and the fan image in the layout

8. After that, export all the widgets in your `Screen01.ui.qml` as alias properties of the root item by clicking on the icons located to the right of the widget name, as follows:

Figure 9.26 – Adding aliases to the widgets

9. Next, we will apply animation and logic to the user interface, but we won't be doing it in `Screen01.ui.qml`. Instead, we will do it all in `App.qml`.

10. In `App.qml`, remove the default code for the mouse area and add in a **width** and **height** for the window so that we get more space to preview, as follows:

```
import QtQuick
import QtQuick.Window
Window {
    visible: true
    width: 480
    height: 550
    Screen01 {
        anchors.fill: parent
    }
}
```

11. After that, add the following code that defines the behavior of the buttons in the **Screen01** widget:

```
        button1 {
            Behavior on y { SpringAnimation { spring: 2;
    damping: 0.2 } }
            onClicked: {
                button1.y = button1.y + (45 * 3)
            }
        }
```

```
            button2 {
                    Behavior on y { SpringAnimation { spring: 2;
    damping: 0.2 } }
                    onClicked: {
                        button2.y = button2.y + (45 * 3)
                    }
            }
```

12. In the following code, we continue to define button3:

```
            button3 {
                    Behavior on y { SpringAnimation { spring: 2;
    damping: 0.2 } }
                    onClicked: {
                        button3.y = button3.y + (45 * 3)
                    }
            }
```

13. Then, follow this with the behavior of the fan image and the mouse area widget it is attached to as follows:

```
            fan {
                    RotationAnimation on rotation {
                        id: anim01
                        loops: Animation.Infinite
                        from: 0
                        to: -360
                        duration: 1000
                    }
            }
```

14. In the following code, we then define mouseArea1:

```
            mouseArea1 {
                    onPressed: {
                        if (anim01.paused)
                            anim01.resume()
                        else
                            anim01.pause()
                    }
            }
```

15. Last but not least, add the behavior of the rectangle and the mouse area widget it's attached to as follows:

```
rectangle2 {
    id: rect2
    state: "BLUE"
    states: [
        State {
            name: "BLUE"
            PropertyChanges {
                target: rect2
                color: "blue"
            }
        },
```

16. In the following code, we continue to add the RED state:

```
        State {
            name: "RED"
            PropertyChanges {
                target: rect2
                color: "red"
            }
        }
    ]
}
```

17. We then finish the code by defining mouseArea2 as follows:

```
mouseArea2 {
    SequentialAnimation on x {
        loops: Animation.Infinite
        PropertyAnimation { to: 150; duration: 1500 }
        PropertyAnimation { to: 50; duration: 500 }
    }
    onClicked: {
        if (rect2.state == "BLUE")
            rect2.state = "RED"
        else
            rect2.state = "BLUE"
    }
}
```

18. If you compile and run the program now, you should see three buttons at the top of the window and a moving rectangle at the bottom left, followed by a spinning fan at the bottom right, as demonstrated in the following screenshot. If you click any of the buttons, they will move slightly downward with a nice, smooth animation. If you click on the rectangle, it will change color from **blue** to **red**.

19. Meanwhile, the fan image will pause its animation if you click on it while it's animating, and it will resume the animation if you click on it again:

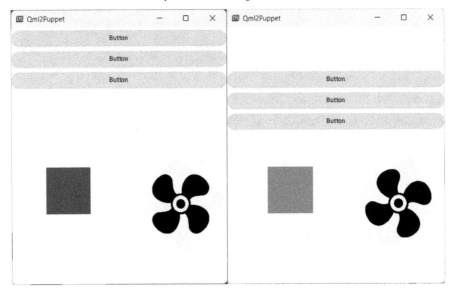

Figure 9.27 – You can now control the animation and color of the widgets

How it works...

Most of the animation elements supported by the C++ version of Qt, such as transition, sequential animation, and parallel animation, are also available in Qt Quick. If you are familiar with the Qt animation framework in C++, you should be able to grasp this pretty easily.

In this example, we added a spring animation element to all three buttons that specifically tracked their respective y-axes. If Qt detects that the y value has changed, the widget will not instantly pop to the new position; instead, it will be interpolated, move across the canvas, and perform a little shaking animation when reaching its destination that simulates the spring effect. We just have to write one line of code and leave the rest to Qt.

As for the fan image, we added a rotation animation element to it and set the duration to `1000 milliseconds`, which means it will complete a full rotation in one second. We also set it to loop its animation infinitely. When we clicked on the mouse area widget it's attached to, we just called `pause()` or `resume()` to enable or disable the animation.

Next, for the rectangle widget, we added two states to it, one called **BLUE** and one called **RED**, each of which carries a **color** property that will be applied to the rectangle upon state change. At the same time, we added **sequential animation group** to the mouse area widget that the rectangle is attached to and then added two **property animation** elements to the group. You can also mix different types of group animation; Qt can handle this very well.

Displaying information using model/view

Qt includes a **model/view framework** that maintains separation between the way data are organized and managed and the way that they are presented to the user. In this section, we will learn how to make use of the model/view; in particular, by using the list view to display information and, at the same time, apply our own customization to make it look slick.

How to do it...

Let's get started by following these steps:

1. Create a new **Qt Quick application** project and open up the **Assets** window in Qt Design Studio. Add six images, home.png, map.png, profile.png, search.png, settings.png, and arrow.png to the project, as follows:

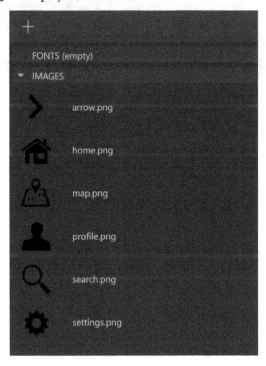

Figure 9.28 – Adding more images to the project

2. After that, create and open `Screen01.ui.qml`, as we did in all previous examples. Drag a **List View** widget from under the **Qt Quick – Views** category in the **Components** window and place it onto the canvas. Then, set its **Anchors** setting to fill the parent size by clicking on the button located in the middle of the **Layout** window, as shown in the following screenshot:

Figure 9.29 – Set the layout anchor as a fill parent

3. Next, switch over to the script editor, as we will define what the list view will look like as follows:

```
import QtQuick
Rectangle {
    id: rectangle1
    property alias listView1: listView1
    property double sizeMultiplier: width / 480
```

4. We will continue to write the code by adding the following list view:

```
ListView {
    id: listView1
    y: 0
    height: 160
    orientation: ListView.Vertical
    boundsBehavior: Flickable.StopAtBounds
    anchors.fill: parent
```

```
                delegate: Item {
                    width: 80 * sizeMultiplier
                    height: 55 * sizeMultiplier
```

5. We will continue to add rows to the list view, as follows:

```
                Row {
                    id: row1
                    Rectangle {
                        width: listView1.width
                        height: 55 * sizeMultiplier
                        gradient: Gradient {
                            GradientStop { position: 0.0; color:
    "#ffffff" }
                            GradientStop { position: 1.0; color:
    "#f0f0f0" }
                        }
                        opacity: 1.0
```

6. We then add a mouse area and an image, as shown in the following code snippet:

```
                        MouseArea {
                            id: mouseArea
                            anchors.fill: parent
                        }
                        Image {
                            anchors.verticalCenter: parent.
    verticalCenter
                            x: 15 * sizeMultiplier
                            width: 30 * sizeMultiplier
                            height: 30 * sizeMultiplier
                            source: icon
                        }
```

7. Then, continue to add two text objects, as follows:

```
                        Text {
                            text: title
                            font.family: "Courier"
                            font.pixelSize: 17 * sizeMultiplier
                            x: 55 * sizeMultiplier
                            y: 10 * sizeMultiplier
                        }
                        Text {
                            text: subtitle
                            font.family: "Verdana"
```

```
                            font.pixelSize: 9 * sizeMultiplier
                            x: 55 * sizeMultiplier
                            y: 30 * sizeMultiplier
                        }
```

8. After that, add an image object, as follows:

```
                    Image {
                        anchors.verticalCenter: parent.
        verticalCenter
                        x: parent.width - 35 * sizeMultiplier
                        width: 30 * sizeMultiplier
                        height: 30 * sizeMultiplier
                        source: "images/arrow.png"
                    }
                }
            }
        }
```

9. Using the following code, we will then define the list model:

```
        model: ListModel {
            ListElement {
                title: "Home"
                subtitle: "Go back to dashboard"
                icon: "images/home.png"
            }
            ListElement {
                title: "Map"
                subtitle: "Help navigate to your destination"
                icon: "images/map.png"
            }
```

10. We will continue to write the code:

```
            ListElement {
                title: "Profile"
                subtitle: "Customize your profile picture"
                icon: "images/profile.png"
            }
            ListElement {
                title: "Search"
                subtitle: "Search for nearby places"
```

```
                    icon: "images/search.png"
                }
```

11. We will now add the final list element, as shown in the following code:

```
                ListElement {
                    title: "Settings"
                    subtitle: "Customize your app settings"
                    icon: "images/settings.png"
                }
            }
        }
    }
```

12. After that, open up App.qml and replace the code with the following:

```
import QtQuick
import QtQuick.Window
Window {
    visible: true
    width: 480
    height: 480
    Screen01 {
        anchors.fill: parent
            MouseArea {
                onPressed: row1.opacity = 0.5
                onReleased: row1.opacity = 1.0
            }
        }
    }
}
```

13. Build and run the program, and now your program should look like this:

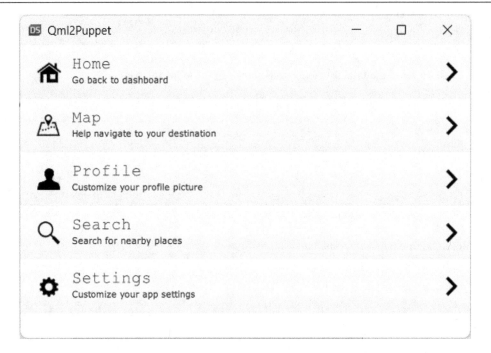

Figure 9.30 – Navigation menu with different fonts and icons

How it works...

Qt Quick allows us to customize the look of each row of the list view with ease. The delegate defines what each row will look like, and the model is where you store the data that will be displayed on the list view.

In this example, we added a background with a gradient on each row, and then we also added an icon on each side of the item, a title, a description, and a mouse area widget that makes each row of the list view clickable. The delegate is not static, as we allow the model to change the title, description, and icon to make each row look unique.

In App.qml, we defined the behavior of the mouse area widget that will halve its own opacity value when pressed and return to fully opaque when released. Since all other elements, such as title and icon, are all the children of the mouse area widget, all will also automatically follow their parent widget's behavior and become semi-transparent.

Additionally, we have finally solved the display problem on mobile devices with high resolution and DPI. It's a very simple trick; first, we defined a variable called sizeMultiplier. The value of sizeMultiplier is the result of dividing the width of the window by a predefined value, say 480, which is the current window width we used for the PC. Then, multiply sizeMultiplier by all the widget variables that are related to size and position, including font size. Do note that, in this case, you should use the `pixelSize` property for text instead of `pointSize`, so that you will get the correct display when multiplying by `sizeMultiplier`. The following screenshot shows you what the app looks like on the mobile device with and without `sizeMultiplier`:

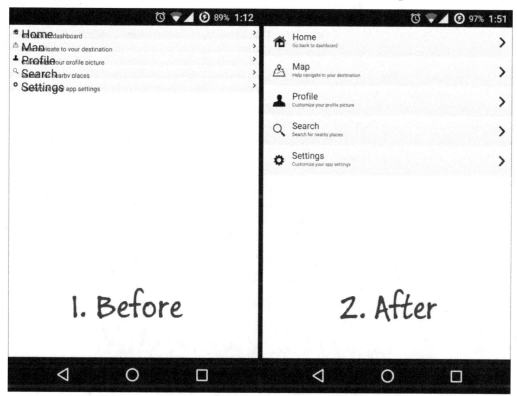

Figure 9.31 – Correcting size using size multiplier

Notice that you may get a messed-up user interface in the editor once you multiply everything by the `sizeMultiplier` variable. This is because the width variable may return as 0 in the editor. Hence, by multiplying 0 by 480, you may get the result 0, which makes the entire user interface look funny. However, it will look fine when running the actual program. If you want to preview the user interface on the editor, temporarily set **sizeMultiplier** to `1`.

Integrating QML and C++

Qt supports bridging between C++ classes with the QML engine. This combination allows developers to take advantage of both the simplicity of QML and the flexibility of C++. You can even integrate features that are not supported by Qt from external components, then pass the resulting data to Qt Quick to be displayed in the UI. In this example, we will learn how to export our user interface components from QML to the C++ framework and manipulate their properties before displaying them on screen.

How to do it...

Let's go through the following steps:

1. Once again, we will start everything from scratch. Therefore, create a new **Qt Quick application** project in Qt Creator and open up Screen01.ui.qml with Qt Design Studio. Then, open up Screen01.ui.qml.

2. We can keep the mouse area and text widget but place the text widget at the bottom of the window. Change the Text property of the text widget to **Change this text** using C++ and set its **font size** to 18. After that, go to the **Layout** tab and enable both **Vertical center anchor** and **Horizontal center anchor** to ensure it's always somewhere in the middle of the window, regardless of how you rescale the window. Set the **Margin** for the **Vertical center anchor** to 120, as shown in the following screenshot:

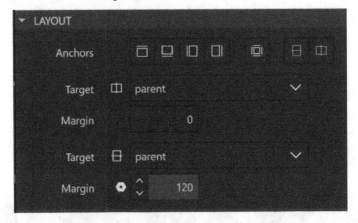

Figure 9.32 – Place it at the center of the layout

3. Next, drag a rectangle widget from the **Components** window to the canvas and set its color to #ff0d0d. Set its **Width** and **Height** to 200 and enable both the vertical and horizontal center anchor. After that, set the **Margin** of the horizontal center anchor to -14. Your UI should now look something like this:

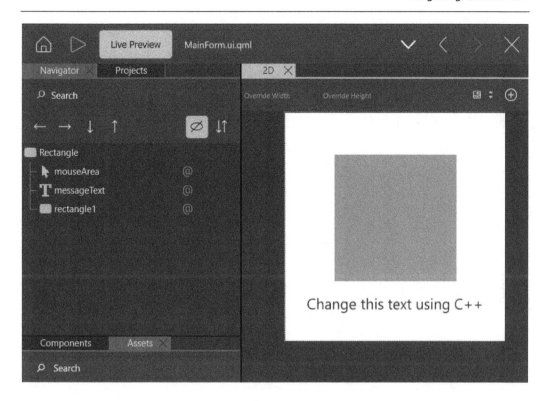

Figure 9.33 – Place the square and text as they are positioned in this image

4. Once you are done with that, right-click on your project directory in **Qt Creator** and choose **File | New File…**. Then, a window will pop up and let you pick a file template. Select **C++ Class** and press **Choose…**. After that, it will ask you to define the C++ class by filling in the information for the class. In this case, insert **MyClass** in the **Class Name** field and select **QObject** as the **Base class**. Then, make sure the **Include QObject** option is ticked, and you can now click the **Next** button, followed by the **Finish** button. Two files—myclass.h and myclass.cpp—will now be created and added to your project:

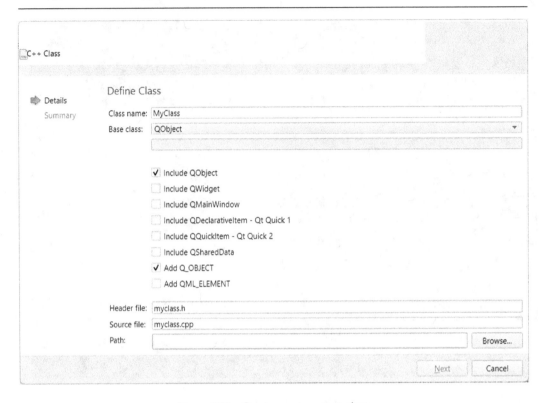

Figure 9.34 – Create a new custom class

5. Now, open up `myclass.h` and add a variable and function under the class constructor, as shown in the following code:

```
#ifndef MYCLASS_H
#define MYCLASS_H
#include <QObject>
class MyClass : public QObject
{
    Q_OBJECT
public:
    explicit MyClass(QObject *parent = 0);
    // Object pointer
    QObject* my Object;
    // Must call Q_INVOKABLE so that this function can be used
in QML
    Q_INVOKABLE void setMyObject(QObject* obj);
};
#endif // MYCLASS_H
```

6. After that, open up `myclass.cpp` and define the `setMyObject()` function, as follows:

```cpp
#include "myclass.h"
MyClass::MyClass(QObject *parent) : Qobject(parent)
{
}
void MyClass::setMyObject(Qobject* obj)
{
    // Set the object pointer
    my Object = obj;
}
```

7. We can now close `myclass.cpp` and open up `App.qml`. At the top of the file, import the `MyClassLib` components that we just created in C++:

```qml
import QtQuick
import QtQuick.Window
import MyClassLib
```

8. Then, define `MyClass` in the `Window` object and call its `setMyObject()` function within the `MainForm` object, as shown in the following code:

```qml
Window {
    visible: true
    width: 480
    height: 320
    MyClass {
        id: myclass
    }
    Screen01 {
        anchors.fill: parent
        mouseArea.onClicked: {
            Qt.quit();
        }
        Component.onCompleted:
    myclass.setMyObject(messageText);
    }
}
```

9. Lastly, open up `main.cpp` and register the custom class to the QML engine. We will also change the properties of the text widget and the rectangle here using C++ code, as follows:

```cpp
#include <QGuiApplication>
#include <QQmlApplicationEngine>
#include <QtQml>
#include <QQuickView>
```

```
#include <QQuickItem>
#include <QQuickView>
#include "myclass.h"
int main(int argc, char *argv[])
{
    // Register your class to QML
    qmlRegisterType<MyClass>("MyClassLib", 1, 0, "MyClass");
```

10. Then, proceed to create the objects, just like the highlighted section in the following code:

```
QGuiApplication app(argc, argv);
QQmlApplicationEngine engine;
engine.load(QUrl(QStringLiteral("qrc:/content/App.qml")));
QObject* root = engine.rootObjects().value(0);
QObject* messageText =
root->findChild<QObject*>("messageText");
    messageText->setProperty("text", QVariant("C++ is now in
control!"));
    messageText->setProperty("color", QVariant("green"));
    QObject* square = root->findChild<QObject*>("square");
    square->setProperty("color", QVariant("blue"));
    return app.exec();
}
```

11. Now, build and run the program, and you should see that the colors of the rectangle and the text are completely different from what you defined earlier in Qt Quick, as shown in the following screenshot. This is because their properties have been changed by the C++ code:

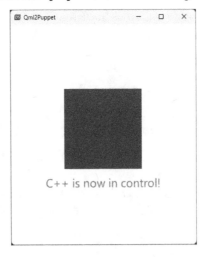

Figure 9.35 – Text and color can now be changed by C++

How it works...

QML is designed to be easily extendable through C++ code. The classes in the Qt QML module enable QML objects to be loaded and manipulated from C++.

Only classes that are inherited from the QObject base class can be integrated with QML, as it is part of the Qt ecosystem. Once the class has been registered with the QML engine, we get the root item from the QML engine and use it to find the objects we want to manipulate.

After that, use the setProperty() function to change any of the properties belonging to the widget. Other than setProperty(), you may also use the Q_PROPERTY() macro in a class that inherits QObject to declare a property. Here is an example:

```
Q_PROPERTY(QString text MEMBER m_text NOTIFY textChanged)
```

Notice that the Q_INVOKABLE macro needs to be placed in front of the function that you intend to call in QML. Without it, Qt will not expose the function to Qt Quick, and you will not be able to call it.

10

JSON Parsing Made Easy

JSON is the file extension of a data format called **JavaScript Object Notation**, which is used to store and transport information in a structured format. The JSON format is used extensively for the web. Most modern web **Application Programming Interfaces** (**APIs**) use JSON format to transfer data to their web clients.

This chapter will cover the following recipes:

- JSON format in a nutshell
- Processing JSON data from a text file
- Writing JSON data to a text file
- Using Google's Geocoding API

Technical requirements

The technical requirements for this chapter include Qt 6.6.1 MinGW 64-bit and Qt Creator 12.0.2. All the code used in this chapter can be downloaded from the following GitHub repository: `https://github.com/PacktPublishing/QT6-C-GUI-Programming-Cookbook---Third-Edition-/tree/main/Chapter10`.

JSON format in a nutshell

JSON is a human-readable text format commonly used for data transmission in web applications, especially **JavaScript** applications. However, it is also used for many other purposes, hence it is independent of JavaScript and can be used for any programming language or platform, despite its name.

In this example, we will learn about JSON format and how to verify whether your JSON data is in a valid format or not.

How to do it...

Let's get started and learn how to write your own JSON data and verify its format:

1. Open up your web browser and go to the **JSONLint Online Validator and Formatter** website at `https://jsonlint.com`.

2. Write the following JSON data in the text editor on the website:

```
{
    "members": [
        {
            "name": "John",
            "age": 29,
            "gender": "male"
        },
        {
            "name": "Alice",
            "age": 24,
            "gender": "female"
        },
        {
            "name": "",
            "age": 26,
            "gender": "male"
        }
    ]
}
```

3. After that, press the **Validate JSON** button. You should get the following result:

```
JSON is valid!
```

4. Now, try to remove the double quote symbols from the `members` variable:

```
{
    members: [
        {
            "name": "John",
            "age": 29,
            "gender": "male"
        },
```

5. Press the **Validate JSON** button again and you should get an error like this:

```
Invalid JSON!
Error: Parse error on line 1:
{    members: [           {
-----^
Expecting 'STRING', '}', got 'undefined'
```

6. Now, revert to the valid JSON format by adding the double quote symbols back to the members variable. Then, press the **Compress** button. You should get the following result, which has no empty space and next lines:

```
{"members":[{"name":"John","age":29,"gender":"male"},
{"name":"Alice","age":24,"gender":"female"},
{"name":"","age":26,"gender":"male"}]}
```

7. You can now press the **Prettify** button to revert it to the previous structure.

How it works...

The curly braces, { and }, contain a set of data as an object. An **object** is an individual data structure that contains its own properties or variables in the form of **key-value pairs**. Keys are unique strings that act as human-readable variable names, and values are represented by either a string, integer, floating-point number, Boolean, or even an entire object or array. JSON supports recursive objects, which is very handy for many different use cases.

The square brackets, [and], indicate that the data is contained in an array. An **array** simply stores a list of values of the same type, which can be manipulated, sorted, or removed from the array by iterating over its content using a standard iterator pattern in any programming language you use for your project.

In the previous example, we first created a nameless object as the main object of the data. You must create either a main object or a main array as a starting point. Then, we added an array called members, which contains individual objects with variables such as name, age, and gender. Do note that if you add double quotes (") around an integer or floating-point number, the variable will be treated as a string instead of a number.

The previous example demonstrated the simplest form of JSON data that can be sent through the network and processed by any modern programming language.

Processing JSON data from a text file

In this recipe, we will learn how to process JSON data taken from a text file and extract it using the stream reader.

How to do it...

Let's create a simple program that reads and processes XML files by following these steps:

1. Create a new **Qt Widgets Application** project at your desired location.

2. Open any text editor and create a JSON file that looks like the following, then save it as `scene.json`:

```
[
    {
        "name": "Library",
        "tag": "building",
        "position": [120.0, 0.0, 50.68],
        "rotation": [0.0, 0.0, 0.0],
        "scale": [1.0, 1.0, 1.0]
    }
]
```

3. Continue to write the JSON code by adding more objects after the `Library` object, as shown in the following code:

```
{
    "name": "Town Hall",
    "tag": "building",
    "position": [80.2, 0.0, 20.5],
    "rotation": [0.0, 0.0, 0.0],
    "scale": [1.0, 1.0, 1.0]
},
{
    "name": "Tree",
    "tag": "prop",
    "position": [10.46, -0.2, 80.2],
    "rotation": [0.0, 0.0, 0.0],
    "scale": [1.0, 1.0, 1.0]
}
```

4. Go back to Qt Creator and open `mainwindow.h`. Add the following headers at the top of the script, right after `#include <QMainWindow>`:

```
#include <QJsonDocument>
#include <QJsonArray>
#include <QJsonObject>
#include <QDebug>
#include <QFile>
#include <QFileDialog>
```

5. Open `mainwindow.ui` and drag a push button from the widget box on the left side to the UI editor. Change the object name of the button to `loadJsonButton` and its display text to `Load JSON`:

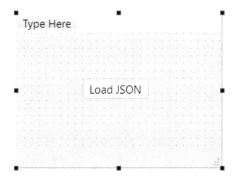

Figure 10.1 – Adding the Load JSON push button

6. Right-click on the button and select **Go to slot…**. A window will pop up with a list of signals available for selection.

7. Choose the default `clicked()` option and press the **OK** button. Qt will now insert a slot function in your header and source files called `on_loadJsonButton_clicked()`.

8. Add the following code to the `on_loadJsonButton_clicked()` function:

```
void MainWindow::on_loadJsonButton_clicked()
{
    QString filename = QFileDialog::getOpenFileName(this, "Open
JSON", ".", "JSON files (*.json)");
    QFile file(filename);
    if (!file.open(QFile::ReadOnly | QFile::Text))
        qDebug() << "Error loading JSON file.";
    QByteArray data = file.readAll();
    file.close();
    QJsonDocument json = QJsonDocument::fromJson(data);
```

9. We continue to write the code. The following code loops through the JSON file and prints out each attribute's name and value:

```
if (json.isArray())
{
    QJsonArray array = json.array();
    if (array.size() > 0)
    {
        for (int i = 0; i < array.size(); ++i)
        {
            qDebug() << "[Object]================================
===";

            QJsonObject object = json[i].toObject();
            QStringList keys = object.keys();
            for (int j = 0; j < keys.size(); ++j)
            {
                qDebug() << keys.at(j) << object.value(keys.
at(j));
            }

            qDebug() << "=======================================
===";
        }
    }
}
```

10. Build and run the project and you will see a window pop up that looks like the one you made in *step 5*:

Figure 10.2 – Building and launching the program

11. Click on the **Load JSON** button and you should see the *file selector* window pop up on the screen. Select the JSON file you created in *step 2* and press the **Select** button. You should see the following debug text appear in the *Application Output* window in Qt Creator, which indicates that the program has successfully loaded the data from the JSON file you just selected:

```
[Object]===================================
"name" QJsonValue(string, "Library")
"position" QJsonValue(array, QJsonArray([120,0,50.68]))
"rotation" QJsonValue(array, QJsonArray([0,0,0]))
"scale" QJsonValue(array, QJsonArray([1,1,1]))
"tag" QJsonValue(string, "building")
==========================================
[Object]===================================
"name" QJsonValue(string, "Town Hall")
"position" QJsonValue(array, QJsonArray([80.2,0,20.5]))
"rotation" QJsonValue(array, QJsonArray([0,0,0]))
"scale" QJsonValue(array, QJsonArray([1,1,1]))
"tag" QJsonValue(string, "building")
==========================================
[Object]===================================
"name" QJsonValue(string, "Tree")
"position" QJsonValue(array, QJsonArray([10.46,-0.2,80.2]))
"rotation" QJsonValue(array, QJsonArray([0,0,0]))
"scale" QJsonValue(array, QJsonArray([1,1,1]))
"tag" QJsonValue(string, "prop")
==========================================
```

Figure 10.3 – The results printed in the Application Output window

How it works...

In this example, we're trying to extract and process data from a JSON file using the QJsonDocument class. Imagine you're making a computer game and you're using JSON files to store the attributes of all the objects in your game scene. In this case, the JSON format plays an important role in storing the data in a structured way, which allows for easy extraction.

We need to add the header of the class related to JSON to our source file, which, in this case, is the QJsonDocument class. The QJsonDocument class is built into Qt's core library, so there is no need to include any additional modules with it, which also means that it's the recommended class to use to process JSON data in Qt. Once we click on the **Load JSON** button, the on_loadJsonButton_clicked() slot will be called; this is where we write the code to process the JSON data.

We use a file dialog to select the JSON file we want to process. Then, we send the selected file's filename, together with its path, to the QFile class to open and read the text data of the JSON file. After that, the file's data is sent to the QJsonDocument class for processing.

We first check whether the main JSON structure is an array. If it is an array, we then check whether the array has any data in it. After that, use a `for` loop to read through the entire array and extract the individual objects stored in the array.

Then, we extract the key-pair data from the objects and print out both the key and value.

There's more...

Besides the web applications, many commercial game engines and interactive applications use the JSON format to store information for in-game scenes, meshes, and other forms of assets used in their products. This is because the JSON format provides many benefits over other file formats, such as compact file size, high flexibility and extendibility, easy file recovery, and a relational tree structure that allows it to be used for highly efficient and performance-critical applications, such as search engines, intelligent data mining servers, and scientific simulations.

> **Note**
>
> To learn more about the XML format, visit `https://www.w3schools.com/js/js_json_intro.asp`.

Writing JSON data to a text file

Since we have learned how to process data obtained from a JSON file in the previous recipe, we will move on to learning how to save data to a JSON file. We will continue with the previous example and add to it.

How to do it...

We will learn how to save data in a JSON file through the following steps:

1. Add another button to `mainwindow.ui`, then set its object name as `saveJsonButton` and its label as `Save JSON`:

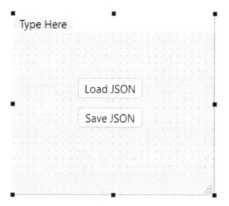

Figure 10.4 – Adding the Save JSON button

2. Right-click on the button and select **Go to slot…**. A window will pop up with a list of signals available for selection. Select the `clicked()` option and click **OK**. A signal function called `on_saveJsonButton_clicked()` will now be automatically added to both your `mainwindow.h` and `mainwindow.cpp` files by Qt:

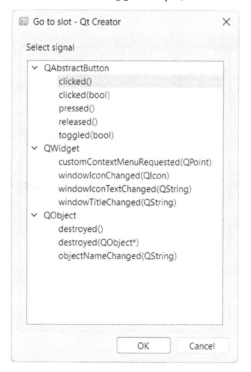

Figure 10.5 – Selecting the clicked() signal and pressing OK

3. Add the following code to the `on_saveJsonButton_clicked()` function:

```
QQString filename = QFileDialog::getSaveFileName(this, "Save
JSON", ".", "JSON files (*.json)");
QFile file(filename);
if (!file.open(QFile::WriteOnly | QFile::Text))
    qDebug() << "Error saving JSON file.";
QJsonDocument json;
QJsonArray array;
```

4. Let's also write the first `contact` element:

```
QJsonObject contact1;
contact1["category"] = "Friend";
contact1["name"] = "John Doe";
contact1["age"] = 32;
contact1["address"] = "114B, 2nd Floor, Sterling Apartment,
Morrison Town";
contact1["phone"] = "0221743566";
array.append(contact1);
```

5. Write the second `contact` element as follows:

```
QJsonObject contact2;
contact2["category"] = "Family";
contact2["name"] = "Jane Smith";
contact2["age"] = 24;
contact2["address"] = "13, Ave Park, Alexandria";
contact2["phone"] = "0025728396";
array.append(contact2);
```

6. Finally, save the data into the text file:

```
json.setArray(array);
    file.write(json.toJson());
    file.close();
}
```

7. Build and run the program and you should see an additional button on the program UI:

Figure 10.6 – Your application should now look like this

8. Click on the **Save JSON** button and a save file dialog will appear on the screen. Type the filename you require and click the **Save** button.

9. Open up the JSON file you just saved with any text editor. The first part of the file should look like this:

```
[
    {
        "address": "114B, 2nd Floor, Sterling Apartment,
Morrison Town",
        "age": 32,
        "category": "Friend",
        "name": "John Doe",
        "phone": "0221743566"
    },
    {
        "address": "13, Ave Park, Alexandria",
        "age": 24,
        "category": "Family",
        "name": "Jane Smith",
        "phone": "0025728396"
    }
]
```

How it works...

The saving process is similar to loading a JSON file in the previous example. The only difference is instead of using the `QJsonDocument::fromJson()` function, we switched to using the `QJsonDocument::toJson()` function. We still used the file dialog and the `QFile` class to save the XML file. This time, we had to change the open mode from `QFile::ReadOnly` to `QFile::WriteOnly` before passing the byte array data to the `QFile` class.

Next, we started writing the JSON file by creating `QJsonDocument` and `QJsonArray` variables followed by creating a `QJsonObject` object for each contact. Then, we filled in the information for each contact and appended it to the `QJsonArray` array.

Finally, we used `QJsonDocument::setArray()` to apply the `QJsonArray` array we created previously as the main array of the JSON data before passing it to the `QFile` class as a byte array data using the `QJsonDocument::toJson()` function.

Using Google's Geocoding API

In this example, we will learn how to obtain the full address of a specific location by using Google's Geocoding API.

How to do it...

Let's create a program that utilizes the Geocoding API by following these steps:

1. Create a new **Qt Widgets Application** project.
2. Open `mainwindow.ui` and add a couple of text labels, input fields, and a button to make your UI look similar to this:

Figure 10.7 – Setting up your UI

3. Open your project (.pro) file and add the network module to your project. You can do that by simply adding the word network after core and gui, as shown in the following code:

```
QT += core gui network
```

4. Open mainwindow.h and add the following headers to the source code:

```
#include <QMainWindow>
#include <QDebug>
#include <QtNetwork/QNetworkAccessManager>
#include <QtNetwork/QNetworkReply>
#include <QJsonDocument>
#include <QJsonArray>
#include <QJsonObject>
```

5. Declare a slot function manually and call it getAddressFinished():

```
private slots:
void getAddressFinished(QNetworkReply* reply);
```

6. Declare a private variable called addressRequest:

```
private:
QNetworkAccessManager* addressRequest;
```

7. Open mainwindow.ui again, right-click on the **Get Address** button, and select **Go to slot....** Then, choose the clicked() option and press **OK**. A slot function will now be added to both the mainwindow.h and mainwindow.cpp source files.

8. Open mainwindow.cpp and add the following code to the class constructor:

```
MainWindow::MainWindow(QWidget *parent) :
QMainWindow(parent),
ui(new Ui::MainWindow) {
ui->setupUi(this);
addressRequest = new QNetworkAccessManager();
connect(addressRequest, &QNetworkAccessManager::finished, this,
&MainWindow::getAddressFinished);
}
```

9. Add the following code to the getAddressFinished() slot function we just declared manually:

```
void MainWindow::getAddressFinished(QNetworkReply* reply) {
QByteArray bytes = reply->readAll();
//qDebug() << QString::fromUtf8(bytes.data(), bytes.size());
QJsonDocument json = QJsonDocument::fromJson(bytes);
```

10. Continue to get the first set of results from the JSON array to obtain the formatted address:

```
QJsonObject object = json.object();
QJsonArray results = object["results"].toArray();
QJsonObject first = results.at(0).toObject();
QString address = first["formatted_address"].toString();
qDebug() << "Address:" << address;
}
```

11. Add the following code to the `clicked()` slot function created by Qt:

```
void MainWindow::on_getAddressButton_clicked() {
QString latitude = ui->latitude->text();
QString longitude = ui->longitude->text();
QNetworkRequest request;
request.setUrl(QUrl("https://maps.googleapis.com/maps/api/
geocode/json?latlng=" + latitude + "," + longitude + "&key=YOUR_
KEY"));
addressRequest->get(request);
}
```

12. Build and run the program and you should be able to obtain the address by inserting the **Longitude** and **Latitude** values and clicking the **Get Address** button:

Figure 10.8 – Inserting the coordinates and pressing the Get Address button

13. Let's try with a longitude of `-73.9780838` and a latitude of `40.6712957`. Click the **Get Address** button and you will see the following result in the application output window:

```
Address: "185 7th Ave, Brooklyn, NY 11215, USA"
```

How it works...

I won't be able to tell you exactly how Google obtains the address from its backend system but I can teach you how to request data from Google by using QNetworkRequest. All you need to do is to set the URL of the network request to the URL I used in the previous source code and append both the latitude and longitude information to the URL.

After that, all we can do is wait for the response from the Google API server. We need to specify JSON as the desired format when sending the request to Google; otherwise, it may return the results in JSON format. This can be done by adding the json keyword within the network request URL, as highlighted here:

```
request.setUrl(QUrl("https://maps.googleapis.com/maps/api/geocode/
xml?keylatlng=" + latitude + "," + longitude + "&key=YOUR_CODE"));
```

When the program receives the response from Google, the getAddressFinished() slot function will be called and we will be able to obtain the data sent by Google through QNetworkReply.

Google usually replies with a long text in JSON format, which contains a ton of data we don't need. All we need is the text stored in the formatted_address element in the JSON data. Since there is more than one element by the name of formatted_address, we just need to find the first one and ignore the rest. You can also do the reverse by providing an address to Google and obtaining the location's coordinates from its network response.

There's more...

Google's **Geocoding API** is part of the **Google Maps APIs** web services, which provide geographical data for your map applications. Besides the Geocoding API, you can also use their **Location API**, **Geolocation API**, and **Time Zone API** to achieve your desired results.

> **Note**
>
> For more information regarding the Google Maps APIs web services, visit https://
> developers.google.com/maps/web-services.

11

Conversion Library

Data kept within our computer environment is encoded in a variety of ways. Sometimes, it can be used directly for a certain purpose; other times, it needs to be converted into another format in order to fit the context of the task. The process of converting data from one format into another also varies depending on the source format as well as the target format.

Sometimes, the process can be very complex, especially when dealing with data that is feature-rich and sensitive, such as image or video conversion. Even a small error during the conversion process may render a file unusable.

This chapter will cover the following recipes:

- Converting data
- Converting images
- Converting videos
- Converting currency

Technical requirements

The technical requirements for this chapter include Qt 6.6.1 MinGW-64-bit and Qt Creator 12.0.2. All the code used in this chapter can be downloaded from the following GitHub repository: `https://github.com/PacktPublishing/QT6-C-GUI-Programming-Cookbook---Third-Edition-/tree/main/Chapter11`.

Converting data

Qt provides a set of classes and functions for easily converting between different types of data. This makes Qt more than just a GUI library; it is a complete platform for software development. The `QVariant` class, which we will use in the following example, makes Qt even more flexible and powerful compared to the similar conversion functionalities provided by the C++ standard library.

How to do it...

Let's learn how to convert various data types in Qt by following these steps:

1. Open **Qt Creator** and create a new **Qt Console Application** project by going to **File | New Project…**:

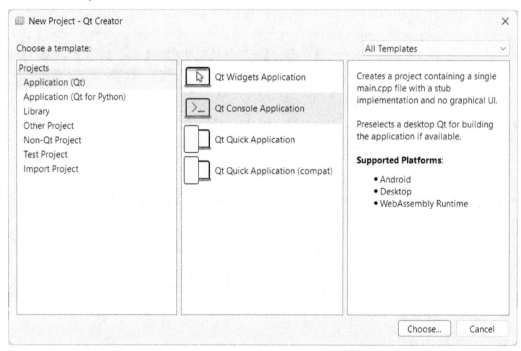

Figure 11.1 – Create a Qt Console Application project

2. Open `main.cpp` and add the following headers to it:

```
#include <QCoreApplication>
#include <QDebug>
#include <QtMath>
#include <QDateTime>
#include <QTextCodec>
#include <iostream>
```

3. In the `main()` function, add the following code to convert a string into a number:

```
int numberA = 2;
QString numberB = "5";
qDebug() << "1) " << "2 + 5 =" << numberA + numberB.toInt();
```

4. Convert the number back into a string:

```
float numberC = 10.25;
float numberD = 2;
QString result = QString::number(numberC * numberD);
qDebug() << "2) " << "10.25 * 2 =" << result;
```

5. Let's see how to round down a value using qFloor():

```
float numberE = 10.3;
float numberF = qFloor(numberE);
qDebug() << "3) " << "Floor of 10.3 is" << numberF;
```

6. Using qCeil(), we are able to round down a number to the smallest integral value not smaller than its initial value:

```
float numberG = 10.3;
float numberH = qCeil(numberG);
qDebug() << "4) " << "Ceil of 10.3 is" << numberH;
```

7. Create a date-time variable by converting it from a piece of date-time data written in the string format:

```
QString dateTimeAString = "2016-05-04 12:24:00";
QDateTime dateTimeA = QDateTime::fromString(dateTimeAString,
"yyyy-MM-dd hh:mm:ss");
qDebug() << "5) " << dateTimeA;
```

8. Convert the date-time variable back into a string with our custom format:

```
QDateTime dateTimeB = QDateTime::currentDateTime();
QString dateTimeBString = dateTimeB.toString("dd/MM/yy
hh:mm");
qDebug() << "6) " << dateTimeBString;
```

9. Call the QString::toUpper() function to convert a string variable into all capital letters:

```
QString hello1 = "hello world!";
qDebug() << "7) " << hello1.toUpper();
```

10. Calling QString::toLower() will convert the string completely into lowercase:

```
QString hello2 = "HELLO WORLD!";
qDebug() << "8) " << hello2.toLower();
```

11. The QVariant class provided by Qt is a very powerful data type that can be easily converted to other types without any effort from the programmer:

```
QVariant aNumber = QVariant(3.14159);
double aResult = 12.5 * aNumber.toDouble();
qDebug() << "9) 12.5 * 3.14159 =" << aResult;
```

12. This demonstrates how a single QVariant variable can be simultaneously converted to multiple data types without any effort from the programmer:

```
qDebug() << "10) ";
QVariant myData = QVariant(10);
qDebug() << myData;
myData = myData.toFloat() / 2.135;
qDebug() << myData;
myData = true;
qDebug() << myData;
myData = QDateTime::currentDateTime();
qDebug() << myData;
myData = "Good bye!";
qDebug() << myData;
```

13. The full source code in main.cpp will now look like this:

```
#include <QCoreApplication>
#include <QDebug>
#include <QtMath>
#include <QDateTime>
#include <QStringConverter>
#include <iostream>
int main(int argc, char *argv[]) {
    QCoreApplication a(argc, argv);
```

14. After that, let's add code to convert a string into a number, and vice versa:

```
// String to number
    int numberA = 2;
    QString numberB = "5";
    qDebug() << "1) " << "2 + 5 =" << numberA +
numberB.toInt();
// Number to string
    float numberC = 10.25;
    float numberD = 2;
    QString result = QString::number(numberC * numberD);
    qDebug() << "2) " << "10.25 * 2 =" << result;
```

15. Write the code to convert floating-point numbers to their nearest succeeding or preceding integer number, respectively:

```
// Floor
    float numberE = 10.3;
    float numberF = qFloor(numberE);
    qDebug() << "3) " << "Floor of 10.3 is" << numberF;
// Ceil
    float numberG = 10.3;
    float numberH = qCeil(numberG);
    qDebug() << "4) " << "Ceil of 10.3 is" << numberH;
```

16. Convert a string into the date-time format, and vice versa:

```
// Date time from string
    QString dateTimeAString = "2016-05-04 12:24:00";
    QDateTime dateTimeA = QDateTime::fromString(dateTimeAString,
"yyyy-MM-dd hh:mm:ss");
    qDebug() << "5) " << dateTimeA;
// Date time to string
    QDateTime dateTimeB = QDateTime::currentDateTime();
    QString dateTimeBString = dateTimeB.toString("dd/MM/yy
hh:mm");
    qDebug() << "6) " << dateTimeBString;
```

17. Continue to add code to convert strings into uppercase or lowercase characters:

```
// String to all uppercase
    QString hello1 = "hello world!";
    qDebug() << "7) " << hello1.toUpper();
// String to all lowercase
    QString hello2 = "HELLO WORLD!";
    qDebug() << "8) " << hello2.toLower();
```

18. Convert the QVariant data type into other types:

```
// QVariant to double
    QVariant aNumber = QVariant(3.14159);
    double aResult = 12.5 * aNumber.toDouble();
    qDebug() << "9) 12.5 * 3.14159 =" << aResult;
// QVariant different types
    qDebug() << "10) ";
    QVariant myData = QVariant(10);
    qDebug() << myData;
    myData = myData.toFloat() / 2.135;
    qDebug() << myData;
```

```
        myData = true;
        qDebug() << myData;
```

19. Convert the `QVariant` data type into `QDateTime` and `QString`:

```
        myData = QDateTime::currentDateTime();
        qDebug() << myData;
        myData = "Good bye!";
        qDebug() << myData;
        return a.exec();
    }
```

20. Compile and run the project, and you should see something like this:

```
1)   2 + 5 = 7
2)   10.25 * 2 = "20.5"
3)   Floor of 10.3 is 10
4)   Ceil of 10.3 is 11
5)   QDateTime(2016-05-04 12:24:00.000 Malay Peninsula Standard Time Qt::LocalTime)
6)   "07/01/24 14:56"
7)   "HELLO WORLD!"
8)   "hello world!"
9) 12.5 * 3.14159 = 39.2699
10)
QVariant(int, 10)
QVariant(double, 4.68384)
QVariant(bool, true)
QVariant(QDateTime, QDateTime(2024-01-07 14:56:06.813 Malay Peninsula Standard Time Qt::LocalTime))
QVariant(QString, "Good bye!")
```

Figure 11.2 – Printing the conversion results on the application output window

How it works...

All the data types provided by Qt, such as `QString`, `QDateTime`, and `QVariant`, contain functions that make conversion to other types easy and straightforward. Qt also provides its own object conversion function, `qobject_cast()`, which doesn't rely on the standard library. It is also more compatible with Qt and works well to convert between Qt's widget types and data types.

Qt also provides you with the `QtMath` class, which helps you to manipulate number variables, such as rounding up a floating-point number or converting an angle from degrees to radians. `QVariant` is a special class that can be used to store data of all kinds of types, such as `int`, `float`, `char`, and `string`. It can automatically determine the data type by examining the value stored in the variable. You can also easily convert the data into any of the types supported by the `QVariant` class by just calling a single function, such as `toFloat()`, `toInt()`, `toBool()`, `toChar()`, or `toString()`.

There's more...

Be aware that each of these conversions takes computing power. Even though modern computers are extremely fast at handling these operations, you should be careful not to overdo it with a large quantity at once. If you're converting a large set of variables for complex calculations, it might slow down your computer significantly, so try to convert variables only when necessary.

Converting images

In this section, we will learn how to build a simple image converter that converts an image from one format into another. Qt supports reading and writing different types of image formats, and this support comes in the form of external DLL files due to licensing issues.

However, you don't have to worry about that because as long as you include those DLL files in your project, it will work seamlessly across different formats. There are certain formats that only support reading and not writing, and some that support both.

> **Note**
>
> You can check out the full details about converting images at `http://doc.qt.io/qt-6/qtimageformats-index.html`.

How to do it...

Qt's built-in image libraries make image conversion really simple:

1. Open Qt Creator and create a new **Qt Widgets Application** project.
2. Open `mainwindow.ui` and add a line edit and push button to the canvas to select image files, a combo box to select the desired file format, and another push button to start the conversion process:

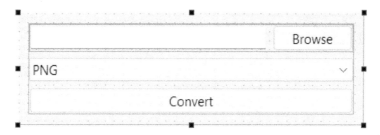

Figure 11.3 – Lay out the UI as shown here

3. Double-click the combobox, and a window will then appear where you can edit the box. We will add three items to the combobox list by clicking the + button three times and renaming the items PNG, JPEG, and BMP:

Figure 11.4 – Adding three options to the combobox

4. Right-click on one of the push buttons, select **Go to slot…**, and then click the **OK** button. A slot function will be automatically added to your source files. Repeat this step for the other push button as well:

Figure 11.5 – Select the clicked() signal and press OK

5. Let's move over to the source code. Open `mainwindow.h` and add the following header:

```
#include <QMainWindow>
#include <QFileDialog>
#include <QMessageBox>
#include <QDebug>
```

6. Open `mainwindow.cpp` and define what will happen when the **Browse** button is clicked, which in this case is opening the file dialog to select an image file:

```
void MainWindow::on_browseButton_clicked() {
    QString fileName = QFileDialog::getOpenFileName(this, "Open
Image", "", "Image Files (*.png *.jpg *.bmp)");
    ui->filePath->setText(fileName);
}
```

7. Define what will happen when the **Convert** button is clicked:

```
void MainWindow::on_convertButton_clicked() {
    QString fileName = ui->filePath->text();
    if (fileName != "") {
        QFileInfo fileInfo = QFileInfo(fileName);
        QString newFileName = fileInfo.path() + "/" + fileInfo.
completeBaseName();
        QImage image = QImage(ui->filePath->text());
        if (!image.isNull()) {
```

8. Check which format is used:

```
// 0 = PNG, 1 = JPG, 2 = BMP
            int format = ui->fileFormat->currentIndex();
            if (format == 0) {
                newFileName += ".png";
            }
            else if (format == 1) {
                newFileName += ".jpg";
            }
            else if (format == 2) {
                newFileName += ".bmp";
            }
```

9. Check whether the image has been converted:

```
            qDebug() << newFileName << format;
            if (image.save(newFileName, 0, -1)) {
                QMessageBox::information(this, "Success", "Image
successfully converted.");
```

```
            }
        else {
            QMessageBox::warning(this, "Failed", "Failed to
convert image.");
        }
    }
```

10. Display the message boxes:

```
        else {
            QMessageBox::warning(this, "Failed", "Failed to open
image file.");
        }
    }
    else {
        QMessageBox::warning(this, "Failed", "No file is
selected.");
    }
}
```

11. Build and run the program now, and we should get a pretty simple image converter that looks like this:

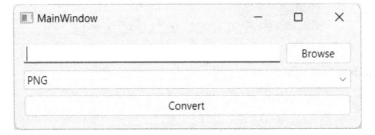

Figure 11.6 – Browse an image, select a format, and press the Convert button

How it works...

The previous example uses the native QImage class from Qt, which contains functions that can access pixel data and manipulate it. It is also used to load an image file and extract its data through different decompression methods, depending on the format of the image.

Once the data is extracted, you can do anything you want with it, such as display the image on screen, manipulate its color information, resize the image, or compress it with another format and save it as a file.

We used `QFileInfo` to separate the filename from the extension so that we could amend the extension name with the new format selected by the user from the combobox. This way, we can save the newly converted image in the same folder as the original image and automatically give it the same filename as well, except in a different format.

As long as you're trying to convert the image to a format supported by Qt, you just need to call `QImage::save()`. Internally, Qt will figure out the rest for you and output the image to the chosen format. In the `QImage::save()` function, there is a parameter that sets the image quality and another that sets the format. In this example, we just set both as the default values, which saves the image at the highest quality and lets Qt figure out the format by checking the extension stated in the output filename.

There's more...

You can also convert an image into a PDF using the `QPdfWriter` class provided by Qt. Essentially, you paint the selected image to the layout of a newly created PDF document and set its resolution accordingly.

> **Note**
>
> For more information about the `QPdfWriter` class, visit `http://doc.qt.io/qt-6/qpdfwriter.html`.

Converting videos

In this recipe, we will create a simple video converter using Qt and **FFmpeg**, a leading multimedia framework that is free and open source. Although Qt supports playing video files through its widget, it does not currently support video conversion. Fear not! You can still achieve the same goal by making your program cooperate with another standalone program, through the `QProcess` class provided by Qt.

How to do it...

Let's make a simple video converter with the following steps:

1. Download `FFmpeg` (a static package) from `http://ffmpeg.zeranoe.com/builds` and extract the contents to your preferred location – for example, `C:/FFmpeg/`.

2. Open Qt Creator and create a new **Qt Widgets Application** project by going to **File | New Project...**.

3. Open `mainwindow.ui` – we're going to work on the program's user interface. Its UI is very similar to the previous example, except that we add an extra text-edit widget to the canvas, just under the combobox:

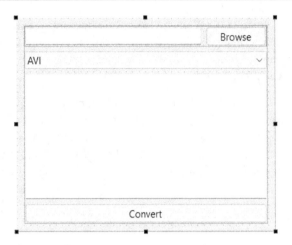

Figure 11.7 – Design your video converter's UI like this

4. Double-click the combobox, and then a window will appear to edit the box. We will add three items to the combobox list by clicking the + button three times, and then rename the items AVI, MP4, and MOV:

Figure 11.8 – Adding three video formats to the combobox

5. Right-click on one of the push buttons, select **Go to slot…**, and then click the **OK** button. A slot function will then be automatically added to your source files. Repeat this step for the other push button as well.

6. Open `mainwindow.h` and add the following headers to the top:

```
#include <QMainWindow>
#include <QFileDialog>
#include <QProcess>
#include <QMessageBox>
#include <QScrollBar>
#include <QDebug>
```

7. Add the following pointers under the `public` keyword:

```
public:
    explicit MainWindow(QWidget *parent = 0);
    ~MainWindow();
QProcess* process;
QString outputText;
QString fileName;
QString outputFileName;
```

8. Add three extra slot functions under the two functions that Qt created for us previously in the *Converting images* recipe:

```
private slots:
    void on_browseButton_clicked();
    void on_convertButton_clicked();
    void processStarted();
    void readyReadStandardOutput();
    void processFinished();
```

9. Open `mainwindow.cpp` and add the following code to the class constructor:

```
MainWindow::MainWindow(QWidget *parent) :
    QMainWindow(parent), ui(new Ui::MainWindow) {
    ui->setupUi(this);
    process = new QProcess(this);
    connect(process, QProcess::started, this,
MainWindow::processStarted);
    connect(process, QProcess::readyReadStandardOutput, this,
MainWindow::readyReadStandardOutput);
    connect(process, QProcess::finished, this,
MainWindow::processFinished);
}
```

10. Define what will happen when the **Browse** button is clicked, which in this case is opening up the file dialog to allow us to choose the video file:

```
void MainWindow::on_browseButton_clicked() {
    QString fileName = QFileDialog::getOpenFileName(this, "Open
Video", "", "Video Files (*.avi *.mp4 *.mov)");
    ui->filePath->setText(fileName);
}
```

11. Define what will happen if the **Convert** button is clicked. Here, we pass the filenames and arguments to FFmpeg, which will then handle the conversion process externally:

```
void MainWindow::on_convertButton_clicked() {
    QString ffmpeg = "C:/FFmpeg/bin/ffmpeg";
    QStringList arguments;
    fileName = ui->filePath->text();
    if (fileName != "") {
        QFileInfo fileInfo = QFileInfo(fileName);
        outputFileName = fileInfo.path() + "/" +
fileInfo.completeBaseName();
```

12. Check for the file's format – specifically, whether it's .avi, .mp4, or .mov:

```
        if (QFile::exists(fileName)) {
            int format = ui->fileFormat->currentIndex();
            if (format == 0) {
                outputFileName += ".avi"; // AVI
            }
            else if (format == 1) {
                outputFileName += ".mp4"; // MP4
            }
            else if (format == 2) {
                outputFileName += ".mov"; // MOV
            }
```

13. Start the conversion using the following code:

```
            qDebug() << outputFileName << format;
            arguments << "-i" << fileName << outputFileName;
            qDebug() << arguments;
            process-
>setProcessChannelMode(QProcess::MergedChannels);
            process->start(ffmpeg, arguments);
        }
```

14. Display the message boxes:

```
        else {
                QMessageBox::warning(this, "Failed", "Failed to open
    video file.");
            }
        }
        else {
            QMessageBox::warning(this, "Failed", "No file is
    selected.");
        }
    }
```

15. Tell the program what to do when the conversion process has started:

```
    void MainWindow::processStarted() {
        qDebug() << "Process started.";
        ui->browseButton->setEnabled(false);
        ui->fileFormat->setEditable(false);
        ui->convertButton->setEnabled(false);
    }
```

16. Write the slot function that gets called during the conversion process whenever FFmpeg returns an output to the program:

```
    void MainWindow::readyReadStandardOutput() {
        outputText += process->readAllStandardOutput();
        ui->outputDisplay->setText(outputText);
        ui->outputDisplay->verticalScrollBar()-
    >setSliderPosition(ui->outputDisplay->verticalScrollBar()-
    >maximum());
    }
```

17. Define the slot function that gets called when the entire conversion process has been completed:

```
    void MainWindow::processFinished() {
        qDebug() << "Process finished.";
        if (QFile::exists(outputFileName)) {
            QMessageBox::information(this, "Success", "Video
    successfully converted.");
        }
        else {
            QMessageBox::information(this, "Failed", "Failed to
    convert video.");
        }
        ui->browseButton->setEnabled(true);
        ui->fileFormat->setEditable(true);
```

```
                    ui->convertButton->setEnabled(true);
        }
```

18. Build and run the project, and you should get a simple, yet workable, video converter:

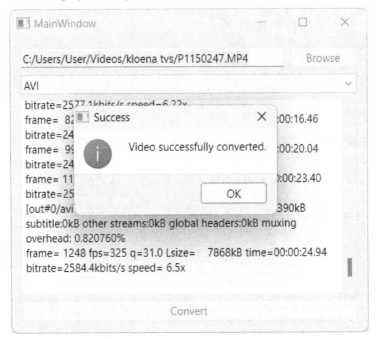

Figure 11.9 – Your own video converter powered by FFmpeg and Qt

How it works...

The QProcess class provided by Qt is used to start external programs and communicate with them. In this case, we started ffmpeg.exe, located in C:/FFmpeg/bin/, as a process and started communicating with it. We also sent it a set of arguments to tell it what to do when it started. The arguments we used in this example are relatively basic – we only told FFmpeg the path to the source image and the output filename.

> **Note**
>
> For more information regarding the argument settings available in FFmpeg, check out www.ffmpeg.org/ffmpeg.html.

FFmpeg does more than just convert video files. You can also use it to convert audio files and images.

> **Note**
>
> For more information regarding all the formats supported by FFmpeg, check out `https://www.ffmpeg.org/general.html#File-Formats`.

Other than that, you can also play a video or audio file by running `ffplay.exe`, located in `C:/FFmpeg/bin`, or print out the information of the video or audio file in a human-readable fashion by running `ffprobe.exe`.

> **Note**
>
> Check out FFmpeg's full documentation at `https://www.ffmpeg.org/about.html`.

There's more...

There are lots of things you can do using this method. You're not limited to what Qt provides, and you can break out of such limitations by carefully selecting a third-party program that provides what you need. One such example is making your own antivirus GUI by utilizing the command-line-only antivirus scanners available on the market, such as **Avira ScanCL**, **Panda Antivirus Command Line Scanner**, **SAV32CLI**, and **ClamAV**. You can build your own GUI using Qt and essentially send commands to the antivirus process to tell it what to do.

Converting currency

In this example, we will learn how to create a simple currency converter using Qt, with the help of an external service provider called **Fixer.io**.

How to do it...

Make yourself a currency converter by following these simple steps:

1. Open Qt Creator and create a new **Qt Widgets Application** project from **File | New Project...**.

2. Open the project file (`.pro`) and add the network module to our project:

   ```
   QT += core gui network
   ```

3. Open `mainwindow.ui` and remove the menu bar, toolbar, and status bar from the UI.

4. Add three horizontal layouts, a horizontal line, and a push button to the canvas. Left-click on the canvas, and continue by clicking the **Lay Out Vertically** button on top of the canvas. Change the label of the push button to Convert. The UI should look something like this:

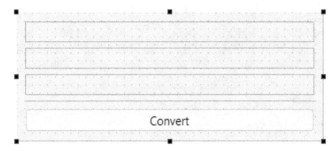

Figure 11.10 – Place three vertical layouts above the Convert button

5. Add two labels to the top layout, and set the text of the left one to From:, followed by the right one to To:. Add two **Line Edit** widgets to the second layout, and set both their default values to 1:

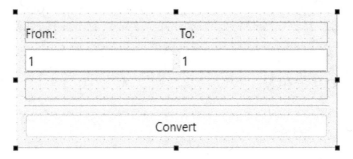

Figure 11.11 – Add labels and Line Edit widgets to the layouts

6. Select the line edit on the right and enable the **readOnly** checkbox located in the **Property** pane:

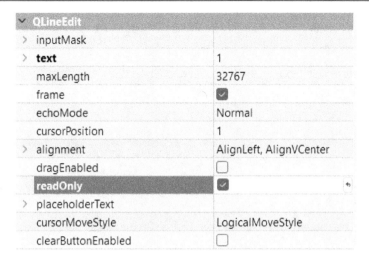

Figure 11.12 – Enable the readOnly property for the second line edit

7. Set the cursor property to **Forbidden** so that users know it's not editable when hovering the mouse over the widget:

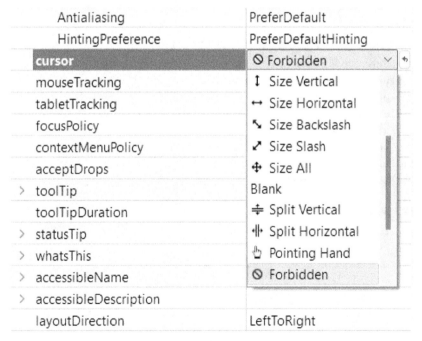

Figure 11.13 – Display the Forbidden cursor to let users know it's disabled

8. Add two comboboxes to the third layout located at the bottom. We will leave them empty for now:

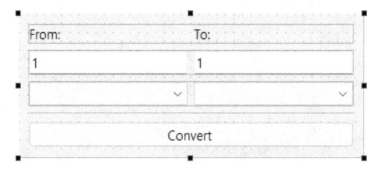

Figure 11.14 – Add two comboboxes to the final layout

9. Right-click on the **Convert** button and select **Go to slot…**. A window will pop up, asking you to select an appropriate signal. Let's keep the default `clicked()` signal as the selection and click **OK**. Qt Creator will automatically add a slot function to both `mainwindow.h` and `mainwindow.cpp`.

10. Open `mainwindow.h` and make sure the following headers are added to the top of the source file:

```
#include <QMainWindow>
#include <QDoubleValidator>
#include <QNetworkAccessManager>
#include <QNetworkRequest>
#include <QNetworkReply>
#include <QJsonDocument>
#include <QJsonObject>
#include <QDebug>
#include <QMessageBox>
```

11. Add another slot function, called `finished()`:

```
private slots:
    void on_convertButton_clicked();
    void finished(QNetworkReply* reply);
```

12. Add two variables under the `private` label:

```
private:
    Ui::MainWindow *ui;
    QNetworkAccessManager* manager;
    QString targetCurrency;
```

13. Open the `mainwindow.cpp` file. Add several currency short code to both comboboxes in the class constructor. Set a validator to the **Line Edit** widget on the left so that it can only accept inputs that are numbers. Initialize the network access manager and connect its `finished()` signal to our `finished()` slot function:

```
MainWindow::MainWindow(QWidget *parent) :
    QMainWindow(parent), ui(new Ui::MainWindow) {
    ui->setupUi(this);
    QStringList currencies;
    currencies.push_back("EUR");
    currencies.push_back("USD");
    currencies.push_back("CAD");
    currencies.push_back("MYR");
    currencies.push_back("GBP");
```

14. We continue from the previous code and insert the currency short forms into the comboboxes. Then, we declare a new network access manager and connect its finished signal to our custom slot function:

```
    ui->currencyFrom->insertItems(0, currencies);
    ui->currencyTo->insertItems(0, currencies);
    QValidator *inputRange = new QDoubleValidator(this);
    ui->amountFrom->setValidator(inputRange);
    manager = new QNetworkAccessManager(this);
    connect(manager, &QNetworkAccessManager::finished, this,
&MainWindow::finished);
}
```

15. Define what will happen if the **Convert** button is clicked by the user:

```
void MainWindow::on_convertButton_clicked() {
    if (ui->amountFrom->text() != "") {
        ui->convertButton->setEnabled(false);
        QString from = ui->currencyFrom->currentText();
        QString to = ui->currencyTo->currentText();
        targetCurrency = to;
        QString url = "http://data.fixer.io/api/latest?base="
+       from + "&symbols=" + to + "&access_key=YOUR_KEY";
```

16. Start the request by calling `get()`:

```
        QNetworkRequest request = QNetworkRequest(QUrl(url));
        manager->get(request);
    }
    else {
        QMessageBox::warning(this, "Error", "Please insert a
```

```
value.");
        }
    }
```

17. Define what will happen when the `finished()` signal is triggered:

```cpp
void MainWindow::finished(QNetworkReply* reply) {
    QByteArray response = reply->readAll();
    qDebug() << response;
    QJsonDocument jsonResponse =
QJsonDocument::fromJson(response);
    QJsonObject jsonObj = jsonResponse.object();
    QJsonObject jsonObj2 = jsonObj.value("rates").toObject();
    double rate = jsonObj2.value(targetCurrency).toDouble();
```

18. Continue to write the code from the preceding code, as shown in the following snippet:

```cpp
    if (rate == 0)
        rate = 1;
    double amount = ui->amountFrom->text().toDouble();
    double result = amount * rate;
    ui->amountTo->setText(QString::number(result));
    ui->convertButton->setEnabled(true);
}
```

19. Compile and run the project, and then you should get a simple currency converter that looks like this:

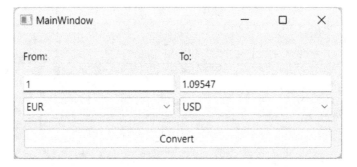

Figure 11.15 – A usable currency converter is complete

How it works...

Similar to the previous example we saw, which uses an external program to achieve a specific task, this time we used an external service provider that provided us with an open **Application Programming Interface** (**API**) that is free for all and easy to use.

This way, we don't have to think about the method used to retrieve the latest currency rate. Instead, the service provider has already done the job for us; we just have to send a polite request for it. Then, we wait for the response from their server and process the data according to our intended purposes.

There are quite a few different service providers you can choose from, besides Fixer.io (`http://fixer.io`). Some are free but come without any advanced features; some provide you with a premium price. Some of these alternatives are **Open Exchange Rates** (`https://openexchangerates.org`), the **currencylayer API** (`https://currencylayer.com`), the **Currency API** (`https://currency-api.appspot.com`), the **XE Currency Data API** (`http://www.xe.com/xecurrencydata`), and **jsonrates** (`http://jsonrates.com`).

In the previous code, you should have noticed an access key being passed to the Fixer.io API, which is a free access key I registered for this tutorial. If you use it for your own project, you should create an account at Fixer.io.

There's more...

Besides currency exchange rates, you can use this method to execute more advanced tasks that are perhaps too complicated to do by yourself, or are simply impossible to access unless you use the services provided by specialists, such as programmable **Short Message Service** (**SMS**) and voice services, web analytics and statistics generation, and online payment gateways. Most of these services are not free, but you can easily achieve those functions in minutes without even setting up the server infrastructure and backend system; it's definitely the cheapest and fastest way to get your product up and running without much hassle.

12

Accessing Databases with SQL Driver and Qt

Structured Query Language (**SQL**) is a special programming language used to manage data held in a relational database management system. A SQL server is a database system designed to use one of the many types of SQL programming languages to manage its data.

In this chapter, we will cover the following recipes:

- Setting up a database
- Connecting to a database
- Writing basic SQL queries
- Creating a login screen with Qt
- Displaying information from a database in model view
- Advanced SQL queries

Technical requirements

The technical requirements for this chapter include Qt 6.6.1 MinGW 64-bit and Qt Creator 12.0.2. All the code used in this chapter can be downloaded from the following GitHub repository: `https://github.com/PacktPublishing/QT6-C-GUI-Programming-Cookbook---Third-Edition-/tree/main/Chapter12`.

Setting up a database

Qt supports several different types of SQL drivers in the form of plugins/add-ons, such as **SQLite**, **ODBC**, **PostgreSQL**, **MySQL**, and so on. However, it's very easy to integrate these drivers into your Qt project. We will learn how to do this in the following example.

How to do it...

In this example, we will learn how to use Qt with **SQLite**. Let's set up our SQLite editor before we dive into Qt:

1. Download **SQLiteStudio** from `https://sqlitestudio.pl` and install it to administrate your SQLite databases:

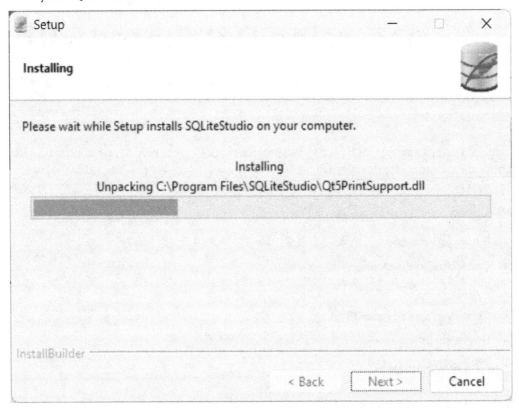

Figure 12.1 – Install SQLiteStudio onto your computer

2.   Open **SQLiteStudio** and you should see something like this:

Figure 12.2 – SQLiteStudio is a handy program for managing SQLite databases

3.   We need to create a new database before we start; go to **Database** | **Add a database**. Select the **SQLite 3** option for your database type, followed by selecting your file name and setting your database name. Then, click the **Test connection** button. You should see a green tick appearing beside the button. After that, click on the **OK** button:

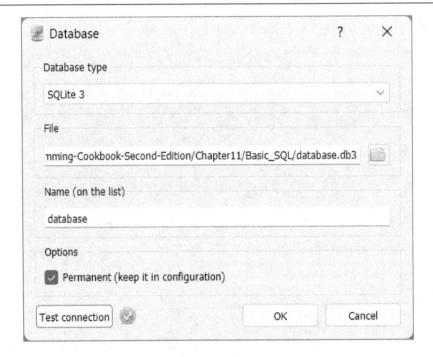

Figure 12.3 – Creating a new SQLite 3 database

4. Once the database has been created, you should see the database appear in the **Databases** window. Then, right-click on **Tables** and select **Create a table** option from the menu that pops up:

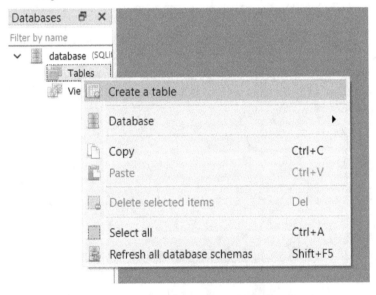

Figure 12.4 – Select the Create a table option from the menu

5. Set the table name as `employee`. Then, click on the **Add column (lns)** button located above the table name input field. The **Column** window will now pop up:

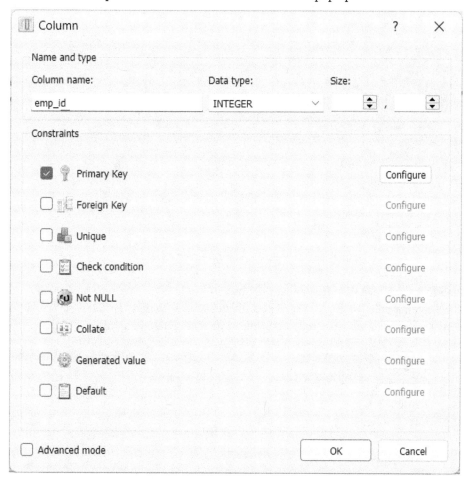

Figure 12.5 – Create a new column called emp_id

6. Set the column name as `emp_id`, set the data type as **INTEGER**, and check the **Primary key** checkbox. Then, click on the **Configure** button at the right of the **Primary key** checkbox. The **Edit constraint** window will now pop up. Check on the **Autoincrement** checkbox and click **Apply**:

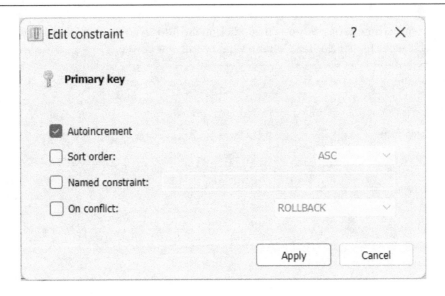

Figure 12.6 – Enable the Autoincrement checkbox

7. After that, press the **OK** button under the **Column** window. We have now successfully created a new column called emp_id. Let's repeat the steps above (without enabling the primary key) to create other columns. You may follow the same settings as seen here:

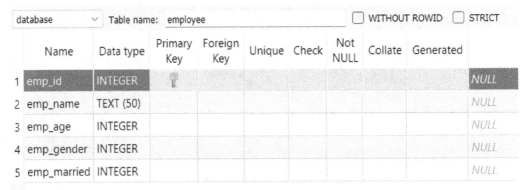

Figure 12.7 – Create all five columns

8. The columns are not actually created at this point. Click on the button with a green tick icon located above the table name. A window will pop up to confirm the creation of the columns. Press **OK** to proceed:

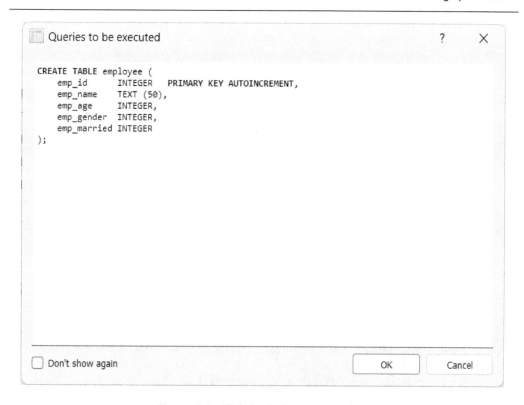

```
Queries to be executed                                          ?    X

CREATE TABLE employee (
    emp_id      INTEGER   PRIMARY KEY AUTOINCREMENT,
    emp_name    TEXT (50),
    emp_age     INTEGER,
    emp_gender  INTEGER,
    emp_married INTEGER
);
```

Don't show again   OK   Cancel

Figure 12.8 – Click the OK button to confirm

9. Now, we have created the `employee` table. Let's move on from the **Structure** tab to the **Data** tab. We can use the **Data** tab to view all the data belonging to the `employee` table, which is currently empty. Let's insert dummy data into the `employee` table by clicking on the **Insert row (Ins)** button, which is the one with a green plus icon. Then, simply insert some dummy data like so:

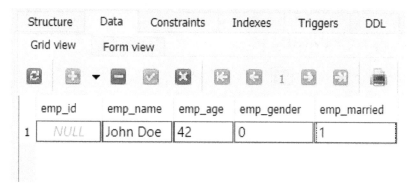

emp_id	emp_name	emp_age	emp_gender	emp_married
1	NULL	John Doe	42	0	1

Figure 12.9 – Insert dummy data into the employee table

10. Let's set up the SQL driver for our Qt project. Just go to your Qt installation folder and look for the `sqldrivers` folder. For example, mine is located at `C:\Qt\6.4.2\mingw_64\plugins\sqldrivers`.

11. Copy the entire `sqldrivers` folder to your project's build directory. You can remove the DLL files that are not relevant to the SQL server you're running. In our case, since we're using **SQLite**, we can delete everything except `qsqlite.dll`.

12. The DLL files mentioned in the previous step are the drivers that enable Qt to communicate with different types of SQL architecture. You may also need the DLL file of the SQL client library in order for the driver to work. In our case, we need `sqlite3.dll` to be located in the same directory as our program's executable. You can either get it from the installation directory of **SQLiteStudio** or from the official website of **SQLite**: `https://www.sqlite.org/download.html`.

How it works...

Qt provides us with SQL drivers so that we can easily connect to different types of SQL servers without implementing them ourselves.

Currently, Qt officially supports SQLite, ODBC, and PostgreSQL. If you need to connect directly to MySQL, you need to recompile Qt drivers by yourself, which is out of the scope of this book. For security reasons, it's not recommended that you connect to MySQL directly from your application. Instead, your application should interact with your MySQL database (or any other SQL servers that are not officially supported by Qt) indirectly by sending an HTTP request using QNetworkAccessManager to your backend script (such as PHP, ASP, and JSP), which can then communicate with the database.

If you only need a simple file-based database and don't plan to use a server-based database, **SQLite** is a good choice for you, which is what we have chosen for this chapter.

In the *Connecting to a database* recipe, we will learn how to connect to our SQL database using Qt's SQL module.

Connecting to a database

In this recipe, we will learn how to connect our Qt 6 application to the SQL server.

How to do it...

Connecting to SQL Server in Qt is really simple:

1. Open Qt Creator and create a new **Qt Widgets Application** project.

2. Open your project file (`.pro`), add the `sql` module to your project, and run qmake like this:

```
QT += core gui sql
```

3. Open `mainwindow.ui` and drag seven label widgets, a combo box, and a checkbox to the canvas. Set the `text` properties of four of the labels to `Name:`, `Age:`, `Gender:`, and `Married:`. Then, set the `objectName` properties of the rest to name, age, gender, and married. There is no need to set the object name for the previous four labels because they're for display purposes only:

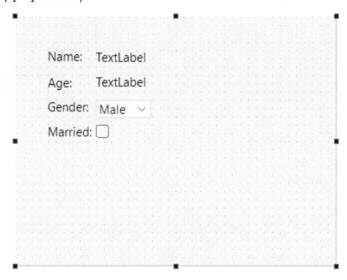

Figure 12.10 – Setting the text properties

4. Open `mainwindow.h` and add the following headers below the `QMainWindow` header:

```
#include <QMainWindow>
#include <QtSql>
#include <QSqlDatabase>
#include <QSqlQuery>
#include <QDebug>
```

5. Open `mainwindow.cpp` and insert the following code into the class constructor:

```
MainWindow::MainWindow(QWidget *parent) :
    QMainWindow(parent), ui(new Ui::MainWindow) {
    ui->setupUi(this);
    QSqlDatabase db = QSqlDatabase::addDatabase("QSQLITE");
    db.setDatabaseName("database.db3");
```

6. Start the SQL query once the database connection has been opened:

```
if (db.open()) {
    QSqlQuery query;
```

```
                    if (query.exec("SELECT emp_name, emp_age, emp_gender,
        emp_married FROM employee")) {
                        while (query.next()) {
                            qDebug() << query.value(0) << query.
        value(1) <<
        query.value(2) << query.value(3);
                                ui->name->setText(query.value(0).
        toString());
                                ui->age->setText(query.value(1).
        toString());
                                ui->gender->setCurrentIndex(query.
        value(2).toInt());
                                ui->married->setChecked(query.value(3).
        toBool());
                        }
                    }
```

7. Print out any error texts:

```
                    else {
                        qDebug() << query.lastError().text();
                    }
                    db.close();
                }
                else {
                    qDebug() << "Failed to connect to database.";
                }
            }
```

8. If you compile and run your project now, you should get something like this:

Figure 12.11 – The data from our database is now showing on the Qt program

How it works...

The previous example shows you how to connect to your SQL database using the `QSqlDatabase` class derived from the SQL module. You won't be able to access any of the classes related to SQL without adding the module to your Qt project.

We must tell Qt which SQL architecture we are running by mentioning it when calling the `addDatabase()` function. The options supported by Qt are **QSQLITE, QODBC, QODBC3, QPSQL**, and **QPSQL7**. If you encounter an error message that says `QSqlDatabase: QMYSQL driver not loaded`, you should check whether the DLL files are placed in the correct directory.

We can send our SQL statements to the database through the `QSqlQuery` class and wait for it to return the results, which are usually either the data you requested or error messages due to invalid statements. If there are any data coming from the database server, they will all be stored in the `QSqlQuery` class. All you need to retrieve these data is to perform a "while" loop on the `QSqlQuery` class to check for all existing records and retrieve them by calling the `value()` function.

Since we used SQLite in the preceding example, we don't need to set the server host, username, and password when connecting to the database. SQLite is a file-based SQL database; therefore, we only need to set the file name when calling `QSqlDatabase::setDatabaseName()`.

> **Important note**
>
> Qt 6 no longer officially supports QMYSQL or QMYSQL3. You can add MySQL support by re-compiling Qt from the source yourself. However, this method is not recommended for beginners. For more information, check out `https://doc.qt.io/qt-6/sql-driver.html#compile-qt-with-a-specific-driver`.

Writing basic SQL queries

In the previous example, we wrote our very first SQL query, which involves the `SELECT` statement. This time, we will learn how to use some other SQL statements, such as `INSERT`, `UPDATE`, and `DELETE`.

How to do it...

Let's create a simple program that demonstrates basic SQL query commands by following these steps:

1. We can use our previous project files, but there are a couple of things we need to change. Open `mainwindow.ui` and replace the labels for **Name** and **Age** with line-edit widgets. Then, add three buttons to the canvas and call them UPDATE, INSERT, and DELETE:

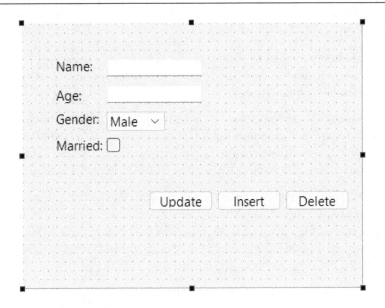

Figure 12.12 – Modify the UI to this

2. Open `mainwindow.h` and add the following variables under the private inheritance:

```
private:
    Ui::MainWindow *ui;
    QSqlDatabase db;
    bool connected;
    int currentID;
```

3. Open `mainwindow.cpp` and go to the class constructor. It is still pretty much the same as the previous example, except we store the database connection status in a Boolean variable called `connected`, and we also obtain the ID of the data from the database and store it in an integer variable called `currentID`:

```
MainWindow::MainWindow(QWidget *parent) :
    QMainWindow(parent), ui(new Ui::MainWindow) {
    ui->setupUi(this);
    db = QSqlDatabase::addDatabase("QSQLITE");
    db.setDatabaseName("database.db3");
    connected = db.open();
```

4. Let's make a query after we have connected to the database:

```
if (connected) {
        QSqlQuery query;
        if (query.exec("SELECT emp_id, emp_name, emp_age,
```

```
emp_gender, emp_married FROM employee")) {
                    while (query.next()) {
                            currentID = query.value(0).toInt();
                            ui->name->setText(query.value(1).
toString());

                            ui->age->setText(query.value(2).
toString());

                            ui->gender->setCurrentIndex(query.
value(3).toInt());

                            ui->married->setChecked(query.value(4).
toBool());

                    }

            }
```

5. Print out any error messages:

```
            else {
                    qDebug() << query.lastError().text();
            }
        }
        else {
            qDebug() << "Failed to connect to database.";
        }
    }
```

6. Go to `mainwindow.ui` and right-click on one of the buttons we added to the canvas in step 1. Select **Go to slot…** and click **OK**. Repeat these steps on the other button, and now you should see three slot functions being added to both your `mainwindow.h` and `mainwindow.cpp`:

```
private slots:
    void on_updateButton_clicked();
    void on_insertButton_clicked();
    void on_deleteButton_clicked();
```

7. Open `mainwindow.cpp` and we will declare what the program will do when we click on the **Update** button:

```
void MainWindow::on_updateButton_clicked() {
    if (connected) {
        if (currentID == 0) {
            qDebug() << "Nothing to update.";
        }
        else {
            QString id = QString::number(currentID);
            QString name = ui->name->text();
            QString age = ui->age->text();
```

```
                QString gender =
QString::number(ui->gender->currentIndex());
                QString married =
QString::number(ui->married->isChecked());
```

8. Make an UPDATE query like so:

```
                qDebug() << "UPDATE employee SET emp_name = '"
+ name + "', emp_age = '" + age + "', emp_gender = " + gender +
", emp_married = " + married + " WHERE emp_id = " + id;
                QSqlQuery query;
                if (query.exec("UPDATE employee SET emp_name =
'" + name + "', emp_age = '" + age + "', emp_gender = " + gender
+ ", emp_married = " + married + " WHERE emp_id = " + id)) {
                        qDebug() << "Update success.";
                }
```

9. Print out the last error message, if any:

```
                else {
                        qDebug() << query.lastError().text();
                }
            }
        }
        else {
            qDebug() << "Failed to connect to database.";
        }
    }
```

10. Declare what will happen when the **INSERT** button is clicked:

```
void MainWindow::on_insertButton_clicked() {
    if (connected) {
        QString name = ui->name->text();
        QString age = ui->age->text();
        QString gender =
QString::number(ui->gender->currentIndex());
        QString married =
QString::number(ui->married->isChecked());
        qDebug() << "INSERT INTO employee (emp_name, emp_age,
emp_gender, emp_married) VALUES ('" + name + "','" + age + "', "
+ gender + "," + married + ")";
```

11. Make an INSERT query like so:

```
                QSqlQuery query;
                if (query.exec("INSERT INTO employee (emp_name, emp_
age, emp_gender, emp_married) VALUES ('" + name + "','" + age +
```

```
"', " + gender + "," + married + ")")) {
            currentID = query.lastInsertId().toInt();
            qDebug() << "Insert success.";
        } else {
            qDebug() << query.lastError().text();
        }
    }
    else {
        qDebug() << "Failed to connect to database.";
    }
}
```

12. Declare what will happen when the **Delete** button is clicked:

```
void MainWindow::on_deleteButton_clicked() {
    if (connected) {
        if (currentID == 0) {
            qDebug() << "Nothing to delete.";
        } else {
            QString id = QString::number(currentID);
            qDebug() << "DELETE FROM employee WHERE emp_id
= " + id;

            QSqlQuery query;
            if (query.exec("DELETE FROM employee WHERE emp_
id = " + id)) {
                currentID = 0;
                qDebug() << "Delete success.";
            } else {
                qDebug() << query.lastError().text();
            }
        }
    }
    else {
        qDebug() << "Failed to connect to database.";
    }
}
```

13. Call `QSqlDatabase::close()` at the class destructor to properly terminate the SQL connection before exiting the program:

```
MainWindow::~MainWindow() {
    db.close();
    delete ui;
}
```

14. If you compile and run the program now, you should be able to select the default data from the database. Then, you can choose to update it or delete it from the database. You can also insert new data into the database by clicking the Insert button. You can use **SQLiteStudio** to check whether the data are being altered correctly:

Structure	Data	Constraints	Indexes	Triggers	DDL

Grid view   Form view

	emp_id	emp_name	emp_age	emp_gender	emp_married
1	1	John Doe	42	0	1
2	2	Jane Smith	26	1	0

Figure 12.13 – Data successfully modified in SQLite

How it works...

It's very important to check whether the database is connected before we proceed to send an SQL query to the database. Therefore, we keep that status in a variable and use it to check before sending out any queries. This, however, is not recommended for complex programs that are kept open for long periods of time, as the database might get disconnected during those periods, and a fixed variable may not be accurate. In that case, it's better to check the actual status by calling QSqlDatabase::isOpen().

The currentID variable is used to save the ID of the current data you obtained from the database. When you want to update the data or delete them from the database, this variable is crucial for letting the database know what data you're trying to update or delete. If you set your database table correctly, SQLite will treat each item of data as a unique entry, so you can be sure that no repeated ID will be produced in the database when new data are being saved.

After inserting new data into the database, we call QSqlQuery::lastInsertId() to obtain the ID of the new data and save it as a currentID variable so that it becomes the current data that we can update or delete from the database. It is a good habit to test your SQL queries on SQLiteStudio before using them in Qt. You can instantly find out whether your SQL statements are correct or incorrect instead of waiting for your project to be built, trying it out, and then rebuilding it. As programmers, we must work in the most efficient way.

Work hard and work smart.

Creating a login screen with Qt

In this recipe, we will learn how put our knowledge to use and create a functional login screen using Qt and SQLite.

How to do it...

Create your first functional login screen by following these steps:

1. Open a web browser and go to **SQLiteStudio**. We will create a new data table called `user`, which looks like this:

Figure 12.14 – Create a new user table

2. Let's insert our first item of data into the newly created table and set `user_employeeID` to the ID of an existing employee. In this way, the user account we create will be linked to the data of one of the employees:

Figure 12.15 – The user_employeeID column is linked to the employee's emp_id column

3. Open **Qt Creator** and create a new **Qt Widgets Application** project. We will start off with `mainwindow.ui`. Place a stacked widget on the canvas and make sure it contains two pages. Then, set up the two pages in the stacked widget as follows:

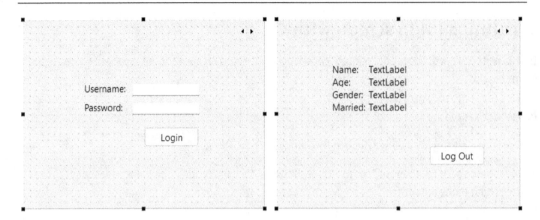

Figure 12.16 – Create a two-page UI inside a stacked widget

4. On the first page of the stacked widget, click the **Edit Tab Order** icon on top of the widget so that you can adjust the order of the widgets in your program:

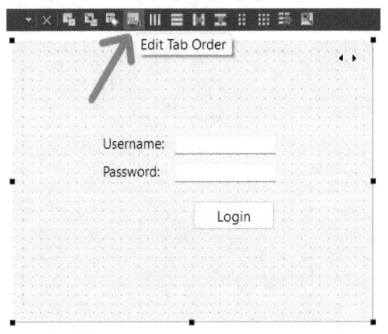

Figure 12.17 – Change the order of the widgets by pressing this button

5.   Once you click the **Edit Tab Order** icon, you will see some numbers appear on top of each widget in the canvas. Make sure the numbers look the same as they do in the screenshot that follows. Otherwise, click on the numbers to change their order. We only do this for the first page of the stacked widget; it's okay to keep the second page as it is:

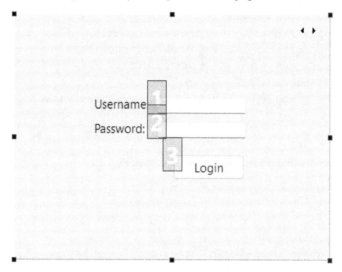

Figure 12.18 – The order of each widget is shown

6.   Right-click on the **Login** button and select **Go to slot…**. Then, make sure the `clicked()` option is selected and press **OK**. Qt will then create a slot function for you in your project source files. Repeat this step for the **Log Out** button as well.

7.   Open `mainwindow.h` and add the following headers after the `#include <QMainWindow>` line:

```
#include <QMainWindow>
#include <QtSql>
#include <QSqlDatabase>
#include <QSqlQuery>
#include <QMessageBox>
#include <QDebug>
```

8.   Add the following variable to `mainwindow.h`:

```
private:
    Ui::MainWindow *ui;
    QSqlDatabase db;
```

9. Open `mainwindow.cpp` and put this code in the class constructor:

```
MainWindow::MainWindow(QWidget *parent) :
    QMainWindow(parent),
    ui(new Ui::MainWindow) {
    ui->setupUi(this);
    ui->stackedWidget->setCurrentIndex(0);
    db = QSqlDatabase::addDatabase("QSQLITE");
    db.setDatabaseName("database.db3");
    if (!db.open()) {
        qDebug() << "Failed to connect to database.";
    }
}
```

10. Define what will happen if the `Login` button is clicked:

```
void MainWindow::on_loginButton_clicked() {
    QString username = ui->username->text();
    QString password = ui->password->text();
    QSqlQuery query;
    if (query.exec("SELECT user_employeeID from user WHERE
user_username = '" + username + "' AND user_password = '" +
password + "'")) {
        int resultSize = 0;
        while (query.next()) {
            QString employeeID = query.value(0).toString();
            QSqlQuery query2;
```

11. Make a SQL query:

```
        if (query2.exec("SELECT emp_name, emp_age,
emp_gender, emp_married FROM employee WHERE emp_id = " +
employeeID)) {
            while (query2.next()) {
                QString name = query2.value(0).
toString();
                QString age = query2.value(1).
toString();
                int gender = query2.value(2).
toInt();
                bool married = query2.value(3).
toBool();
                ui->name->setText(name);
                ui->age->setText(age);
```

12. We continue with the preceding code, and we set the gender and married texts before switching the stacked widget to its second page:

```
                                    if (gender == 0)
                                            ui->gender->setText("Male");
                                    else
                                            ui->gender-
        >setText("Female");

                                    if (married)
                                            ui->married->setText("Yes");
                                    else
                                            ui->married->setText("No");
                                    ui->stackedWidget-
        >setCurrentIndex(1);
                                    }
                            }
                            resultSize++;
                    }
```

13. Print an error message if the login fails:

```
                    if (resultSize == 0)
                    {
                            QMessageBox::warning(this, "Login failed",
        "Invalid username or password.");
                    }
            }
            else
            {
                    qDebug() << query.lastError().text();
            }
    }
```

14. Define what will happen if the **Log Out** button is clicked:

```
    void MainWindow::on_logoutButton_clicked() {
        ui->stackedWidget->setCurrentIndex(0);
    }
```

15. Close the database when the main window is closed:

```
    MainWindow::~MainWindow() {
        db.close();
        delete ui;
    }
```

16. Compile and run the program, and you should be able to log in with the dummy account. After you have logged in, you should be able to see the dummy employee information linked to the user account. You can also log out by clicking on the **Log Out** button:

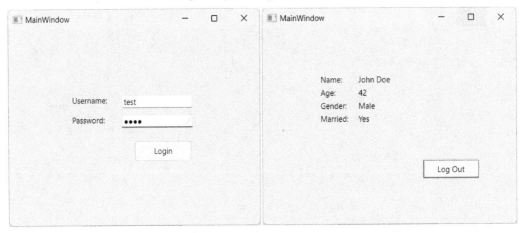

Figure 12.19 – A simple, working login screen

How it works...

In this example, we select data from the user table that matches the username and password that we inserted into the text fields. If nothing is found, it means we have provided an invalid username or password. Otherwise, obtain the `user_employeeID` data from the user account and do another SQL query to look for information from the `employee` table that matches the `user_employeeID` variable. Then, display the data according to the UI of your program.

We must set the widget order in the **Edit Tab Order** mode so that when the program has started, the first widget that gets focused on is the username line-edit widget. If the user presses the *Tab* key on the keyboard, the focus should switch to the second widget, which is the password line edit. An incorrect widget order will ruin the user experience and drive away any potential users. Make sure that the **echoMode** option of the password line edit is set to **Password**. That setting will hide the actual password inserted into the line edit and replace it with dot symbols for security purposes.

Since SQLite does not support returning the query size, we cannot use the `QSqlQuery::size()` function to determine how many results are being returned; the result will always be `-1`. Therefore, we declared a `resultSize` variable to count the result within the while loop operation.

Displaying information from a database in model view

Follow these steps to display information from a database on a model view widget:

How to do it...

In this recipe, we will learn how to display multiple sets of data obtained from our SQL database in a model view in our program:

1. We will be using the database table called `employee`, which we used in the previous example in *Creating a login screen with Qt*. This time, we need a lot more data in the employee table. Open up your **SQLiteStudio** control panel. Add data for a few more employees so that we can display it later in our program:

Grid view   Form view

	emp_id	emp_name	emp_age	emp_gender	emp_married
1	1	John Doe	42	0	1
2	2	Jane Smith	26	1	0
3	3	Larry King	32	0	1
4	4	Jason Freeman	28	0	0
5	5	Laura Jordan	38	1	1

Figure 12.20 – Add more dummy data to the employee table

2. Open Qt Creator, create a new **Qt Widgets Application** project, and then add the **SQL** module to your project.

3. Open `mainwindow.ui` and add a table widget (not a table view) from **Item Widget** (item-based) under the **Widget** box pane. Select the main window on the canvas and click on either the **Lay Out Vertically** or **Lay Out Horizontally** button to make the table widget stick to the size of the main window even when it's resized:

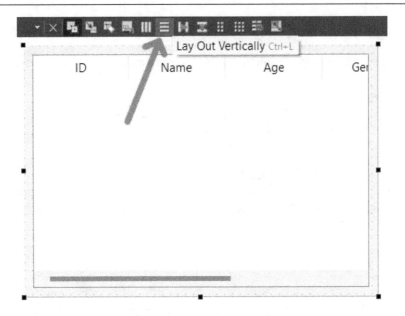

Figure 12.21 – Click on the Lay Out Vertically button

4. Double-click on the table widget and a window will appear. Under the **Columns** tab, add five items by clicking on the + button in the top-left corner. Name the items **ID**, **Name**, **Age**, **Gender**, and **Married**. Click **OK** when you're done:

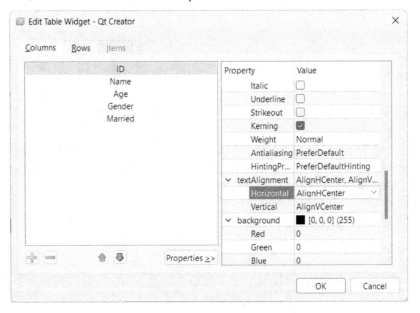

Figure 12.22 – We also set the text alignment to center

5. Right-click on the table widget and select **Go to slot...** in the pop-up menu. Scroll all the way down, select the `itemChanged(QTableWidgetItem*)` option in the pop-up window, and press **OK**. A slot function will be created in both of your source files.

6. Open `mainwindow.h` and add these private variables to the `MainWindow` class:

```
private:
    Ui::MainWindow *ui;
    bool hasInit;
    QSqlDatabase db;
```

7. Add the following class headers to `mainwindow.h`:

```
#include <QtSql>
#include <QSqlDatabase>
#include <QSqlQuery>
#include <QMessageBox>
#include <QDebug>
#include <QTableWidgetItem>
```

8. Open `mainwindow.cpp`; we're going to write tons of code there. We need to declare what will happen when the program is started. Add the following code to the constructor of the `MainWindow` class:

```
MainWindow::MainWindow(QWidget *parent) :
    QMainWindow(parent),
    ui(new Ui::MainWindow)
{
    hasInit = false;
    ui->setupUi(this);
    db = QSqlDatabase::addDatabase("QSQLITE");
    db.setDatabaseName("database.db3");
    ui->tableWidget->setColumnHidden(0, true);
```

9. The SQL query code looks like this:

```
if (db.open()) {
    QSqlQuery query;
    if (query.exec("SELECT emp_id, emp_name, emp_age,
emp_gender, emp_married FROM employee")) {
        while (query.next()) {
            qDebug() << query.value(0) << query.
value(1) << query.value(2) << query.value(3) << query.value(4);
            QString id = query.value(0).toString();
            QString name = query.value(1).toString();
            QString age = query.value(2).toString();
```

```
                              int gender = query.value(3).toInt();
                              bool married = query.value(4).toBool();
```

10. Create several `QTableWidgetItem` objects:

```
                        ui->tableWidget->setRowCount(ui-
>tableWidget->rowCount() + 1);
                        QTableWidgetItem* idItem = new
QTableWidgetItem(id);
                        QTableWidgetItem* nameItem = new
QTableWidgetItem(name);
                        QTableWidgetItem* ageItem = new
QTableWidgetItem(age);
                        QTableWidgetItem* genderItem = new
QTableWidgetItem();

                        if (gender == 0)
                              genderItem->setData(0, "Male");
                        else
                              genderItem->setData(0, "Female");
                        QTableWidgetItem* marriedItem = new
QTableWidgetItem();

                        if (married)
                              marriedItem->setData(0, "Yes");
                        else
                              marriedItem->setData(0, "No");
```

11. Move those objects to the table widget:

```
                        ui->tableWidget->setItem(ui->tableWidget-
>rowCount() - 1, 0, idItem);
                        ui->tableWidget->setItem(ui->tableWidget-
>rowCount() - 1, 1, nameItem);
                        ui->tableWidget->setItem(ui->tableWidget-
>rowCount() - 1, 2, ageItem);
                        ui->tableWidget->setItem(ui->tableWidget-
>rowCount() - 1, 3, genderItem);
                        ui->tableWidget->setItem(ui->tableWidget-
>rowCount() - 1, 4, marriedItem);
                        }
                  hasInit = true;
            }
            else {
                  qDebug() << query.lastError().text();
            }
      }
      else {
            qDebug() << "Failed to connect to database.";
```

```
        }
    }
```

12. Declare what will happen when an item of the table widget has been edited. Add the following code to the on_tableWidget_itemChanged() slot function:

```cpp
void MainWindow::on_tableWidget_itemChanged(QTableWidgetItem
*item) {
    if (hasInit) {
            QString id = ui->tableWidget->item(item->row(),
0)->data(0).toString();
            QString name = ui->tableWidget->item(item->row(),
1)->data(0).toString();
            QString age = QString::number(ui->tableWidget-
>item(item->row(), 2)->data(0).toInt());
            ui->tableWidget->item(item->row(), 2)->setData(0,
age);
            QString gender;
            if (ui->tableWidget->item(item->row(), 3)->data(0).
toString() == "Male") {
                gender = "0";
            } else {
                ui->tableWidget->item(item->row(),
3)->setData(0,"Female");
                gender = "1";
            }
            QString married;
            if (ui->tableWidget->item(item->row(), 4)->data(0).
toString() == "No") {
                married = "0";
            } else {
                ui->tableWidget->item(item->row(),
4)->setData(0, "Yes");
                married = "1";
            }
            qDebug() << id << name << age << gender << married;
            QSqlQuery query;
            if (query.exec("UPDATE employee SET emp_name = '" +
name + "', emp_age = '" + age + "', emp_gender = '" + gender +
"', emp_married = '" + married + "' WHERE emp_id = " + id)) {
                QMessageBox::information(this, "Update
Success", "Data updated to database.");
            } else {
                qDebug() << query.lastError().text();
            }
    }
}
```

13. Close the database at the class destructor:

```
MainWindow::~MainWindow() {
    db.close();
    delete ui;
}
```

14. If you compile and run the example now, you should get something like this:

Figure 12.23 – We have created our own SQL editor

How it works...

The table widget is similar to the one you see in spreadsheet applications such as **Microsoft Excel** and **OpenOffice Calc**. In contrast to other types of model viewers, such as list view or tree view, table view (or table widget) is a two-dimensional model viewer, which displays data in the form of rows and columns.

The main difference between a table view and a table widget in Qt is that a table widget is built on top of a table view class, which means a table widget is easier to use and more suitable for beginners. However, a table widget is less flexible and tends to be less scalable than a table view, which is not the best choice if you want to customize your table. After retrieving data from SQLite, we created a `QTableWidgetItem` item for each of the data items and set which column and row should be added to the table widget. Before adding an item to the table widget, we must increase the row count of the table by calling `QTableWidget::setRowCount()`. We can also get the current row count of the table widget by simply calling `QTableWidget::rowCount()`.

The first column from the left is hidden from view because we only use it to save the ID of the data so that we can use it to update the database when one of the data items in its row has changed. The `on_tableWidget_itemChanged()` slot function will be called when the data in one of the cells has changed. It will not only get called when you edit the data in the cell but also when the data are first added to the table after being retrieved from the database. To ensure that this function is only triggered when we edit the data, we use a Boolean variable called `hasInit` to check whether we have done the initialization process (adding the first batch of data to the table). If `hasInit` is false, ignore the function call.

To prevent users from entering a totally irrelevant type of data, such as inserting letters into a numerical-only data cell, we manually check whether the data are anything close to what we'd expected when they were being edited. Revert it to a default value if it doesn't come close to anything considered valid. This is, of course, a simple hack, which does the job but is not the most professional method. Alternatively, you can try to create a new class that inherits the `QItemDelegate` class and defines how your model view should behave. Then, call `QTableWidget::setItemDelegate()` to apply the class to your table widget.

Advanced SQL queries

By following this recipe, you will learn how to use advanced SQL statements such as `INNER JOIN`, `COUNT`, `LIKE`, and `DISTINCT`.

How to do it...

You can do a lot more than just perform simple queries on the SQL database. Let's follow these steps to learn how:

1. We need to add a few tables to our database before we can dive into the programming part. Open your **SQLiteStudio**. We need several tables for this example to work:

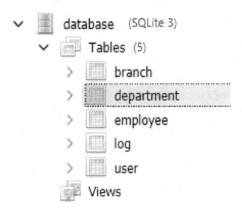

Figure 12.24 – Additional tables that we need to create for this example

2. I will show you the structure of each of the tables required for this project and the dummy data inserted into the tables for testing. The first table is called branch, which is used to store the IDs and names of different branches of the dummy company:

Figure 12.25 – The branch table

3. Secondly, we have the `department` table, which stores the IDs and names of different departments of the dummy company, which is also linked to the `branch` data by the branch IDs:

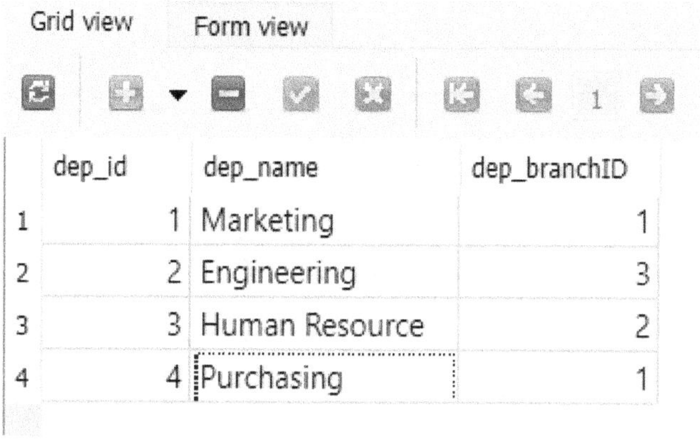

	dep_id	dep_name	dep_branchID
1	1	Marketing	1
2	2	Engineering	3
3	3	Human Resource	2
4	4	Purchasing	1

Figure 12.26 – The department table, which links to the branch table

4. We also have an `employee` table, which stores information on all the employees in the dummy company. This table is similar to the one we used in the previous examples, except it has two extra columns, `emp_birthday` and `emp_departmentID`:

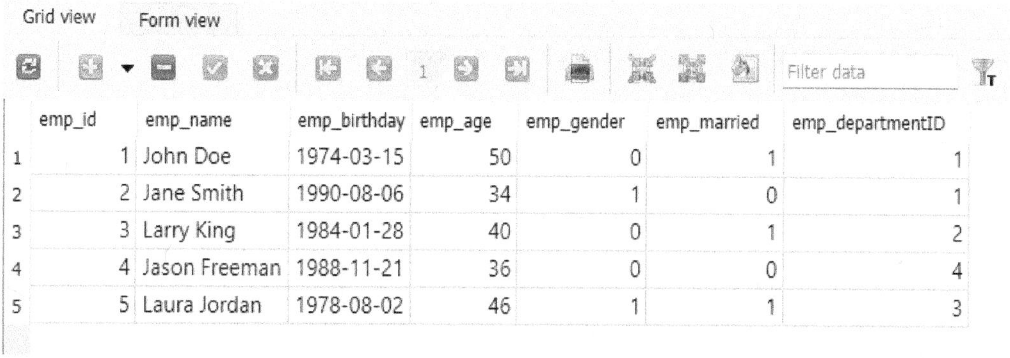

	emp_id	emp_name	emp_birthday	emp_age	emp_gender	emp_married	emp_departmentID
1	1	John Doe	1974-03-15	50	0	1	1
2	2	Jane Smith	1990-08-06	34	1	0	1
3	3	Larry King	1984-01-28	40	0	1	2
4	4	Jason Freeman	1988-11-21	36	0	0	4
5	5	Laura Jordan	1978-08-02	46	1	1	3

Figure 12.27 – The employee table, which links to the department table

5. We also have a table called `log`, which contains dummy records of the login time for each employee. `log_loginTime` will be set as a date-time variable type:

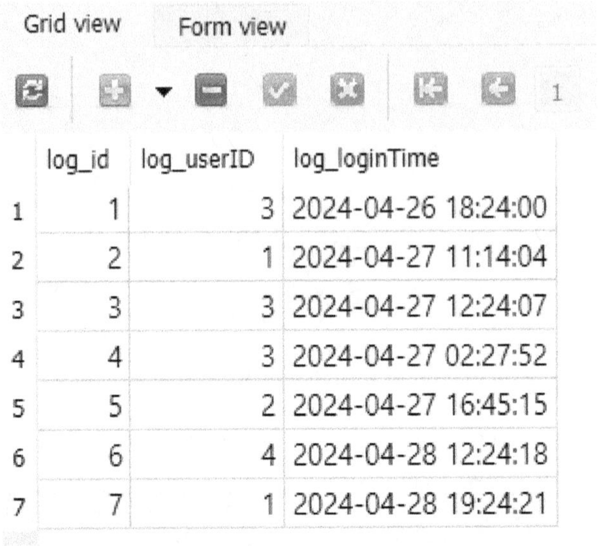

Grid view   Form view

log_id	log_userID	log_loginTime
1	1	3 2024-04-26 18:24:00
2	2	1 2024-04-27 11:14:04
3	3	3 2024-04-27 12:24:07
4	4	3 2024-04-27 02:27:52
5	5	2 2024-04-27 16:45:15
6	6	4 2024-04-28 12:24:18
7	7	1 2024-04-28 19:24:21

Figure 12.28 – The log table, which links to the user table

6. We have the `user` table that we also used in the previous examples:

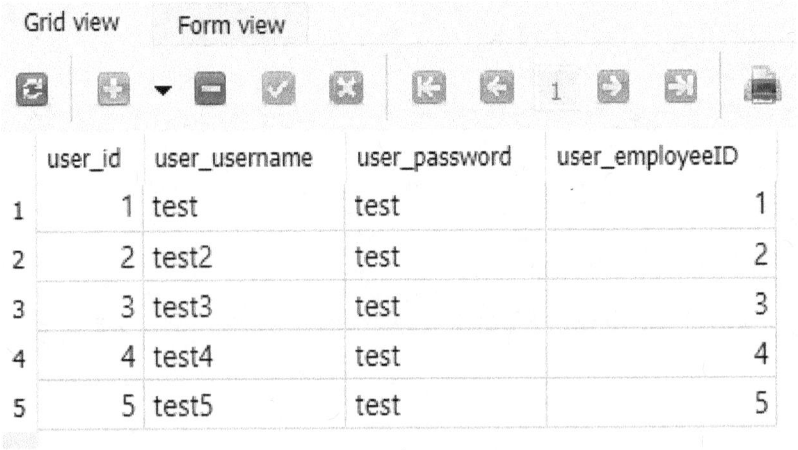

Grid view   Form view

user_id	user_username	user_password	user_employeeID
1	1 test	test	1
2	2 test2	test	2
3	3 test3	test	3
4	4 test4	test	4
5	5 test5	test	5

Figure 12.29 – The user table

7. Open Qt Creator. This time, instead of choosing **Qt Widgets Application**, we select **Qt Console Application**:

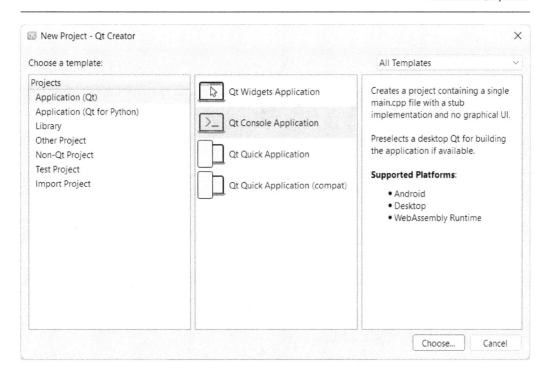

Figure 12.30 – Create a Qt Console Application project

8. Open your project file (.pro) and add the `sql` module to your project:

```
QT += core sql
QT -= gui
```

9. Open `main.cpp` and add the following header files to the top of the source file:

```
#include <QSqlDatabase>
#include <QSqlQuery>
#include <QSqlError>
#include <QDate>
#include <QDebug>
```

10. Add the following function to display employees who are more than 30 years old:

```
void filterAge() {
    qDebug() << "== Employees above 40 year old =============";
    QSqlQuery query;
    if (query.exec("SELECT emp_name, emp_age FROM employee
WHERE emp_age > 40")) {
        while (query.next()) {
            qDebug() << query.value(0).toString() << query.
```

```
value(1).toString();
            }
    }
    else {
    qDebug() << query.lastError().text();
    }
}
```

11. Add the following function to display the `department` and `branch` information of each employee:

```
void getDepartmentAndBranch() {
    qDebug() << "== Get employees' department and branch
==============";
    QSqlQuery query;
    if (query.exec("SELECT emp_name, dep_name, brh_name FROM
(SELECT emp_name, emp_departmentID FROM employee) AS myEmployee
INNER JOIN department ON department.dep_id = myEmployee.emp_
departmentID INNER JOIN branch ON branch.brh_id = department.
dep_branchID")) {
            while (query.next()) {
                    qDebug() << query.value(0).toString() << query.
value(1).toString() << query.value(2).toString();
            }
    }
    else {
            qDebug() << query.lastError().text();
    }
}
```

12. Add the following function, which displays employees who are working in the New York branch and are under 40 years old:

```
void filterBranchAndAge() {
    qDebug() << "== Employees from New York and age below 40
=============";
    QSqlQuery query;
    if (query.exec("SELECT emp_name, emp_age, dep_name, brh_
name FROM (SELECT emp_name, emp_age, emp_departmentID FROM
employee) AS myEmployee INNER JOIN department ON department.dep_
id = myEmployee.emp_departmentID INNER JOIN branch ON branch.
brh_id = department.dep_branchID WHERE branch.brh_name = 'New
York' AND myEmployee.emp_age < 40")) {
            while (query.next()) {
                    qDebug() << query.value(0).toString() << query.
value(1).toString() << query.value(2).toString() << query.
value(3).toString();
            }
```

```
        }
        else {
        qDebug() << query.lastError().text();
        }

    }
```

13. Add the following function, which counts the total number of female employees in the dummy company:

```
void countFemale() {
    qDebug() << "== Count female employees =============";
    QSqlQuery query;
    if (query.exec("SELECT COUNT(emp_gender) FROM employee
WHERE emp_gender = 1")) {
        while (query.next()) {
            qDebug() << query.value(0).toString();
        }
    }
    else {
        qDebug() << query.lastError().text();
    }

}
```

14. Add the following function, which filters the employee list and only displays those names that start with Ja:

```
void filterName() {
    qDebug() << "== Employees name start with 'Ja'
=============";
    QSqlQuery query;
    if (query.exec("SELECT emp_name FROM employee WHERE emp_
name LIKE '%Ja%'")) {
        while (query.next()) {
            qDebug() << query.value(0).toString();
        }
    }
    else {
        qDebug() << query.lastError().text();
    }

}
```

15. Add the following function, which displays employees who have birthdays in August:

```
void filterBirthday() {
    qDebug() << "== Employees birthday in August
=============";
```

```
        QSqlQuery query;
        if (query.exec("SELECT emp_name, emp_birthday FROM employee
WHERE strftime('%m', emp_birthday) = '08'")) {
                while (query.next()) {
                        qDebug() << query.value(0).toString() << query.
value(1).toDate().toString("d-MMMM-yyyy");
                }
        }
        else {
                qDebug() << query.lastError().text();
        }
}
```

16. Add the following function, which checks who logged into the dummy system on 27 April 2024 and displays their names on the terminal:

```
void checkLog() {
        qDebug() << "== Employees who logged in on 27 April 2024
==============";
        QSqlQuery query;
        if (query.exec("SELECT DISTINCT emp_name FROM (SELECT emp_
id, emp_name FROM employee) AS myEmployee INNER JOIN user ON
user.user_employeeID = myEmployee.emp_id INNER JOIN log ON log.
log_userID = user.user_id WHERE DATE(log.log_loginTime) = '2024-
04-27'")) {
                while (query.next()) {
                        qDebug() << query.value(0).toString();
                }
        }
        else {
                qDebug() << query.lastError().text();
        }
}
```

17. In the main() function, connect the program to the SQLite database and call all the functions that we defined in the previous steps. Close the database connection, and we're done:

```
int main(int argc, char *argv[]) {
        QCoreApplication a(argc, argv);
        QSqlDatabase db = QSqlDatabase::addDatabase("QSQLITE");
        db.setDatabaseName("database.db3");
        if (db.open()) {
                filterAge();
                getDepartmentAndBranch();
                filterBranchAndAge();
                countFemale();
```

```
            filterName();
            filterBirthday();
            checkLog();
            db.close();
    }
    else {
            qDebug() << "Failed to connect to database.";
    }
    return a.exec();
}
```

18. If you compile and run the project now, you should see a terminal window that displays the filtered results:

```
== Employees above 40 year old =============
"John Doe" "50"
"Laura Jordan" "46"
== Get employees' department and branch =============
"John Doe" "Marketing" "New York"
"Jane Smith" "Marketing" "New York"
"Larry King" "Engineering" "Bangalore"
"Jason Freeman" "Purchasing" "New York"
"Laura Jordan" "Human Resource" "California"
== Employees from New York and age below 40 =============
"Jane Smith" "34" "Marketing" "New York"
"Jason Freeman" "36" "Purchasing" "New York"
== Count female employees =============
"2"
== Employees name start with 'Ja' =============
"Jane Smith"
"Jason Freeman"
== Employees birthday in August =============
"Jane Smith" "6-August-1990"
"Laura Jordan" "2-August-1978"
== Employees who logged in on 27 April 2024 =============
"John Doe"
"Larry King"
"Jane Smith"
```

Figure 12.31 – Printing the results on the Application Output window

How it works...

A console application does not have a GUI and only shows you a text display in a terminal window. This is usually used in a backend system, as it uses fewer resources compared to a widget application. We used it in this example because it's faster to display the result without the need to place any widgets in the program, which we don't need in this case.

We separated the SQL queries into different functions so that it's easier to maintain the code and it doesn't become too messy. Do note that in C++, the functions have to be located before the main() function; otherwise, they will not be able to be called by main().

There's more...

The INNER JOIN statement used in the preceding example joins two tables together and selects all rows from both tables, as long as there is a match between the columns in both tables. There are many other types of JOIN statements that you can use in SQLite (and some other types of SQL architecture), such as LEFT JOIN, RIGHT JOIN, and FULL OUTER JOIN.

The following diagram shows the different types of JOIN statements and their effects:

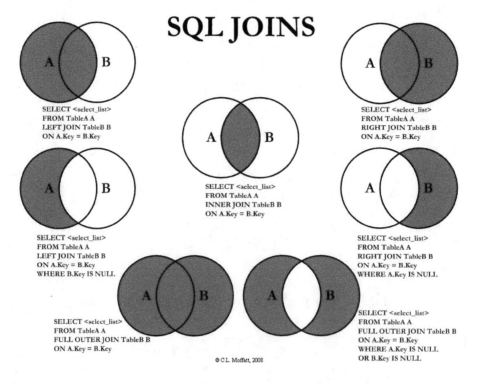

Figure 12.32 – Different types of JOIN statements

The following bullet points explain the `LIKE` and `DISTINCT` statements, which we used in our example code in this recipe:

- The `LIKE` statement is normally used to search for a string variable in the database without the full word. Notice that there are two % symbols located before and after the search keyword.

- The `DISTINCT` statement used in the previous example filters out results that have the exact same variable. For example, without the `DISTINCT` statement, you will see two versions of Larry King appear in the terminal because there are two records of him logging into the system on the same day. By adding the `DISTINCT` statement, SQLite will eliminate one of the results and ensure every result is unique.

- You may be wondering what `d-MMMM-yyyy` stands for and why we used it in the preceding example. That is actually an expression supplied to the `QDateTime` class in Qt to display the date-time result using a given format. In this case, it will change the date-time data that we get from SQLite, 2024-08-06, to the format that we specified, resulting in 6-August-2024.

For more information, check out Qt's documentation at `http://doc.qt.io/qt-6/qdatetime. html#toString`, which has the full list of expressions that can be used to determine the format of the date and time string.

SQL provides an easy and efficient way to save and load user data without reinventing the wheel. Qt provides you with an out-of-the-box solution for connecting your application with a SQL database; in this chapter, we have learned how to do this by using a step-by-step approach, and we were able to load and save our user's data into the SQL database.

13

Developing Web Applications Using Qt WebEngine

Qt includes a module called **Qt WebEngine** that allows us to embed a web browser widget into our program and use it to display web pages or local HTML content. Prior to version 5.6, Qt used another similar module called **Qt WebKit**, which is now deprecated and has since been replaced by the Chromium-based **WebEngine** module. Qt also allows communication between JavaScript and C++ code through **Qt WebChannel**, which enables us to make use of this module in a much more effective fashion.

In this chapter, we will cover the following recipes:

- Introducing **Qt WebEngine**
- Using webview and web settings
- Embedding Google maps in your project
- Calling C++ functions from JavaScript
- Calling JavaScript functions from C++

Technical requirements

The technical requirements for this chapter include Qt 6.6.1 MSVC 2019 64 bit, Qt Creator 12.0.2, and Microsoft Visual Studio. All the code used in this chapter can be downloaded from the following GitHub repository: https://github.com/PacktPublishing/QT6-C-GUI-Programming-Cookbook---Third-Edition-/tree/main/Chapter13.

Introducing Qt WebEngine

In this example project, we will explore the basic features of the **WebEngine** module in Qt and try building a simple working web browser. Since Qt 5.6, Qt's **WebKit** module has been deprecated and replaced by the **WebEngine** module, which is based on Google's Chromium engine.

How to do it...

First, let's set up our **WebEngine** project:

1. At the moment, Qt's **WebEngine** module only works with the Visual C++ compiler and not others, such as **MinGW** or **Cygwin**. This might change in the future, but it all depends on whether Qt developers want to port it to other compilers or not. Make sure that the Qt version you installed on your computer supports the Visual C++ compiler. You can add the **MSVC 2019 64-bit** component to your Qt installation using Qt's maintenance tool. Also, make sure that you have installed the **Qt WebEngine** component in your Qt version:

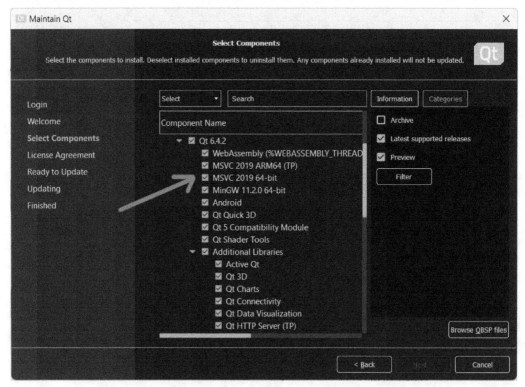

Figure 13.1 – Making sure MSVC 2019 and Qt WebEngine are installed

2. Open up Qt Creator and create a new **Qt Widgets Application** project. Select a kit that uses the Visual C++ compiler:

Manage Kits...	☐ 🖥 **Desktop Qt 5.15.2 MSVC2015 64bit**
	☐ 🖥 **Desktop Qt 5.15.2 MSVC2019 32bit**
Active Project	☐ 🖥 **Desktop Qt 5.15.2 MSVC2019 64bit**
WebEngine_Basic ⌄	
Import Existing Build...	☐ 🖥 **Desktop Qt 6.4.2 MinGW 64-bit**
	☑ 🖥 **Desktop Qt 6.4.2 MSVC2019 64bit**
Build & Run	☐ 🖥 **Desktop Qt 6.4.2 MSVC2019 ARM64**
⊙ Android Qt 5.15.2 Clang Multi-Abi	
⊙ Android Qt 6.4.2 Clang arm64-v8a	☐ 🖥 **Desktop Qt 6.5.3 MinGW 64-bit**
⊙ Android Qt 6.4.2 Clang armeabi-v7a	
⊙ Android Qt 6.4.2 Clang x86	☐ 🖥 **Desktop Qt 6.5.3 MSVC2019 64bit**
⊙ Android Qt 6.4.2 Clang x86_64	
⊙ Android Qt 6.5.3 Clang arm64-v8a	

Figure 13.2 – Only MSVC is officially supported by Qt WebEngine

3. Open up your project file (`.pro`) and add the following modules to your project. After that, you must run qmake to apply the changes:

```
QT += core gui webenginewidgets
```

4. Open up `mainwindow.ui` and remove the **menuBar**, **mainToolBar**, and **statusBar** objects, as we don't need those in this project:

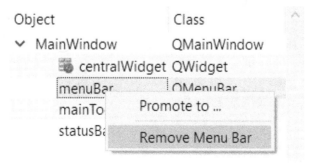

Figure 13.3 – Removing the menu bar, main toolbar, and status bar

5. Place two horizontal layouts on the canvas, then place a **Line Edit** widget and a push button for the layout at the top:

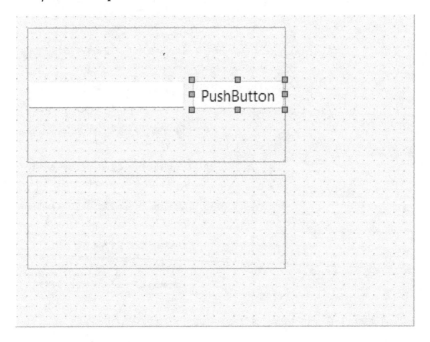

Figure 13.4 – Placing the line edit widget and push button in a layout

6. Select the canvas and click on the **Lay Out Vertically** button located at the top of the editor:

Figure 13.5 – Clicking on the Lay Out Vertically button

7. The layouts will expand and follow the size of the main window. The line edit will also expand horizontally, based on the width of the horizontal layout:

Figure 13.6 – The line edit is now expanding horizontally

8. Add two buttons to the left side of the line edit. We'll use these two buttons to move backward and forward between page histories. Add a **Progress Bar** widget at the bottom of the main window so that we can find out whether the page has finished loading or is still in progress. We don't have to worry about the horizontal layout in the middle at this point as we'll be adding webview to it later at *step 15* using C++ code, and the space will be occupied:

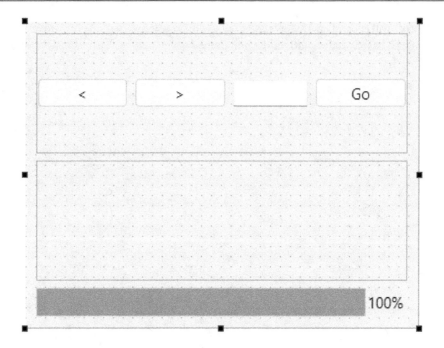

Figure 13.7 – Adding two more buttons and a progress bar to the UI

9.   Right-click on one of the buttons and select **Go to slot…**, then select `clicked()` and click **OK**. A slot function will be automatically created for you in `mainwindow.h` and `mainwindow.cpp`. Repeat this step for all the other buttons as well.

10. Right-click on the line edit and select **Go to slot…**, then select `returnPressed()` and click **OK**. Another slot function will now be automatically created for you in `mainwindow.h` and `mainwindow.cpp`.

11. Let's hop over to `mainwindow.h`. The first thing we need to do is to add the following header to `mainwindow.h`:

```
#include <QtWebEngineWidgets/QtWebEngineWidgets>
```

12. Declare a `loadUrl()` function under the class destructor:

```
public:
    explicit MainWindow(QWidget *parent = 0);
    ~MainWindow();
    void loadUrl();
```

13. Add a custom slot function called `loading()` to `mainwindow.h`:

```
private slots:
    void on_goButton_clicked();
    void on_address_returnPressed();
    void on_backButton_clicked();
    void on_forwardButton_clicked();
    void loading(int progress);
```

14. Declare a QWebEngineView object and call it `webview`:

```
private:
    Ui::MainWindow *ui;
    QWebEngineView* webview;
```

15. Open the `mainwindow.cpp` file and initiate the WebEngine view. Add it to the second horizontal layout and connect its `loadProgress()` signal to the `loading()` slot function we just added to `mainwindow.h`:

```
MainWindow::MainWindow(QWidget *parent) :
    QMainWindow(parent),
    ui(new Ui::MainWindow)
{

    ui->setupUi(this);
    webview = new QWebEngineView;
    ui->horizontalLayout_2->addWidget(webview);
    connect(webview, &QWebEngineView::loadProgress, this,
&MainWindow::loading);
}
```

16. Declare what will happen when the `loadUrl()` function is called:

```
void MainWindow::loadUrl() {
    QUrl url = QUrl(ui->address->text());
    url.setScheme("http");
    webview->page()->load(url);
}
```

17. Call the `loadUrl()` function when the **Go** button is clicked or when the *Enter* key is pressed:

```
void MainWindow::on_goButton_clicked() {
    loadUrl();
}
MainWindow::on_address_returnPressed() {
    loadUrl();
}
```

18. As for the other two buttons, we'll ask `webview` to load the previous page or the next page if it is available in the history stack:

```
void MainWindow::on_backButton_clicked() {
    webview->back();
}
void MainWindow::on_forwardButton_clicked() {
    webview->forward();
}
```

19. Change the value of `progressBar` when the web page is being loaded:

```
void MainWindow::loading(int progress) {
    ui->progressBar->setValue(progress);
}
```

20. Build and run the program now, and you will get a very basic but functional web browser:

Figure 13.8 – We have created a simple web browser from scratch!

How it works...

The old `webview` system was based on Apple's **WebKit** engine and is only available in Qt 5.5 and its predecessor. Since 5.6, **WebKit** has been completely abandoned by Qt and replaced with Google's **Chromium** engine. The API has been completely changed, and therefore all the code related to **Qt WebKit** will not work correctly once migrated to 5.6. If you're new to Qt, it's recommended you skip **WebKit** and learn the **WebEngine** API since it is becoming the new standard in Qt.

> **Note**
>
> If you have used Qt's **WebKit** in the past, this web page teaches you how to port your old code over to **WebEngine**: `https://wiki.qt.io/Porting_from_QtWebKit_to_QtWebEngine`

In *step 15* in the previous section, we connected the `loadProgress()` signal that belongs to the `webview` widget to the `loading()` slot function. The signal will be called automatically when `webview` is loading the web page you requested by calling `QWebEnginePage::load()` in *step 17*. You can also connect the `loadStarted()` and `loadFinished()` signals if you need to.

In *step 17*, we used the `QUrl` class to convert the text obtained from the line edit to URL format. By default, the address we inserted will lead to the local path if we do not specify the URL scheme (HTTP, HTTPS, FTP, and so on). We may not be able to load the page if, say, we gave it `google.com` instead of `http://google.com`. Therefore, we manually specified a URL scheme for it by calling `QUrl::setScheme()`. This ensured the address is properly formatted before passing it to `webview`.

There's more...

If for some reason you need the **WebKit** module for your project instead of **WebEngine**, you can obtain the module code from GitHub and build it by yourself: `https://github.com/qt/qtwebkit`

Using webview and web settings

In this recipe, we will dive deeper into the features available in Qt's **WebEngine** module and explore the settings that we can use to customize our `webview`. We will use the source files from the previous example and add more code to it.

How to do it...

Let's explore some of the basic features of the **Qt WebEngine** module:

1. Open `mainwindow.ui` and add a vertical layout under the progress bar. Add a **Plain Text Edit** widget (under the **Input Widgets** category) and a push button to the vertical layout. Change the display of the push button to **Load HTML** and set the `plaintext` property of the **Plain Text Edit** widget to the following:

```
<Img src="https://www.google.com/images/branding/googlelogo/1x/
googlelogo_color_272x92dp.png"></img>
<h1>Hello World!</h1>
<h3>This is our custom HTML page.</h3>
<script>alert("Hello!");</script>
```

This is how it should look after you have added the code on top of the **Plain Text Edit** widget:

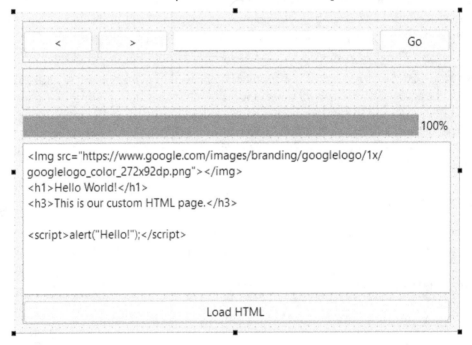

Figure 13.9 – Adding a Plain Text Edit widget and a push button to the bottom

2. Go to **File | New File**. A window will pop up and ask you to choose a file template. Select **Qt Resource File** under the **Qt** category and click on the **Choose...** button. Type in your desired filename and click **Next**, followed by **Finish**:

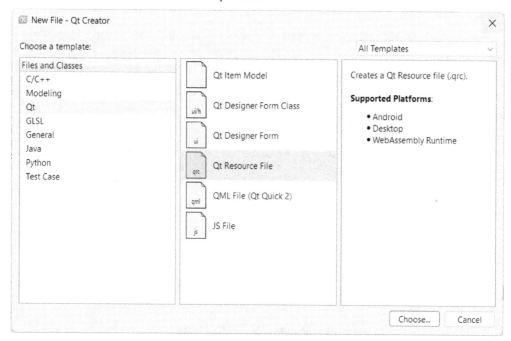

Figure 13.10 – Creating a Qt resource file

3. Open the resource file we just created by right-clicking on it in the **Projects** pane and selecting the **Open in Editor** option. Once the file is opened by the editor, click on the **Add** button, followed by **Add Prefix**. Set the prefix as / and click **Add**, followed by **Add Files**. A file browser window will appear, and we will select the tux.png image file and click **Open**. The image file is now added to our project, where it will be embedded into the executable file (.exe) once it's compiled:

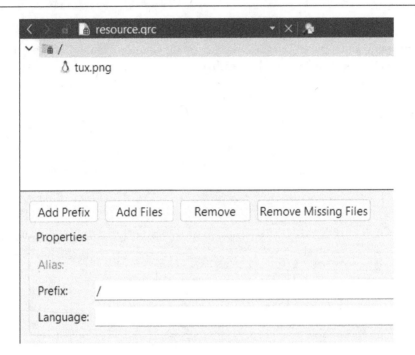

Figure 13.11 – Adding the tux.png image file to our resource file

4. Open `mainwindow.h` and add the following headers to it:

```
#include <QMainWindow>
#include <QtWebEngineWidgets/QtWebEngineWidgets>
#include <QDebug>
#include <QFile>
```

5. Make sure the following functions and pointers have been declared in `mainwindow.h`:

```
public:
    explicit MainWindow(QWidget *parent = 0);
    ~MainWindow();
    void loadUrl();
private slots:
    void on_goButton_clicked();
    void on_address_returnPressed();
    void on_backButton_clicked();
    void on_forwardButton_clicked();
    void startLoading();
    void loading(int progress);
    void loaded(bool ok);
    void on_loadHtml_clicked();
```

```
private:
    Ui::MainWindow *ui;
    QWebEngineView* webview;
```

6. Open `mainwindow.cpp` and add the following code to the class constructor:

```
MainWindow::MainWindow(QWidget *parent) :
    QMainWindow(parent),
    ui(new Ui::MainWindow)
{
    ui->setupUi(this);
    webview = new QWebEngineView;
    ui->horizontalLayout_2->addWidget(webview);
    //webview->page()->settings()->setAttribute(QWebEngineSetting
s::JavascriptEnabled, false);
    //webview->page()->settings()->setAttribute(QWebEngineSetting
s::AutoLoadImages, false);
    //QString fontFamily = webview->page()->settings()->fontFamil
y(QWebEngineSettings::SerifFont);
    QString fontFamily = webview->page()->settings()->fontFamily
(QWebEngineSettings::SansSerifFont);
    int fontSize = webview->page()->settings()->fontSize(QWebEng
ineSettings::MinimumFontSize);
    QFont myFont = QFont(fontFamily, fontSize);
    webview->page()->settings()->setFontFamily(QWebEngineSetting
s::StandardFont, myFont.family());
```

7. Load the image file and place it on `webview`:

```
        QFile file(":://tux.png");
        if (file.open(QFile::ReadOnly)) {
            QByteArray data = file.readAll();
            webview->page()->setContent(data, "image/png");
        }
        else {
            qDebug() << "File cannot be opened.";
        }
        connect(webview, &QWebEngineView::loadStarted, this,
&MainWindow::startLoading()));
        connect(webview, &QWebEngineView::loadProgress, this,
&MainWindow::loading(int)));
        connect(webview, &QWebEngineView::loadFinished, this,
&MainWindow::loaded(bool)));
    }
```

8. The `MainWindow::loadUrl()` function stays the same as in the previous example in the *Introducing Qt WebEngine* recipe, which sets the URL scheme to HTTP before loading the page:

```
void MainWindow::loadUrl() {
    QUrl url = QUrl(ui->address->text());
    url.setScheme("http");
    webview->page()->load(url);
}
```

9. The same goes for the following functions, which also remain the same as the previous example in the *Introducing Qt WebEngine* recipe:

```
void MainWindow::on_goButton_clicked() {
    loadUrl();
}
void MainWindow::on_address_returnPressed() {
    loadUrl();
}
void MainWindow::on_backButton_clicked() {
    webview->back();
}
void MainWindow::on_forwardButton_clicked() {
    webview->forward();
}
```

10. Add the `MainWindow::startLoading()` and `MainWindow::loaded()` slot functions, which will be called by the `loadStarted()` and `loadFinished()` signals. These two functions basically show a progress bar when a page is starting to load and hide the progress bar when the page has finished loading:

```
void MainWindow::startLoading() {
    ui->progressBar->show();
}
void MainWindow::loading(int progress) {
    ui->progressBar->setValue(progress);
}
void MainWindow::loaded(bool ok) {
    ui->progressBar->hide();
}
```

11. Call `webview->loadHtml()` to convert the plain text to HTML content when the **Load HTML** button is clicked:

```
void MainWindow::on_loadHtml_clicked() {
    webview->setHtml(ui->source->toPlainText());
}
```

12. Build and run the program, and you should see something like the following:

Figure 13.12 –webview will now display the result generated from your HTML code

How it works...

In this example, we used C++ to load an image file and set it as `webview` default content (instead of a blank page). We could achieve the same result by loading a default HTML file with an image at startup.

Some of the code in the class constructor has been commented out. You can remove the double slashes (`//`) and see the difference it makes – the JavaScript alert will no longer appear (since JavaScript is disabled) and images will no longer appear in your `webview`.

Another thing you can try is to change the font family from `QWebEngineSettings::SansSerifFont` to `QWebEngineSettings::SerifFont`. You will notice a slight difference in the font as it appears in `webview`:

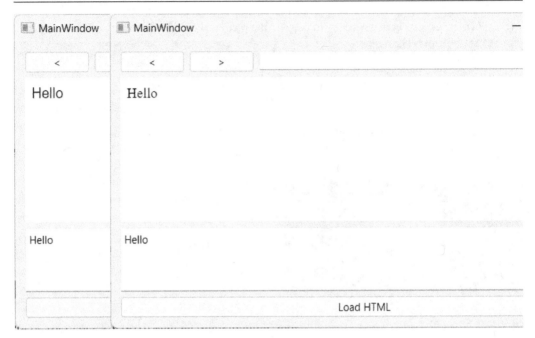

Figure 13.13 – Different types of font showing in webview

By clicking the **Load HTML** button, we ask `webview` to treat the content of the **Plain Text Edit** widget as HTML code and load it as an HTML page. You can use this to make a simple HTML editor powered by Qt!

Embedding Google maps in your project

In this recipe, we will learn how to embed Google maps in our project through Qt's **WebEngine** module. This example doesn't focus much on Qt and C++, but rather on the **Google Maps** API in HTML code.

How to do it...

Let's create a program that displays Google maps by following these steps:

1. Create a new **Qt Widgets Application** project and remove the **statusBar**, **menuBar**, and **mainToolBar** objects.

2. Open your project file (`.pro`) and add the following modules to your project:

```
QT += core gui webenginewidgets
```

3. Open `mainwindow.ui` and add a vertical layout to the canvas. Then, select the canvas and click the **Lay Out Vertically** button on top of the canvas. You will get the following:

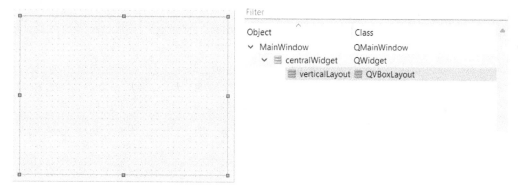

Figure 13.14 – Adding a vertical layout to the central widget

4. Open `mainwindow.cpp` and add the following header to the top of the source code:

```
#include <QtWebEngineWidgets/QWebEngineView>
```

5. Add the following code to the `MainWindow` constructor:

```
MainWindow::MainWindow(QWidget *parent) :
    QMainWindow(parent),
    ui(new Ui::MainWindow)
{
    ui->setupUi(this);
    QWebEngineView* webview = new QWebEngineView;
    QUrl url = QUrl("qrc:/map.html");
    webview->page()->load(url);
    ui->verticalLayout->addWidget(webview);
}
```

6. Go to **File | New File** and create a Qt resource file (`.qrc`). We will add an HTML file to our project, called `map.html`:

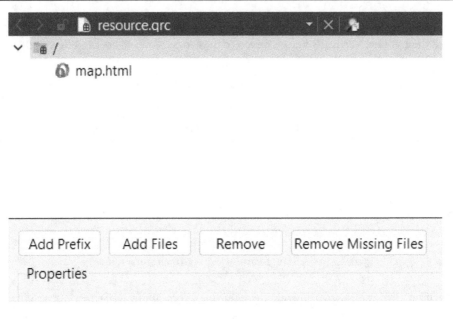

Figure 13.15 – Adding map.html to the resource file

7. Open map.html with your favorite text editor. It's not recommended to open an HTML file using Qt Creator as it does not provide any color coding for HTML syntax.

8. Start writing the HTML code by declaring important tags, such as <html>, <head>, and <body>:

```
<!DOCTYPE html>
<html>
  <head>
  </head>
  <body ondragstart="return false">
  </body>
</html>
```

9. Add a <div> tag to the body and set its ID as map-canvas:

```
<body ondragstart="return false">
  <div id="map-canvas" />
</body>
```

10. Add the following code to the head of the HTML document:

```
<meta name="viewport" content="initial-scale=1.0,
userscalable=no" />
<style type="text/css">
html { height: 100% }
```

```
     body { height: 100%; margin: 0; padding: 0 }
     #map-canvas { height: 100% }
     </style>
     <script type="text/javascript" src="https://maps.googleapis.
com/maps/api/js?key=YOUR_KEY_HERE&libraries=drawing"></script>
```

11. Add the following code, also to the head of the HTML document, beneath the code we inserted in the previous step:

```
     <script type="text/javascript">
         var map;
         function initialize() {
// Add map
             var mapOptions =
             {
                 center: new google.maps.LatLng(40.705311,
-74.2581939), zoom: 6
             };
             map = new google.maps.Map(document.
getElementById("mapcanvas"),mapOptions);
// Add event listener
             google.maps.event.addListener(map, 'zoom_changed',
    function() {
        //alert(map.getZoom());
             });
```

12. Create a marker and place it on the map:

```
// Add marker
             var marker = new google.maps.Marker({
                 position: new google.maps.LatLng(40.705311,
-74.2581939),
                 map: map,
                 title: "Marker A",
});
             google.maps.event.addListener (marker, 'click',
function()
             {
                 map.panTo(marker.getPosition());
             });
             marker.setMap(map);
```

13. Add a polyline to the map:

```
// Add polyline
        var points = [ new google.maps.LatLng(39.8543,
-73.2183), new google.maps.LatLng(41.705311, -75.2581939), new
google.maps.LatLng(40.62388, -75.5483) ];
        var polyOptions = {
        path: points,
        strokeColor: '#FF0000',
        strokeOpacity: 1.0,
        strokeWeight: 2
        };
        historyPolyline = new google.maps.
Polyline(polyOptions);
        historyPolyline.setMap(map);
```

14. Add a polygon shape:

```
// Add polygon
        var points = [ new google.maps.LatLng(37.314166,
-75.432), new google.maps.LatLng(40.2653, -74.4325), new google.
maps.LatLng(38.8288, -76.5483) ];
        var polygon = new google.maps.Polygon({
        paths: points,
        fillColor: '#000000',
        fillOpacity: 0.2,
        strokeWeight: 3,
        strokeColor: '#fff000',
        });
        polygon.setMap(map);
```

15. Create a drawing manager and apply it to the map:

```
// Setup drawing manager
        var drawingManager = new google.maps.drawing.
DrawingManager();
        drawingManager.setMap(map);
        }
    google.maps.event.addDomListener(window, 'load',
initialize);
    </script>
```

16. Compile and run the project. You should see the following:

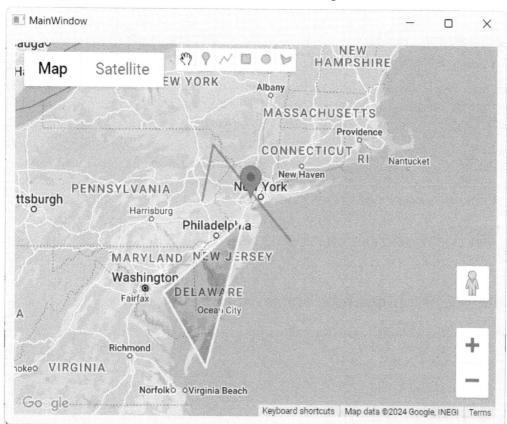

Figure 13.16 – You should see a marker, a polyline, and a triangle on the Google map

How it works...

Google allows you to embed Google maps in a web page using its JavaScript library, called the **Google Maps** API. Through Qt's **WebEngine** module, we can embed Google maps in our C++ project by loading an HTML file to our `webview` widget, which uses the **Google Maps** API. The only downside of this method is that we cannot load maps when there is no internet connection.

The **Google Maps** API can be called by your website as Google allows it. Choose the free API if your plan is for heavier traffic.

Go to `https://console.developers.google.com` to get a free key and replace `YOUR_KEY_HERE` in the JavaScript source path with the API key you obtained from Google.

We must define a `<div>` object, which serves as a container for the map. Then, when we initialize the map, we specify the ID of the `<div>` object so that the **Google Maps** API knows which HTML element to look for when embedding the map. By default, we set the center of the map to the coordinates of New York and set the default zoom level to 6. Then, we add an event listener that gets triggered when the zoom level of the map changes.

Remove the double slashes (//) from the code to see it in action. After that, we add a marker to the map through JavaScript. The marker also has an event listener attached to it, which will trigger the `panTo()` function when the marker is clicked.

It basically pans the map view to the marker that has been clicked. Although we have added the drawing manager to the map (the icon buttons beside the **Map** and **Satellite** buttons), which allows users to draw any type of shape on top of the map, it's also possible to add shapes manually using JavaScript, similar to how we added a marker in *step 12*, in the *How to do it...* section.

Lastly, you may have noticed that headers are added to `mainwindow.cpp` instead of `mainwindow.h`. This is totally fine unless you are declaring class pointers in `mainwindow.h`—then, you have to include those headers in it.

Calling C++ functions from JavaScript

In this recipe, we will learn how to put our knowledge to use and create a functional login screen using Qt and SQLite.

How to do it...

Let's learn how to call C++ functions from JavaScript using the following steps:

1. Create a **Qt Widgets Application** project. Open the project file (`.pro`) and add the following modules to the project:

   ```
   QT += core gui webenginewidgets
   ```

2. Open `mainwindow.ui` and delete the **mainToolBar**, **menuBar**, and **statusBar** objects, as we don't need any of these in this example program.

3. Add a vertical layout to the canvas, then select the canvas and click on the **Lay Out Vertically** button on top of the canvas. Add a text label to the top of the vertical layout and set its text to `Hello!`. Make its font bigger by setting its `styleSheet` property as follows:

   ```
   font: 75 26pt "MS Shell Dlg 2";
   ```

This is what it looks like after we applied the font properties to our style sheet:

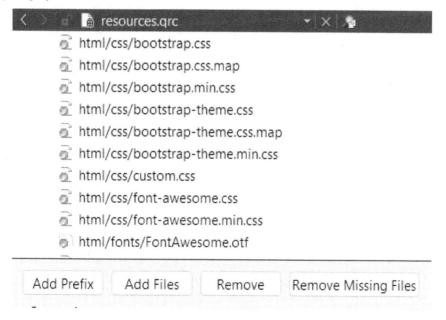

Hello!

Figure 13.17 – Applying the font property to the "Hello!" text

4. Go to **File | New File…** and create a resource file. Add an empty HTML file and all the JavaScript files, CSS files, font files, and so on that belong to **jQuery**, **Bootstrap**, and **Font Awesome** to your project resources:

resources.qrc

html/css/bootstrap.css
html/css/bootstrap.css.map
html/css/bootstrap.min.css
html/css/bootstrap-theme.css
html/css/bootstrap-theme.css.map
html/css/bootstrap-theme.min.css
html/css/custom.css
html/css/font-awesome.css
html/css/font-awesome.min.css
html/fonts/FontAwesome.otf

Add Prefix   Add Files   Remove   Remove Missing Files

Figure 13.18 – Adding all the files to the project's resource

5. Open your HTML file, which in this case is called `test.html`. Link all the necessary JavaScript and CSS files to the HTML source code, between the `<head>` tags:

```html
<!DOCTYPE html>
<html>
<head>
    <script src="qrc:///qtwebchannel/qwebchannel.js"></script>
    <script src="js/jquery.min.js"></script>
    <script src="js/bootstrap.js"></script>
    <link rel="stylesheet" type="text/css" href="css/bootstrap.
css">
    <link rel="stylesheet" type="text/css" href="css/
fontawesome.css">
</head>
<body>
</body>
</html>
```

6. Add the following JavaScript to the `<head>` element, wrapped between the `<script>` tags:

```html
<script>
    $(document).ready(function()
    {
        new QWebChannel(qt.webChannelTransport,
function(channel)
        {
            mainWindow = channel.objects.mainWindow;
        });
        $("#login").click(function(e) {
            e.preventDefault();
            var user = $("#username").val();
            var pass = $("#password").val();
            mainWindow.showLoginInfo(user, pass);
        });
```

7. Print **Good bye!** when clicking on the **changeText** button with the following code:

```html
        $("#changeText").click(function(e)
        {
            e.preventDefault();
            mainWindow.changeQtText("Good bye!");
        });
    });
</script>
```

8. Add the following code to the `<body>` element:

```
<div class="container-fluid">
    <form id="example-form" action="#" class="container-
fluid">
        <div class="form-group">
            <div class="col-md-12"><h3>Call C++ Function
from Javascript</h3></div>
            <div class="col-md-12">
            <div class="alert alert-info" role="alert"><i
class="fa fa-info-circle"></i>
            <span id="infotext">Click "Login" to send username
and password variables to C++. Click "Change Cpp Text" to change
the text label on Qt GUI.</span>
            </div>
            </div>
```

9. Continuing from the previous code, this time, we create input fields for username and password, with two buttons at the bottom called **Login** and **Change Cpp Text**:

```
            <div class="col-md-12"><label>Username:</
label><input id="username" type="text"><p />
            </div>
            <div class="col-md-12">
            <label>Password:</label> <input id="password"
type="password"><p />
            </div>
            <div class="col-md-12">
            <button id="login" class="btn btn-success"
type="button"><i class="fa fa-check"></i> Login</button>
            <button id="changeText" class="btn btn-primary"
type="button">
            <i class="fa fa-pencil"></i> Change Cpp Text</
button>
            </div>
        </div>
    </form>
</div>
```

10. Open `mainwindow.h` and add the following public functions to the `MainWindow` class:

```
public:
    explicit MainWindow(QWidget *parent = 0);
    ~MainWindow();
    Q_INVOKABLE void changeQtText(QString newText);
    Q_INVOKABLE void showLoginInfo(QString user, QString pass);
```

11. Open `mainwindow.cpp` and add the following headers to the top of the source code:

```
#include <QtWebEngineWidgets/QWebEngineView>
#include <QtWebChannel/QWebChannel>
#include <QMessageBox>
```

12. Add the following code to the `MainWindow` constructor:

```
MainWindow::MainWindow(QWidget *parent) :
    QMainWindow(parent),
    ui(new Ui::MainWindow)
{

    qputenv("QTWEBENGINE_REMOTE_DEBUGGING", "1234");
    ui->setupUi(this);
    QWebEngineView* webview = new QWebEngineView();
    ui->verticalLayout->addWidget(webview);
    QWebChannel* webChannel = new QWebChannel();
    webChannel->registerObject("mainWindow", this);
    webview->page()->setWebChannel(webChannel);
    webview->page()->load(QUrl("qrc:///html/test.html"));

}
```

13. Declare what happens when `changeQtText()` and `showLoginInfo()` are called:

```
void MainWindow::changeQtText(QString newText) {
    ui->label->setText(newText);
}
void MainWindow::showLoginInfo(QString user, QString pass) {
    QMessageBox::information(this, "Login info", "Username is "
+ user + " and password is " + pass);
}
```

14. Compile and run the program; you should see something similar to the following screenshot. If you click on the **Change Cpp Text** button, the word **Hello!** at the top will change to **Goodbye!** If you click on the **Login** button, a message box will appear and show you exactly what you typed in the **Username** and **Password** input fields:

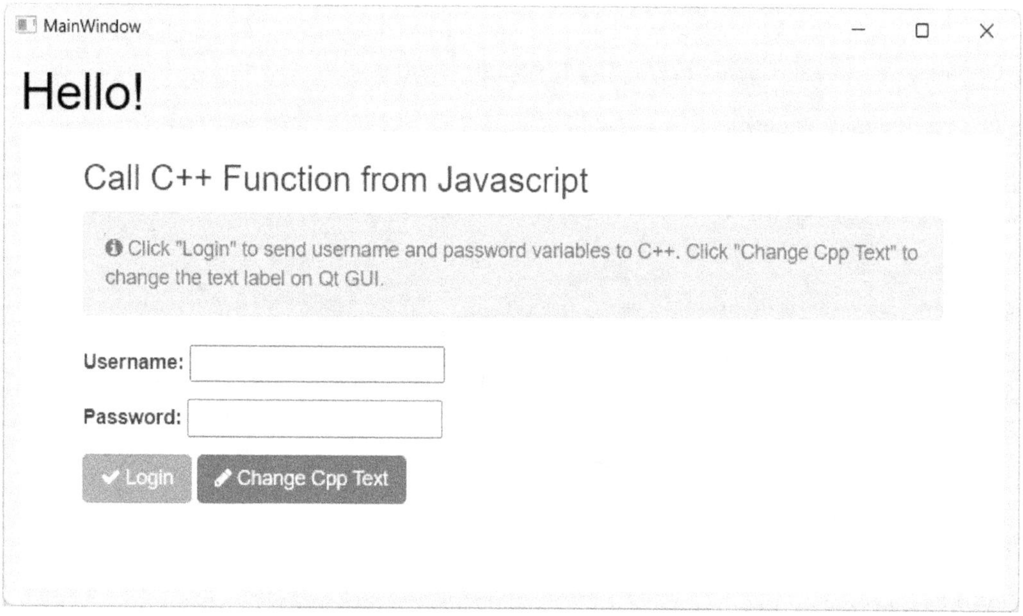

Figure 13.19 – Clicking on the buttons to call C++ functions

How it works...

In this example, we used two JavaScript libraries: **jQuery** and **Bootstrap**. We also used an iconic font package called **Font Awesome**. These third-party add-ons were used to make the HTML UI more interesting and responsive to different screen resolutions.

We also used **jQuery** to detect the document's ready status, as well as to obtain the values of input fields.

> **Note**
>
> You can download **jQuery** from `https://jquery.com/download`, **Bootstrap** from `http://getbootstrap.com/getting-started/#download`, and **Font Awesome** from `http://fontawesome.io`.

Qt's **WebEngine** module uses a mechanism called **WebChannel**, which enables **peer-to-peer** (**P2P**) communication between the C++ program and the HTML page. The **WebEngine** module provides a JavaScript library that makes integration a lot easier. The JavaScript is embedded in your project's resource by default, so you don't need to import it into your project manually. You just have to include it in your HTML page by calling the following:

```
<script src="qrc:///qtwebchannel/qwebchannel.js"></script>
```

Once you have included qwebchannel.js, you can initialize the QWebChannel class and assign the Qt object we registered earlier in C++ to a JavaScript variable.

In C++, this is done as follows:

```
QWebChannel* webChannel = new QWebChannel();
webChannel->registerObject("mainWindow", this);
webview->page()->setWebChannel(webChannel);
```

Then, in JavaScript, this is done as follows:

```
new QWebChannel(qt.webChannelTransport, function(channel) {
mainWindow = channel.objects.mainWindow;
});
```

You may be wondering what this line means:

```
qputenv("QTWEBENGINE_REMOTE_DEBUGGING", "1234");
```

Qt's **WebEngine** module uses the remote debugging method to check for JavaScript errors and other problems. The number 1234 defines the port number you want to use for remote debugging.

Once you have enabled remote debugging, you can access the debugging page by opening up a Chromium-based web browser, such as Google Chrome (this will not work in Firefox and other browsers), and typing in http://127.0.0.1:1234. You will then see a page that looks like this:

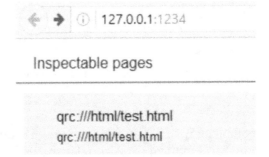

Figure 13.20 – Inspectable pages allow you to debug more easily

The first page will display all HTML pages that are currently running in your program, which in this case is test.html. Click on the page link, and it will take you to another page for inspection. You can use this to check for CSS errors, JavaScript errors, and missing files.

Note that you should disable remote debugging once your program is bug-free and ready for deployment. This is because remote debugging takes time to initialize and will increase your program's startup time.

If you want to call a C++ function from JavaScript, you must place the Q_INVOKABLE macro in front of the function's declaration; otherwise, it will not work:

```
Q_INVOKABLE void changeQtText(QString newText);
```

Calling Javascript functions from C++

In the previous recipe, we learned how to call C++ functions from JavaScript through Qt's **WebChannel** system. In this example, we will try to do the reverse: call JavaScript functions from C++ code.

How to do it...

We can call JavaScript functions from C++ through the following steps:

1. Create a new **Qt Widgets Application** project and add the webenginewidgets module to your project.

2. Open mainwindow.ui and remove the **mainToolBar**, **menuBar**, and **statusBar** objects.

3. Add a vertical layout and a horizontal layout to the canvas. Select the canvas and click **Lay Out Vertically**. Make sure the horizontal layout is located at the bottom of the vertical layout.

4. Add two push buttons to the horizontal layout; one is called **Change HTML Text** and the other is called **Play UI Animation**. Right-click on one of the buttons and click **Go to slot...**. A window will pop up and ask you to pick a signal. Select the clicked() option and click **OK**. Qt will automatically add a slot function to your source code. Repeat this step for the other button:

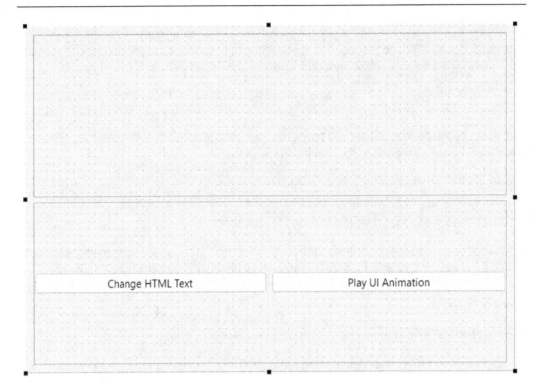

Figure 13.21 – Placing the buttons in the bottom layout

5. Open `mainwindow.h` and add the following headers to it:

```
#include <QtWebEngineWidgets/QWebEngineView>
#include <QtWebChannel/QWebChannel>
#include <QMessageBox>
```

6. Declare the class pointer of a `QWebEngineView` object called `webview`:

```
public:
    explicit MainWindow(QWidget *parent = 0);
    ~MainWindow();
    QWebEngineView* webview;
```

7. Open `mainwindow.cpp` and add the following code to the `MainWindow` constructor:

```
MainWindow::MainWindow(QWidget *parent) :
    QMainWindow(parent),
    ui(new Ui::MainWindow)
{

    //qputenv("QTWEBENGINE_REMOTE_DEBUGGING", "1234");
```

```
ui->setupUi(this);
webview = new QWebEngineView();
ui->verticalLayout->addWidget(webview);
QWebChannel* webChannel = new QWebChannel();
webChannel->registerObject("mainWindow", this);
webview->page()->setWebChannel(webChannel);
webview->page()->load(QUrl("qrc:///html/test.html"));
}
```

8. Define what will happen when the changeHtmlText button and the playUIAnimation button are clicked:

```
void MainWindow::on_changeHtmlTextButton_clicked() {
    webview->page()->runJavaScript("changeHtmlText('Text has
been replaced by C++!');");
}
void MainWindow::on_playUIAnimationButton_clicked() {
    webview->page()->runJavaScript("startAnim();");
}
```

9. Let's create a resource file for our project by going to **File | New File…**. Select **Qt Resource File** under the **Qt** category and click **Choose…**. Insert your desired filename and click **Next**, followed by **Finish**.

10. Add an empty HTML file and all the required add-ons (**jQuery**, **Bootstrap**, and **Font Awesome**) to the project resources. Add the tux.png image file to the resources file as well, as we'll be using it in a short while in *step 14*.

11. Open the HTML file we just created and add it to the project resources; in our case, it's called test.html. Add the following HTML code to the file:

```
<!DOCTYPE html>
<html>
  <head>
    <script src="qrc:///qtwebchannel/qwebchannel.js"></script>
    <script src="js/jquery.min.js"></script>
    <script src="js/bootstrap.js"></script>
    <link rel="stylesheet" type="text/css" href="css/bootstrap.
css">
    <link rel="stylesheet" type="text/css" href="css/
fontawesome.css">
  </head>
<body>
</body>
</html>
```

12. Add the following JavaScript code, which is wrapped within the `<script>` tags, to the `<head>` element of our HTML file:

```
<script>
  $(document).ready(function()
  {
    $("#tux").css({ opacity:0, width:"0%", height:"0%" });
    $("#listgroup").hide();
    $("#listgroup2").hide();
    new QWebChannel(qt.webChannelTransport,
function(channel)
    {
      mainWindow = channel.objects.mainWindow;
    });
  });
  function changeHtmlText(newText)
  {
    $("#infotext").html(newText);
  }
```

13. Define a `startAnim()` function:

```
  function startAnim() {
  // Reset
    $("#tux").css({ opacity:0, width:"0%", height:"0%" });
    $("#listgroup").hide();
    $("#listgroup2").hide();
    $("#tux").animate({ opacity:1.0, width:"100%",
height:"100%" }, 1000, function()
    {
// tux animation complete
      $("#listgroup").slideDown(1000, function() {
      // listgroup animation complete
        $("#listgroup2").fadeIn(1500);
      });
    });
  }
</script>
```

14. Add the following code to the `<body>` element of our HTML file:

```
<div class="container-fluid">
  <form id="example-form" action="#" class="container-fluid">
    <div class="form-group">
    <div class="col-md-12"><h3>Call Javascript Function from
```

```
C++</h3></div>
      <div class="col-md-12">
      <div class="alert alert-info" role="alert"><i class="fa
fa-info-circle"></i> <span id="infotext"> Change this text using
C++.</span></div>
      </div>
      <div class="col-md-2">
        <img id="tux" src="tux.png"></img>
      </div>
```

15. Continue writing the following code, to which we've added a list:

```
<div class="col-md-5">
  <ul id="listgroup" class="list-group">
  <li class="list-group-item">Cras justoodio</li>
  <li class="list-group-item">Dapibus acfacilisis in</li>
  <li class="list-group-item">Morbi leorisus</li>
  <li class="list-group-item">Porta acconsectetur ac</li>
  <li class="list-group-item">Vestibulum ateros</li>
  </ul>
</div>
<div id="listgroup2" class="col-md-5">
  <a href="#" class="list-group-item active">
  <h4 class="list-group-item-heading">Item heading</h4>
  <p class="list-group-item-text">Cras justo odio</p>
  </a>
```

16. The code continues as we add the remaining items to a second list:

```
      <a href="#" class="list-group-item">
        <h4 class="list-group-item-heading">Item heading</h4>
        <p class="list-group-item-text">Dapibus ac facilisis
in</p>
      </a>
      <a href="#" class="list-group-item">
        <h4 class="list-group-item-heading">Item heading</h4>
        <p class="list-group-item-text">Morbi leo risus</p>
      </a>
    </div>
  </div>
 </form>
</div>
```

17. Build and run the program; you should get a similar result to that in the following screenshot. When you click on the **Change HTML Text** button, the information text is located within the top panel. If you click on the **Play UI Animation** button, penguin images, alongside the two sets of widgets, will appear one after the other, with different animations:

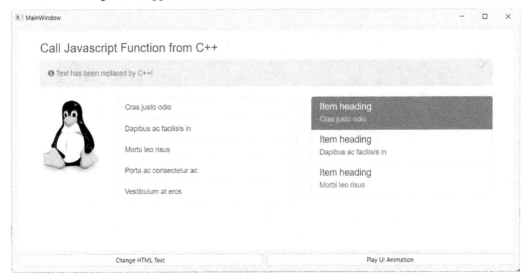

Figure 13.22 – Clicking on the buttons at the bottom to see the results

How it works...

This example is similar to the previous one in the *Calling C++ functions from JavaScript* recipe. Once we have included the **WebChannel** JavaScript library and initiated the QWebChannel class, we can call any of the JavaScript functions from C++ by calling webview->page()->runJavascript("jsFunctionNameHere();"). Don't forget to apply the web channel created in C++ to webview page as well; otherwise, it will not be able to communicate with the QWebChannel class in your HTML file.

By default, we change the CSS properties of the penguin image and set its opacity to 0, width to 0%, and height to 0%. We also hide the two list groups by calling the hide() **jQuery** function. When the **Play UI Animation** button is clicked, we repeat the steps just in case the animations have been played before (that is, the same button has been clicked before), and then we hide the list groups again in order for the animations to be replayed.

One powerful feature of **jQuery** is that you can define what happens after an animation finishes, which allows us to play animations in sequence. In this example, we started with the penguin image and interpolated its CSS properties to a targeted setting within a second (1,000 milliseconds). Once that was done, we started another animation, which made the first list group slide from top to bottom in 1 second. After that, we ran the third animation, which made the second list group fade in from nowhere within 1.5 seconds.

To replace the information text located in the top panel, we created a JavaScript function called `changeHtmlText()` within the function itself, and we got the HTML element by referring to its ID and calling `html()` to change its contents.

14

Performance Optimization

Qt 6 is known for its optimized performance. However, performance issues may still occur if your code is poorly written. There are many ways we can identify these issues and fix them before releasing the software to our users.

In this chapter, we will cover the following recipes:

- Optimizing forms and C++
- Profiling and optimizing QML
- Rendering and animation

Technical requirements

The technical requirements for this chapter include Qt 6.6.1 MinGW 64 bit, Qt Creator 12.0.2, and Windows 11. All the code used in this chapter can be downloaded from the following GitHub repository at https://github.com/PacktPublishing/QT6-C-GUI-Programming-Cookbook---Third-Edition-/tree/main/Chapter14.

Optimizing forms and C++

It's very important to learn how to optimize your form-based Qt 6 applications that are built with C++. The best way to do that is to learn how to measure and compare the different methods that are used and decide which one works the best for you.

How to do it...

Let's get started by following these steps:

1. Let's create a **Qt Widgets Application** project and open up `mainwindow.cpp`. After that, add the following headers to the top of the source code:

```
#include <QPushButton>
#include <QGridLayout>
#include <QMessageBox>
#include <QElapsedTimer>
#include <QDebug>
```

2. Create a `QGridLayout` object and set its parent to `centralWidget`:

```
MainWindow::MainWindow(QWidget *parent) : QMainWindow(parent),
ui(new Ui::MainWindow)
{
    ui->setupUi(this);
    QGridLayout *layout = new QGridLayout(ui->centralWidget);
```

3. Create a `QElapsedTimer` object. We will be using this to measure the performance of our next operation:

```
QElapsedTimer* time = new QElapsedTimer;
time->start();
```

4. We will use two loops to add 600 push buttons to our grid layout and connect all of them to a lambda function when clicked. We will then measure the elapsed time and print out the result, as follows:

```
for (int i = 0; i < 40; ++i) {
    for (int j = 0; j < 15; ++j) {
        QPushButton* newWidget = new QPushButton();
        newWidget->setText("Button");
        layout->addWidget(newWidget, i, j);
        connect(newWidget, QPushButton::clicked, [this]() {
            QMessageBox::information(this, "Clicked", "Button
has been clicked!");
        });
    }
}
qDebug() << "Test GUI:" << time->elapsed() << "msec";
```

5. If we build and run the project now, we will see a window filled with lots of buttons. When we click on one of them, a message box will pop up on the screen. It only took around nine milliseconds on my computer to create and lay out all of the 600 buttons on the main window. There is also no performance issue when we move the window around or resize it, which is quite impressive. It proves that Qt 6 can handle this pretty well. However, please be aware that your users might be using older machines, and you might want to be extra careful when designing your user interface:

Figure 14.1 – Spawn 600 buttons on a Qt window

6.   Let's add a style sheet to each of the buttons, like so:

```
QPushButton* newWidget = new QPushButton();
newWidget->setText("Button");
newWidget->setStyleSheet("background-color: blue; color:
white;");
layout->addWidget(newWidget, i, j);
```

7.   Build and run the program again. This time, it took roughly 75 milliseconds to set up the GUI. This means that the style sheet does have some impact on the performance of your program:

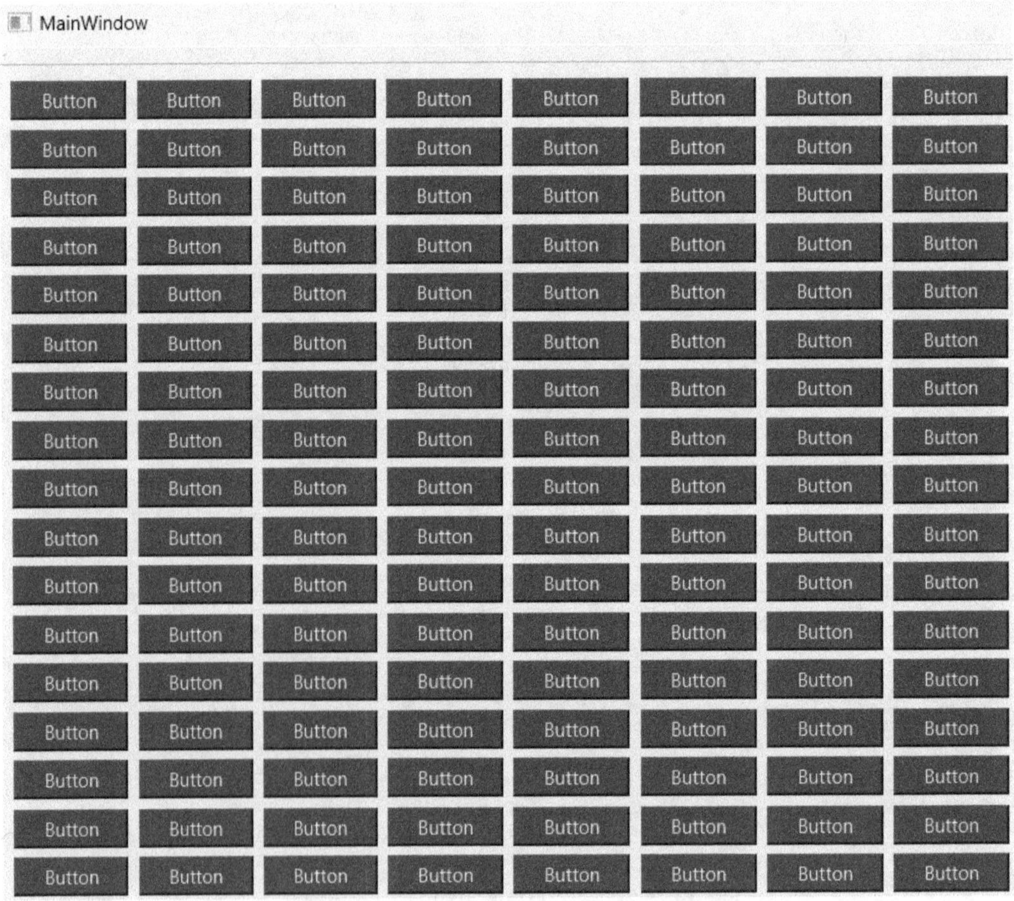

Figure 14.2 – Apply the style sheet to all 600 buttons

8. Once you are done with that, let's do some performance tests on different types of C++ containers. Open up main.cpp and add the following headers:

```cpp
#include "mainwindow.h"
#include <QApplication>
#include <QDebug>
#include <QElapsedTimer>
#include <vector>
#include <QVector>
```

9. Create a testArray() function before the main() function:

```cpp
int testArray(int count) {
    int sum = 0;
    int *myarray = new int[count];
    for (int i = 0; i < count; ++i)
        myarray[i] = i;
    for (int j = 0; j < count; ++j)
        sum += myarray[j];
    delete [] myarray;
    return sum;
}
```

10. Create another function called testVector(), as follows:

```cpp
int testVector(int count) {
    int sum = 0;
    std::vector<int> myarray;
    for (int i = 0; i < count; ++i)
        myarray.push_back(i);
    for (int j = 0; j < count; ++j)
        sum += myarray.at(j);
    return sum;
}
```

11. Once you are done with that, proceed to create yet another function called testQtVector():

```cpp
int testQtVector(int count) {
    int sum = 0;
    QVector<int> myarray;
    for (int i = 0; i < count; ++i)
        myarray.push_back(i);
    for (int j = 0; j < count; ++j)
        sum += myarray.at(j);
    return sum;
}
```

12. Inside the `main()` function, define a `QElapsedTimer` object and an integer variable called `lastElapse`:

```
int main(int argc, char *argv[]) {
    QApplication a(argc, argv);
    MainWindow w;
    w.show();
    QElapsedTimer* time = new QElapsedTimer;
    time->start();
    int lastElapse = 0;
```

13. We will call the three functions we created in the previous steps to test their performance:

```
    int result = testArray(100000000);
    qDebug() << "Array:" << (time->elapsed() - lastElapse) <<
"msec";
    lastElapse = time->elapsed();
    int result2 = testVector(100000000);
    qDebug() << "STL vector:" << (time->elapsed() - lastElapse)
<< "msec";
    lastElapse = time->elapsed();
    int result3 = testQtVector(100000000);
    qDebug() << "Qt vector:" << (time->elapsed() - lastElapse)
<< "msec";
    lastElapse = time->elapsed();
```

14. Build and run the program now; we will see the performance differences between these containers. On my computer, the array took 650 milliseconds to execute, while the STL vector took roughly 3,830 milliseconds, and the Qt vector took around 5,400 milliseconds to execute.

> **Note**
>
> As a result, the array is still the container that yields the best performance, despite its lack of features compared to the other two. Surprisingly, Qt's own vector class works slightly slower than the vector container provided by the C++ standard library.

How it works...

When creating a **Qt Widgets Application** project, try to do the following to improve performance:

- Avoid adding too many pages to a stacked widget and filling them with widgets, as Qt needs to find all of them recursively during the rendering process and event handling, which will highly impact the program's performance.

- Do note that the `QWidget` class uses the Raster Engine, a software renderer, to render the widgets instead of using the GPU. However, it is lightweight enough to keep the performance good most of the time. Alternatively, you could consider using QML for your program's GUI instead, since it is fully hardware accelerated.

- Turn off **mouseTracking**, **tabletTracking**, and other event catching for your widgets if they do not need it. This tracking and catchings adds to the CPU usage costs of your program:

MainWindow : QMainWindow	
Property	**Value**
Strikeout	☐
Kerning	☑
Antialiasing	PreferDefault
cursor	⬚ Arrow
mouseTracking	☐
tabletTracking	☐
focusPolicy	NoFocus
contextMenuPol...	DefaultContextMenu
acceptDrops	☐
> **windowTitle**	MainWindow
> windowIcon	

Figure 14.3 – Disable mouseTracking and tabletTracking for optimization

- Keep your style sheets as simple as possible. A large style sheet needs a longer time for Qt to parse the information into the rendering system, which will also impact performance.

- Different C++ containers produce different speeds, as we showed in the preceding example. Surprisingly, Qt's vector container is slightly slower than STL's (the C++ standard library) vector container. Overall, the good old C++ array is still the fastest, but does not provide sorting functionality. Use what is best for your requirements.

- For large operations, use *asynchronous* methods whenever possible as it will not stall the main process and will keep your program running smoothly.

- *Multi-threading* is really good for running different operations in parallel event loops. However, it can also become quite ugly if not done right, for example, creating and destroying threads frequently, or with inter-thread communications that are not planned well.

- Try to avoid using the web engine unless absolutely necessary. This is because embedding a full web browser on your program is really heavy overkill, especially for a small application. You can consider using QML instead of making a hybrid application if you want to create user interface-centric software.

- By doing performance tests as we did in the preceding example project, you can easily determine which method is the best choice for your project and how to make your program perform better.

> **Note**
>
> In Qt 5, we can use the `QTime` class to do the test as seen in this section. However, functions such as `start()` and `elapsed()` have been deprecated from the `QTime` class in Qt 6. Since Qt 6, the player must use `QElapsedTimer` to handle this.

Profiling and optimizing QML

The QML engine in Qt 6 took advantage of hardware acceleration to make its rendering capability and performance superior to the old widgets user interface. However, this does not mean that you do not need to worry about optimization, because small performance issues may snowball into bigger problems over time and cause damage to your product's reputation.

How to do it...

Follow these steps to start profiling and optimizing a QML application:

1. Let's create a **Qt Quick Application** project:

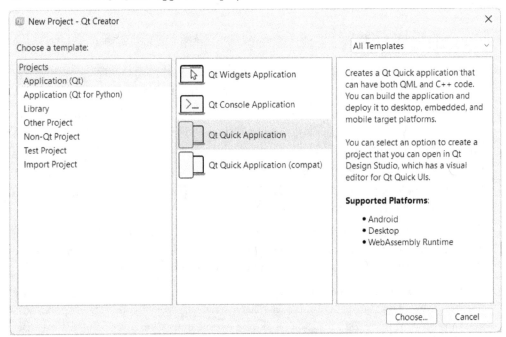

Figure 14.4 – Create a Qt Quick Application project

2.   Then, go to **Analyze | QML Profiler** and run the **QML Profiler** tool:

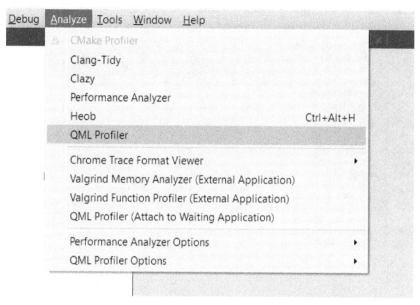

Figure 14.5 – Run the QML Profiler to check the QML performance

3.   Your Qt Quick project will then be run by the QML Profiler. The **QML Profiler** window will also appear under the code editor. Click the **Stop** button located at the top bar of the **QML Profiler** window after the program has passed the test point, which in this case meant successfully creating the empty window:

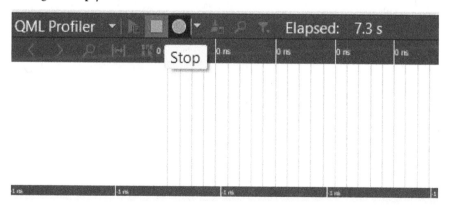

Figure 14.6 – Stop the QML Profiler by pressing the button with the red rectangle icon

4. After you stop the profiler analysis, a timeline will be displayed in the **Timeline** tab under the **QML Profiler** window. There are four tabs that you can switch between, namely **Timeline**, **Flame Graph**, **Quick3D Frame**, and **Statistics**, at the bottom of the **QML Profiler** window:

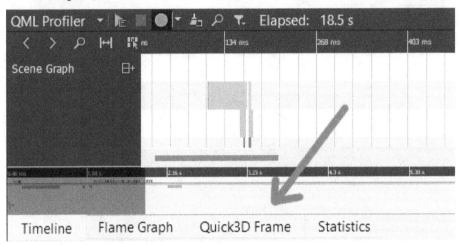

Figure 14.7 – You can look at different data on different tabs

5. Let's check out the **Timeline** tab. We can see six different categories under the timeline display: **Scene Graph**, **Memory Usage**, **Input Events**, **Compiling**, **Creating**, and **Binding**. These categories give us an overview of the different stages and processes of our program throughout its execution. We can also see some colorful bars displayed on the timeline. Let's click on one of the bars under the **Creating** category that says **QtQuick/Window**. Once clicked, we will see the total duration for this operation and the location of the code displayed in a rectangular window located at the top of the QML Profiler window:

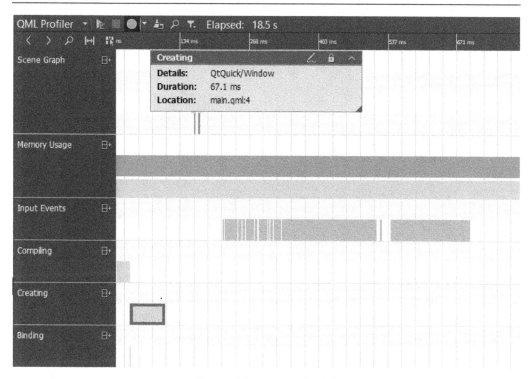

Figure 14.8 – The Timeline tab

6. Once you are done with that, let's move on and open up the **Flame Graph** tab instead. Under the **Flame Graph** tab, you will see the visualization of the total time, memory, and allocation of your application in the form of percentages. You can switch between total time, memory, and allocation by clicking on the selection box that's located at the top-right corner of the **QML Profiler** window:

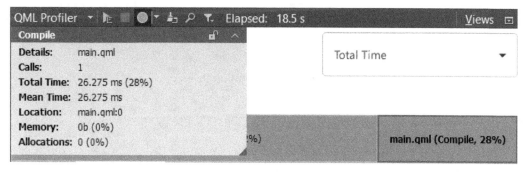

Figure 14.9 – The Flame Graph tab

7. Not only that, you will also see the percentage value displayed on your QML code editor:

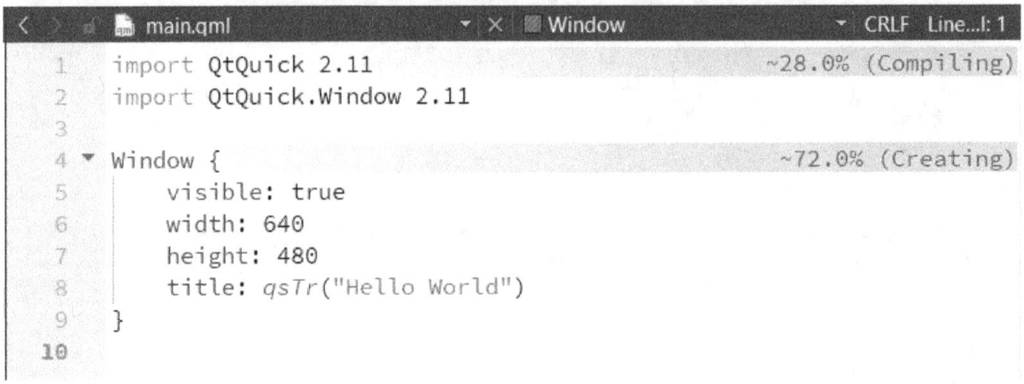

```
main.qml                              ▼ × ■ Window                    ▼ CRLF  Line...l: 1
1   import QtQuick 2.11                                        ~28.0% (Compiling)
2   import QtQuick.Window 2.11
3
4 ▼ Window {                                                   ~72.0% (Creating)
5       visible: true
6       width: 640
7       height: 480
8       title: qsTr("Hello World")
9   }
10
```

Figure 14.10 – Percentage values are shown on the right

8. Open up the **Quick3D Frame** category under the **QML Profiler** window. This tab is where you check the performance of 3D rendering. It is currently empty because we are not doing any 3D rendering.

9. Next, let's open up the **Statistics** category. This tab basically shows us information about the processes in table form:

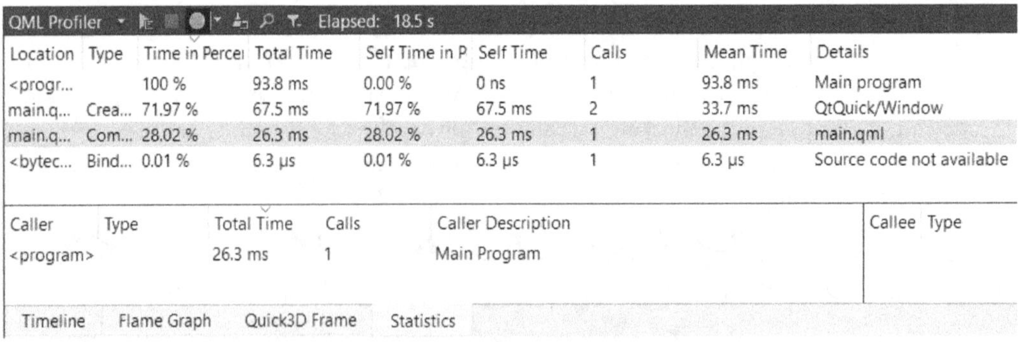

QML Profiler ▼ ▶ ■ ● ▼ ▲ ♪ ▼ Elapsed: 18.5 s

Location	Type	Time in Percer	Total Time	Self Time in P	Self Time	Calls	Mean Time	Details
<progr...		100 %	93.8 ms	0.00 %	0 ns	1	93.8 ms	Main program
main.q...	Crea...	71.97 %	67.5 ms	71.97 %	67.5 ms	2	33.7 ms	QtQuick/Window
main.q...	Com...	28.02 %	26.3 ms	28.02 %	26.3 ms	1	26.3 ms	main.qml
<bytec...	Bind...	0.01 %	6.3 µs	0.01 %	6.3 µs	1	6.3 µs	Source code not available

Caller	Type	Total Time	Calls	Caller Description	Callee	Type
<program>		26.3 ms	1	Main Program		

Timeline   Flame Graph   Quick3D Frame   Statistics

Figure 14.11 – The Statistics tab

How it works...

This is similar to what we did in the previous example project that used C++ and widgets except, this time, it is automatically analyzed by the **QML Profiler** tool that's provided by Qt 6.

The QML Profiler not only produces the total time used for running a specific process, but also displays the memory allocation, the execution timeline of your application, and other information that gives you insight into the performance of your software.

By looking at the data that was analyzed by the QML Profiler, you will be able to find out which part of your code slows down the program, allowing you to fix any problems quickly.

There are some rules that you need to be aware of when writing QML to avoid performance bottlenecks. For instance, type conversion can sometimes be expensive, especially between types that are not closely matched (string to number, for example). Small issues like this will likely snowball into bottlenecks as your project grows larger over time.

Other than that, try not to use `id` for an item lookup multiple times in blocks of code that are run often, as in the following example:

```
Item {
    width: 400
    height: 400
    Rectangle {
    id: rect
    anchors.fill: parent
    color: "green"
    }
    Component.onCompleted: {
        for (var i = 0; i < 1000; ++i) {
            console.log("red", rect.color.r);
            console.log("green", rect.color.g);
            console.log("blue", rect.color.b);
            console.log("alpha", rect.color.a);
        }
    }
}
```

Instead, we can use a variable to cache the data and avoid multiple look-ups on the same item over and over again:

```
Component.onCompleted: {
    var rectColor = rect.color;
    for (var i = 0; i < 1000; ++i) {
        console.log("red", rectColor.r);
        console.log("green", rectColor.g);
        console.log("blue", rectColor.b);
        console.log("alpha", rectColor.a);
    }
}
```

Besides, if you change the property of a binding expression, especially in a loop, Qt will be forced to re-evaluate it repeatedly. This will cause some performance issues. Instead of doing this, the user should follow the next code snippet:

```
Item {
    id: myItem
    width: 400
    height: 400
    property int myValue: 0
    Text {
        anchors.fill: parent
        text: myItem.myValue.toString()
    }
    Component.onCompleted: {
        for (var i = 0; i < 1000; ++i) {
            myValue += 1;
        }
    }
}
```

Instead, we can use a temporary variable for storing the data of myValue, then apply the final result back to myValue once the loop has been completed:

```
Component.onCompleted: {
    var temp = myValue;
    for (var i = 0; i < 1000; ++i) {
        temp += 1;
    }
    myValue = temp;
}
```

Consider using an anchor to position your UI items instead of using bindings. Item positioning with bindings is really slow and inefficient, although it allows for maximum flexibility.

Rendering and animation

When it comes to an application that renders graphics and animation, good performance is critical. Users can easily notice performance issues when graphics are not animated smoothly on screen. In the following example, we will look at how we can further optimize a graphics-heavy Qt Quick application.

How to do it...

To learn how to render animation in QML, follow this example:

1. Create a **Qt Quick Application** project. Then, right-click on the **Resources** icon under our project panel and add tux.png to our project's resources:

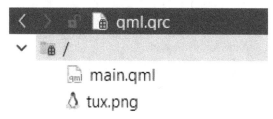

Figure 14.12 – Include main.qml and tux.png into your project resources

2. Open up **main.qml** and change the window size to 650 x 650. We will also add id to the window item and name it window:

```
Window {
    id: window
    visible: true
    width: 650
    height: 650
```

3. Add the following code inside the window item:

```
property int frame: 0;
onAfterRendering: { frame++; }
Timer {
id: timer
interval: 1000
running: true
repeat: true
onTriggered: { frame = 0; }
}
```

4. Right after that, add Repeater and Image under it:

```
Repeater {
    model: 10
    delegate:
    Image {
    id: tux
    source: "tux.png"
```

```
sourceSize.width: 50
sourceSize.height: 60
width: 50
height: 60
smooth: false
antialiasing: false
asynchronous: true
```

5. We will proceed and add the following code:

```
property double startX: Math.random() * 600;
property double startY: Math.random() * 600;
property double endX: Math.random() * 600;
property double endY: Math.random() * 600;
property double speed: Math.random() * 3000 + 1000;
RotationAnimation on rotation{
loops: Animation.Infinite
from: 0
to: 360
duration: Math.random() * 3000 + 1000;
}
```

6. Once you are done with that, add the following code below the previous code:

```
SequentialAnimation {
    running: true
    loops: Animation.Infinite
    ParallelAnimation {
    NumberAnimation {
    target: tux
    property: "x"
    from: startX
    to: endX
    duration: speed
    easing.type: Easing.InOutQuad
}
```

7. The preceding code animates the x property of the image. We need another NumberAnimation property to animate the y property:

```
NumberAnimation {
    target: tux
    property: "y"
    from: startY
    to: endY
```

```
            duration: speed
            easing.type: Easing.InOutQuad
        }
    }
```

8. After that, we repeat the entire code of `ParallelAnimation`, except this time, we swap the `from` and `to` values, like so:

```
ParallelAnimation {
    NumberAnimation {
        target: tux
        property: "x"
        from: endX
        to: startX
        duration: speed
        easing.type: Easing.InOutQuad
    }
```

9. The same goes for `NumberAnimation` for the `y` property:

```
    NumberAnimation {
        target: tux
        property: "y"
        from: endY
        to: startY
        duration: speed
        easing.type: Easing.InOutQuad
    }
}
```

10. Then, we add a `Text` item for displaying the frame rate of our application:

```
Text {
    property int frame: 0
    color: "red"
    text: "FPS: 0 fps"
    x: 20
    y: 20
    font.pointSize: 20
```

11. Let's add `Timer` under `Text` and update the frame rate to display every second:

```
    Timer {
        id: fpsTimer
        repeat: true
        interval: 1000
```

```
                    running: true
                    onTriggered: {
                    parent.text = "FPS: " + frame + " fps"
                    }
                }
            }
```

12. If we build and run the program now, we will be able to see several penguins moving around the screen with a steady 60 fps:

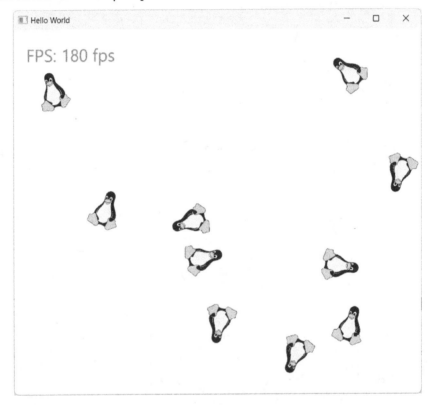

Figure 14.13 – 10 penguins floating around the window

13. Let's go back to our code and change the model property of the Repeater item to 10000. Build and run the program again; you should see that your window is full of moving penguins and that the frame rate has significantly dropped to roughly 39 fps, which is not too bad, considering the amount of penguins we have:

Figure 14.14 – 10,000 penguins floating around the window

14. Next, let's go back to our source code and comment out both of the `sourceSize` properties. We also set the `smooth` and `antialiasing` properties to `false`, while setting the asynchronous property to `false`:

```
Image {
    id: tux
    source: "tux.png"
    //sourceSize.width: 50
```

```
//sourceSize.height: 60
width: 50
height: 60
smooth: true
antialiasing: false
asynchronous: false
```

15. Let's build and run the program again. This time, the frame rate dropped slightly to 32 fps, but the penguins look smoother and are of better quality, even when moving:

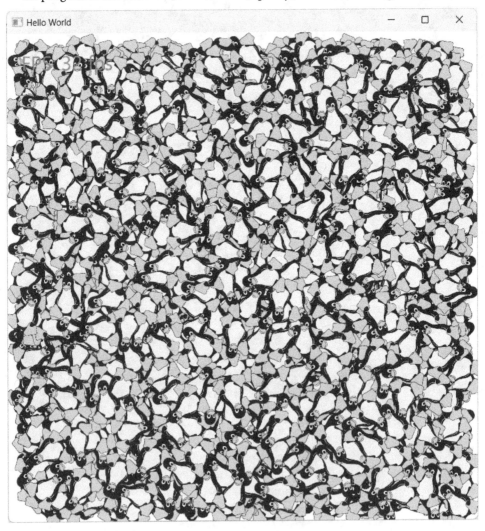

Figure 14.15 – Our penguins look much smoother now without slowing down too much

How it works...

The QML engine that powers Qt Quick applications is very optimized and powerful when it comes to rendering animated graphics on screen. However, there are still some tips that we can follow to make it even faster.

Try and make use of the built-in features provided by Qt 6 instead of implementing your own, such as `Repeater`, `NumberAnimation`, and `SequentialAnimation`. This is because Qt 6 developers have put great effort into optimizing these features so that you don't have to.

The `sourceSize` properties tell Qt to resize the image before loading it into memory so that large images do not use more memory than necessary.

The `smooth` property, when enabled, tells Qt to filter the image to make look it smoother when scaled or transformed from its natural size. It will not make any difference if the image is rendered at the same as its `sourceSize` value. This property will impact the performance of your application on some older hardware.

The `antialiasing` property tells Qt to remove the aliasing artifacts around the edge of the image and make it look smoother. This property will also impact the performance of your program.

The `asynchronous` property tells Qt to load the image under a low-priority thread, which means that your program will not stall when loading huge image files.

We used the frame rate to indicate the performance of our program. Since `onAfterRendering` always gets called on every frame, we can then accumulate the frame variable on every render. Then, we used `Timer` to reset the frame value every second.

Finally, we displayed the value on screen using a `Text` item.

Index

Symbols

A

B

C

`packtpub.com`

Subscribe to our online digital library for full access to over 7,000 books and videos, as well as industry leading tools to help you plan your personal development and advance your career. For more information, please visit our website.

Why subscribe?

- Spend less time learning and more time coding with practical eBooks and Videos from over 4,000 industry professionals

- Improve your learning with Skill Plans built especially for you

- Get a free eBook or video every month

- Fully searchable for easy access to vital information

- Copy and paste, print, and bookmark content

Did you know that Packt offers eBook versions of every book published, with PDF and ePub files available? You can upgrade to the eBook version at `packtpub.com` and as a print book customer, you are entitled to a discount on the eBook copy. Get in touch with us at `customercare@packtpub.com` for more details.

At `www.packtpub.com`, you can also read a collection of free technical articles, sign up for a range of free newsletters, and receive exclusive discounts and offers on Packt books and eBooks.

Other Books You May Enjoy

If you enjoyed this book, you may be interested in these other books by Packt:

Expert C++

Marcelo Guerra Hahn, Araks Tigranyan, John Asatryan, Vardan Grigoryan, Shunguang Wu

ISBN: 978-1-80461-783-0

- Go beyond the basics to explore advanced C++ programming techniques
- Develop proficiency in advanced data structures and algorithm design with C++17 and C++20
- Implement best practices and design patterns to build scalable C++ applications
- Master C++ for machine learning, data science, and data analysis framework design
- Design world-ready applications, incorporating networking and security considerations
- Strengthen your understanding of C++ concurrency, multithreading, and optimizing performance with concurrent data structures

Modern CMake for C++

Rafał Świdziński

ISBN: 978-1-80107-005-8

- Understand best practices for building C++ code

- Gain practical knowledge of the CMake language by focusing on the most useful aspects

- Use cutting-edge tooling to guarantee code quality with the help of tests and static and dynamic analysis

- Discover how to manage, discover, download, and link dependencies with CMake

- Build solutions that can be reused and maintained in the long term

- Understand how to optimize build artifacts and the build process itself

Packt is searching for authors like you

If you're interested in becoming an author for Packt, please visit authors.packtpub.com and apply today. We have worked with thousands of developers and tech professionals, just like you, to help them share their insight with the global tech community. You can make a general application, apply for a specific hot topic that we are recruiting an author for, or submit your own idea.

Share Your Thoughts

Now you've finished *Qt 6 C++ GUI Programming Cookbook*, we'd love to hear your thoughts! Scan the QR code below to go straight to the Amazon review page for this book and share your feedback or leave a review on the site that you purchased it from.

https://packt.link/r/1805122630

Your review is important to us and the tech community and will help us make sure we're delivering excellent quality content.

Download a free PDF copy of this book

Thanks for purchasing this book!

Do you like to read on the go but are unable to carry your print books everywhere?

Is your eBook purchase not compatible with the device of your choice?

Don't worry, now with every Packt book you get a DRM-free PDF version of that book at no cost.

Read anywhere, any place, on any device. Search, copy, and paste code from your favorite technical books directly into your application.

The perks don't stop there, you can get exclusive access to discounts, newsletters, and great free content in your inbox daily

Follow these simple steps to get the benefits:

1. Scan the QR code or visit the link below

https://packt.link/free-ebook/978-1-80512-263-0

2. Submit your proof of purchase
3. That's it! We'll send your free PDF and other benefits to your email directly

www.ingramcontent.com/pod-product-compliance
Lightning Source LLC
LaVergne TN
LVHW081511050326
832903LV00025B/1444